The Oxford Introductions to U.S. Law

Income Tax Law

The Oxford Introductions to U.S. Law

Income Tax Law

Exploring the Capital-Labor Divide

EDWARD J. MCCAFFERY

OXFORD
UNIVERSITY PRESS

OXFORD
UNIVERSITY PRESS

Oxford University Press, Inc., publishes works that further Oxford University's objective of excellence in research, scholarship, and education.

Oxford   New York
Auckland   Cape Town   Dar es Salaam   Hong Kong   Karachi   Kuala Lumpur   Madrid   Melbourne
Mexico City   Nairobi   New Delhi   Shanghai   Taipei   Toronto

With offices in
Argentina   Austria   Brazil   Chile   Czech Republic   France   Greece   Guatemala   Hungary   Italy
Japan   Poland   Portugal   Singapore   South Korea   Switzerland   Thailand   Turkey   Ukraine
Vietnam

Library of Congress Cataloging-in-Publication Data

McCaffery, Edward J.
   Oxford introductions to U.S. law. Income tax law / Edward J. McCaffery.
      p. cm. — (Oxford introductions to U.S. law)
   Includes bibliographical references.
   ISBN 978-0-19-537671-5 ((pbk.) : alk. paper)
      1. Taxation—Law and legislation—United States. I. Title.
      2. II. Title: Income tax law.
   KF6289.85.M38 2011
   343.7305'2—dc23   2011024679

1 2 3 4 5 6 7 8 9
Printed in the United States of America on acid-free paper

Note to Readers
This publication is designed to provide accurate and authoritative information in regard to the subject
matter covered. It is based upon sources believed to be accurate and reliable and is intended to be
current as of the time it was written. It is sold with the understanding that the publisher is not engaged
in rendering legal, accounting, or other professional services. If legal advice or other expert assistance
is required, the services of a competent professional person should be sought. Also, to confirm that the
information has not been affected or changed by recent developments, traditional legal research
techniques should be used, including checking primary sources where appropriate.

*(Based on the Declaration of Principles jointly adopted by a Committee of the
American Bar Association and a Committee of Publishers and Associations.)*

You may order this or any other Oxford University Press publication by
visiting the Oxford University Press website at www.oup.com

To my teachers, especially
William D. Andrews and Louis Kaplow

Contents

Introduction xvii

PART I A Taste of Theory 1

CHAPTER 1 A View of the Forest 3

    1.1 The Basic Logic of Tax 3

    1.2 Three Kinds of Tax 4

    1.3 An Income Tax 6

    1.4 Two Kinds of Consumption Taxes 8

    1.5 A Common View: The Income
       Tax as a "Hybrid" 10

    1.6 The Real Story: The Income Tax as
       a Wage Tax 11

        1.6.1 Tax Planning 101 12

        1.6.2 Beyond Tax Planning 101 15

        1.6.3 The Income Tax, Take Two: Ad Hoc
           Deviations 17

    1.7 Tax Rates 20

    1.8 Following the Tax Form 21

    1.9 The Goals of Tax Planning 22

    1.10 The Capital-Labor Divide, Redux 24

    1.11 Summary 25

PART II   The Details 29

CHAPTER 2   The "What" of Taxation, Part One: Inclusions in the Tax Base 31

2.1 Three Definitions of Income 32
   2.1.1 Constitutional and Statutory Definitions 33
   2.1.2 Judicial Definitions 36
   2.1.3 Academic Definitions 47
2.2 *Macomber* and Why It Matters 48
   2.2.1 Tax versus Economics 48
   2.2.2 On Basis and "Tax Time Bombs" 50
   2.2.3 Rule: Sooner or Later, Part I: Tax Time Bombs Go Off 51
2.3 Four Conceptual Items of *Non*Income 54
   2.3.1 Psychic Income 55
   2.3.2 Imputed Income 55
   2.3.3 Unrealized Income 58
   2.3.4 Borrowing 58
2.4 Tax Planning 101 59
   2.4.1 Note: Tax Planning 102 59
2.5 Statutory Exclusions 62
2.6 Gifts 64
   2.6.1 Definitions 64
   2.6.2 Gifts of Appreciated Property 70
2.7 Beyond Cash 73
   2.7.1 An Important Example 73
   2.7.2 Valuation Principles 75
2.8 "Fringe" or Noncash Benefits 77
   2.8.1 Exclusions Matter 78
   2.8.2 Plugging Up the Leaks 79
2.9 Other Oddities 80
2.10 Debt and Its Discharge 81
2.11 A Small Taste of Theory 83
2.12 Other Taxes 84
2.13 Summary 84

CHAPTER 3 The "What" of Taxation, Part Two: Deductions
from the Tax Base 87

    3.1 General Principles 87

    3.2 The Mechanics of Deductions 89

        3.2.1 The Math of the Matter 91

        3.2.2 Following the Form (Again) 92

        3.2.3 An Important Case Study: The Earned
Income Tax Credit 93

    3.3 Personal Expenditures 94

        3.3.1 Note on Standard Deduction and
Personal Dependency Exemptions 98

        3.3.2 Note on "Phase-outs" and Itemized
Deductions 99

    3.4 Business Expenditures (With Notes
on Timing) 99

        3.4.1 Rule: Sooner or Later, Part II: You
Get Your (Business or Investment)
Basis Back 100

        3.4.2 Question One: Now or Later (Ordinary
or Capital)? 102

        3.4.3 Question Two: If Later, Does the
Deduction Come over Time or "Way
Later"? 103

        3.4.4 Tracking Basis 104

    3.5 Business-Personal Expenditures 105

        3.5.1 Two Senses of Mixed Matters 108

        3.5.2 A Note on Using the Wrong Tools 110

    3.6 The Tripartite Distinction in Action: Interest
Deduction Rules 111

        3.6.1 Losses 113

        3.6.2 A Quick Note on Gambling Losses 114

    3.7 A Note on the AMT 115

    3.8 Summary 117

CHAPTER 4 The "When" of Taxation: Timing with a Capital
and Lowercase T 121

4.1 Realization, Vel Non 122
    4.1.1 A Note on Valuation 124
    4.1.2 Looking at Both Sides 124
    4.1.3 Strange Bedfellows, and a Note on
           Losses 125
    4.1.4 A Note on Nothing 126
4.2 Recognition, Vel Non 127
    4.2.1 Note on Davis, Section 1041, and
           Divorce 129
4.3 A Case Study: Starker and Like-Kind Exchanges,
     with a Note on Boot 130
4.4 Small t Timing: Matters of Accounting 132
4.5 Methods of Accounting, Including Installment
     Sales and Inventory 133
4.6 Constructive Receipt, Cash Equivalence,
     Economic Benefit 135
4.7 Annual Accounting Rule 137
4.8 Claim of Right and Tax Benefit Rules 139
4.9 Note on Depreciation and Capitalization 141
4.10 Summary 141

CHAPTER 5 The "Who" of Taxation: Questions of Attribution
and the Appropriate Filing Unit 145

5.1 General Themes 145
5.2 Husbands and Wives (With Some Historical
     Notes) 147
    5.2.1 Marriage Penalties, Bonuses ... and the
           Real Issue 150
    5.2.2 Note on Head of Household Status 151
    5.2.3 Note on Marriage for Federal Income
           Tax Purposes 151
5.3 Kids 152
5.4 Fruits and Trees 153
    5.4.1 A Note on Economics 155

5.5 Note on Divorce 156

5.6 A Statutory Response: The "Kiddie Tax" 157

5.7 Shifting To and Through Entities 158

    5.7.1 Note on Shifting to a Later Self 159

5.8 Summary 160

CHAPTER 6 **The "How Much" of Taxation: Characterization of Ordinary Income and Capital Gains** 163

6.1 The Math of the Matter: A Question of Rates 163

6.2 The Policy (If Any) of It All 164

6.3 Statutory Scheme 167

6.4 Two Big Examples of Section 1221(1): Real Estate and Securities 170

6.5 Playing with Definitions: *Corn Products* and *Arkansas Best* 171

    6.5.1 A Further Note on Capital Property 173

6.6 Anticipatory Income, or Fruits and Trees, Again 174

6.7 A Modern Day Issue: Carried Interest 176

6.8 Summary 177

CHAPTER 7 **A Summary, of Sorts: Anatomy of a Tax Shelter** 181

7.1 General Strategy of Tax Shelters 182

7.2 Some Quick and Dirty Examples 183

7.3 *Crane, Tufts*, the Role of Debt, and a Deeper Look 185

    7.3.1 A Quick Look to Hollywood 189

7.4 What the Tax Reform Act of 1986 Did, and Did Not Do 190

    7.4.1 What the Law Did 190

    7.4.2 What the Law Did Not Do 192

7.5 Common Law and Judicial Doctrines 193

7.6 Ethics 198

7.7 Summary 199

PART III   **Whither Tax?**   203

CHAPTER 8   **The Once and Future Tax System**   205

    8.1   The Lay of the Land   206

    8.2   Incremental Reform   207

    8.3   More Taxes?   209

    8.4   Comprehensive Reform:
        A Better Direction   211

    8.5   A New View: Three Types of Tax   212

        8.5.1   A New Look at Savings   214

        8.5.2   Putting It All Together: Three Bases,
               Three Types of Savings   218

    8.6   The Case for a Progressive Spending Tax   219

        8.6.1   The Progressive Spending Tax and Tax
               Planning 101   222

        8.6.2   The New Achilles' Heel   222

    8.7   Summary   223

Appendix   227

Table of Cases   233

Glossary of Key Terms   237

Notes for Further Reading   243

Index   245

About the Editor

DENNIS PATTERSON HOLDS the chair in Legal Philosophy and Legal Theory at the European University Institute in Florence, Italy. He is also Board of Governors Professor of Law and Philosophy at Rutgers University School of Law, Camden, New Jersey, and chair in Jurisprudence and International Trade at Swansea University, UK. Patterson is the author of *Law and Truth* (Oxford University Press 1996) and *The New Global Trading Order* with Ari Afilalo (2008). He is general editor of *The Blackwell Companion to the Philosophy of Law and Legal Theory*. He has published widely in commercial law, trade law, and legal philosophy.

About the Author

EDWARD J. MCCAFFERY HOLDS the Robert C. Packard Trustee Chair in Law, Economics and Political Science at the University of Southern California, Los Angeles, and is a Visiting Professor of Law and Economics at the California Institute of Technology, Pasadena, California. McCaffery is the author of *Taxing Women* (1997), *Fair Not Flat: How to Make the Tax System Better and Simpler* (2002), and co-editor, with Joel Slemrod, of *Behavioral Public Finance* (2006). He has published widely about the law, economics, psychology and philosophy of tax.

Introduction

I DECIDED TO BE BOLD. I am taking this opportunity given to me by Oxford University Press to write a truly short introduction to the United States individual income tax,[1] one that also touches on matters of deep philosophic and political importance. *Mirabile dictu.*

There are plenty of guides to the income tax for students, practitioners, and even for do-it-yourselfers. Few of these are short. I wrote this book to show that tax is essentially a simple subject and one that is important for every citizen to comprehend to some extent. Tax matters too much to leave to the too few people who presently understand it.

If you believe that in order to comprehend the income tax, you must master all of its trees and shrubs and even weeds, the task seems hopeless. It is. The U. S. income tax is mindlessly complex. Even professional practitioners operate in limited areas of tax's vast

---

1. This book focuses on the individual income tax. It does not consider the corporate income tax, which is a separate tax, nor does it consider matters of advanced business taxation within the individual income tax, such as partnership tax (partnerships do not pay tax themselves, but pass on tax liabilities and benefits to their individual partners). Individuals act as employees and sole proprietors, however, so many aspects of business taxation are relevant, especially in Chapter 3. Some readers may consider that other off-stage taxes, such as the corporate income tax, undercut this book's principal theme, namely that the tax system has become a highly burdensome wage tax that largely exempts the income from capital. That conclusion, however, is far from certain. *See* Edward J. McCaffery, "The Uneasy Case for Capital Taxation," in Ellen Frankel Paul, Fred D. Miller, Jr., and Jeffrey Paul, eds., *Taxation, Economic Prosperity, and Distributive Justice,* Cambridge University Press (2006).

forest, fearing malpractice if they stray afield. But I believe that it is not necessary to grasp all of the details to see what is important and essential in tax, to understand the choices we have made and might one day make regarding tax system design.

Thus I have two limited goals for this book. One is to give an outline of tax's forest, where there is a logic, even a simple one. Two is to get across the important theoretical themes that will help the reader understand tax and its wide-ranging effects on society today, and to consider possible futures for tax. To do so, we must keep the basics simple, lest we get blinded by minutia.

Many policy matters will arise along the journey. The most central theme turns on the distinction between *capital* and *labor*, financial property and wages. As Karl Marx knew, all wealth comes from one of these two major factors of production, one's own or someone else's in the case of gifts and other transfers.

Here is the key theme of this book:

The so-called income tax does a reasonably good job at getting at labor income or wages. But it does a very poor job at getting at the returns to capital or savings.

Therein lies a considerable rub. The current U.S. "income" tax is increasingly a wage tax. When combined with other aspects of the tax system—most significantly, the important social security or payroll tax—the income tax puts a large burden on working Americans. At the same time, those with financial capital can escape all taxation with basic planning that you will learn shortly. This is an essential point for understanding not just tax but also social, economic, and political life in America over at least the last half century: it points to the middle-class squeeze and the increasingly luxurious life of the rich, our lack of savings and our excessive borrowing, as well as to the rather severe limitations on political options to change these phenomena.

It is *not* my central ambition to explain how to avoid paying taxes. But I will do so, and with remarkable brevity. Throughout this book, descriptions of the way tax is merge with considerations of tax planning, and both planning and description factor into discussions of tax policy. This is the way it should be. The facts of tax today are in large part responses to planning opportunities past and present. Understanding tax means understanding how taxpayers plan around tax. And any responsible consideration of tax policy must take into account the likely planning reactions of taxpayers to any change.

In fact, let us get started now with some basic tax planning advice. I call Tax Planning 101 the simple advice to:

- Buy,
- Borrow,
- Die.

That is it. I teach my students Tax Planning 101 on the first day of class, in part to prove that I can do so—to show how easy it is for those with financial capital to avoid taxes. Details can follow. The point is that Tax Planning 101 is a handy road map for living a life without taxation—for those with capital. Again, this is not a financial planning book. But if any reader does not understand how easy it is for people with wealth to avoid the income tax, she will not understand tax today. She will also not have meaningful, practicable, and hopeful ideas for tax's reform tomorrow.

The book has three parts.

Part I offers a taste of theory and, with it, a brief overview of the whole of tax.

Part II canvasses the essence of the details of tax. It proceeds, in a logical fashion, to discuss the "journalistic questions":

- *what* (presented both in terms of positive inclusions in "taxable income" and negative deductions or subtractions from it),
- *when*,
- *who*, and
- *how much.*

As we move through this logical progression, I focus on connections: for example, the *what* and the *when* questions often intersect. Timing is also a central dimension of the capital-labor divide. The final chapter in Part II presents the anatomy of a tax shelter, bringing together various doctrinal tools to consider taxpayer attempts to avoid taxes and the tax system's diverse responses to these attempts. Here again, the capital-labor divide will help shed what light there is in tax today.

Part III turns to the future, giving an overview of key issues in contemporary tax policy. The capital-labor divide features prominently once more in potential and likely reforms.

I have tried to keep things simple throughout, even to maintain a conversational tone. Tax is enormously interesting, and can even be fun to learn (keep telling yourself that: it helps). Obviously, many details—trees as well as shrubs and weeds in tax's vast forest—are given short shrift or left missing altogether. Still, you will find all of the important principles to enable you to see the forest. There is a glossary of basic terms at the end of the book. I also list a handful of suggestions for further reading. Finally, I would like to thank my colleague, Ed Kleinbard, for reading a draft of the manuscript, and various research assistants and readers, including Stephan Airapetian, Nicholas Hangca, Kaleb Keller, Rebekah Strawn, June Yang and Olga Zolotnik. All errors of commission and omission are of course mine.

I hope this book inspires readers to learn more about this critically important legal and economic system. Lord knows, tax needs all the help it can get.

⚙ PART ONE

A Taste of Theory

ONE

A View of the Forest

MANY PEOPLE WANT TO CUT to the chase, to get into the details and avoid all abstractions. That is all right sometimes. In trying to understand tax, it is a disaster.

The details of tax are dizzying. You cannot learn the whole by stumbling through the parts and subparts without a map. A basic understanding of tax theory is essential to unlocking the big picture, to see where we are, how we got here, and where we can and might go next.

In this chapter, we take a look at the most important and relevant theoretical aspects of tax, focusing on the tax *base*, or what it is that we are attempting to tax in the first place. We will see how the capital-labor divide sets the major fault line in tax today, between wage earners and property owners. There are two principal sources of income, capital and labor, and the income tax is very porous at getting at capital. The capital-labor divide will be central to most of what we discuss in the pages ahead.

✺ 1.1 The Basic Logic of Tax

Let us start at the beginning. Any tax consists of the product of a base, or the "what" of taxation, and a rate structure, or the "how much" of tax. In short:

$$\text{Tax} = \text{Base} \times \text{Rate}$$

Rates are surprisingly offstage in much of the analysis of tax, in part because their application is pretty much mechanical and comes late in the day on a tax form, after taxable income has been computed (in Section 1.8, below, we will take a quick look at how the annual tax return, Form 1040, organizes matters), and in part, no doubt, because many tax students and even tax lawyers are afraid of numbers. No bother: We will look at tax rates a bit in this chapter, to get some core terms and concepts down, and then again in Chapter 6, when we consider the ordinary income-capital gains distinction, which turns on a difference in tax rates. For the most part, you can learn tax perfectly well with a simple constant rate, such as 30 or 50 percent, in mind.

We also want to know "who" pays taxes, the concept of attribution explored in Chapter 5, and "when" taxes are triggered and due, the matters of timing that feature in Chapter 4. What-when-who-and-how-much forms the basic organization of Part II, where we go systematically through the forest, looking at trees.

Here, in getting a first view of the forest with an emphasis on theory, we focus on the tax base. It turns out that this is where most of the action lies.

🎵 1.2 Three Kinds of Tax

It is time now for some theory. The taxation of capital, or savings, is central to any meaningful consideration of tax today. An income tax is meant to tax savings and its yield. But America and Americans need savings, and so the actual income tax has backed off from its theoretical commitment to always taxing capital. The result is confusion and worse – inefficiency and unfairness result, too.

Let us take a step back. There are three principal *bases* to consider for a comprehensive individual-level tax: wages, spending, and income. There are also wealth and property taxes, and taxes on businesses and entities like the corporate income tax. But by far the bulk of tax revenue in any jurisdiction comes from one of the three former types of taxes—wages, income or spending—each of which falls on a *flow* (as opposed to a *stock* or *store*) of value into or out of a household.

The increasingly important payroll or social security and Medicare tax is a wage tax: it falls only on labor earnings.

State and local sales taxes and value-added taxes (VATs) around the world are spending taxes.

An income tax, the main focus of this book, is meant to fall on *both* wages *and* financial returns: that is, on all flows into a household, from labor or capital or both combined.

Among people who think and write about tax policy, the big fault line is between an income and some form of consumption tax. This has been true for centuries. Now for a surprise: There is an important finding in the tax policy literature that, *at flat or constant tax rates*, and *with normal rates of return,*[1] wage and spending taxes are equivalent: neither tax in effect burdens the returns to savings or capital. Both wage and spending taxes are forms of a consumption tax. They are single taxes on a household's income, whether consumed or saved.

An income tax in contrast is generally considered a "double tax" on savings or capital, because both the initial receipt of the sums that get saved *and* the subsequent yield to savings bear a tax. (If you spend everything you make, you do not get taxed again on the returns to that value.) John Stuart Mill most famously set out this point as a criticism of an income tax in 1848.

Because many economists and policymakers consider a bias against savings to be a large problem with the income tax, for reasons of both fairness and efficiency, critics propose flat wage or sales taxes

---

1. The point about normal rates of returns is more complex than the one about flat or constant tax rates. The idea is that "normally" one gets a return on savings equal to the risk-adjusted rate that everyone else can get. Sometimes people get lucky, however, and receive a "windfall" return, like winning a lottery or buying a spectacularly successful stock at just the right time. A wage tax like the payroll tax ignores these windfall returns; a spending tax captures them.

as a replacement. The "flat tax" popularized in a book written by Robert Hall and Alvin Rabushka[2] is essentially a flat wage tax. The "fair tax" recently touted in a book by Neal Boortz and John Linder[3] is a flat national sales or retail tax. The two taxes are, from an economic point of view, equivalent. Both systems exempt the yield to savings. I explain this a bit more in Section 1.4, below, with an example. In Part III, when we return to tax policy in considering future options for tax, I explain how the use of *progressive marginal rates* changes the analysis. Under such rates, a spending tax is not equivalent to a wage tax.

Here is another important point to understand now: A spending tax need not be levied on transactions, such as sales at cash registers. We can have a spending tax based on an annual form, like the 1040, using progressive rates. We will see that soon, as we continue to consider more thoroughly an income tax.

⁂ 1.3 An Income Tax

An income tax falls on all present period earnings, from "whatever source derived," in the language of the Sixteenth Amendment to the U.S. Constitution and Section 61 of the U.S. Internal Revenue Code (IRC). As Henry Simons put it in an influential definition named after him and his predecessor Robert Murray Haig:

> Income may be defined as the algebraic sum of the market value of the rights exercised in consumption plus the change in value of the store of property rights between the beginning and end of the period in question.[4]

---

2. Robert E. Hall and Alvin Rabushka, *The Flat Tax, 2d edition,* Hoover Institute Press (2007).

3. Neal Boortz and John Linder, *The Fair Tax Book: Saying Goodbye to the Income Tax and the IRS,* Harper Paperbacks (2006).

4. Henry Simons, *The Personal Income Taxation: The Definition of Income as a Problem of Fiscal Policy,* University of Chicago Press (1938), at 50.

There is no need to panic. We can restate the celebrated Haig-Simons definition, in reality a simple accounting relation or tautology, as:

$$Income = Consumption + Savings$$

Fitting this shorthand into the longer verbal definition, consumption is the "market value of the rights exercised in consumption"; savings is "the change in value of the store of property rights between the beginning and end of the period in question."

This basic definition means simply that inputs must equal outputs; sources must equal uses; or that all wealth (Income) must be either spent (Consumption) or not spent (Savings). This is not rocket science.

Nonetheless, great edifices are built on simple foundations. The basic definition identifies sources with uses. The income tax is a classic source-based tax: it looks to add up all receipts into a household. Consider what the sources of income might be, in broad terms: ultimately, payments for labor or for capital, the two great factors of production. (Gifts and other oddities, such as found money, must come from someone else's labor or capital.) We can widen the basic definition to include where the income might have come from:

$$Labor + Capital \rightarrow Income = Consumption + Savings$$

The left-hand side of this expanded basic definition consists of the *sources* that lead to household income, labor and capital; the right-hand side, consumption plus savings, consists of the *uses* which must, again by definition, equal these sources. Note, therefore, that an ideal income tax taxes all *uses* just as much as it taxes all *sources* of individual wealth: the two are equal. Thus certain common objections to any "consumption" tax, such as that consumption is important, the "engine of our economy," or that it is not fair to tax consumption, miss the critical point that the income tax *includes consumption within its base.* Indeed, for the many Americans living paycheck to paycheck, not saving at all, *income is consumption.* We really do not have a choice of taxing consumption or not – we have to, in order to meet the government's vast revenue needs. The real question is how we should tax consumption, not if we should.

҉ 1.4 Two Kinds of Consumption Taxes

As John Stuart Mill first pointed out, an ideal income tax double-taxes savings or capital. You pay tax when you get income. Then when you invest it, and the investment yields additional value, an income tax includes that yield as well. Present consumption avoids this second tax, and thus is favored under a pure income tax over savings.

Tax policy experts consider both wage and spending taxes to be forms of a consumption tax, because each is a *single* tax on wealth that flows through a household. This also explains why, if tax rates are constant and the return on investments is normal, they are equivalent.

A wage tax gets to be a single-tax on savings by exempting capital as a source of income on the left-hand side of the basic definition; it, like an income tax, is source-based, but systematically ignores the returns to financial capital as a source. Recall that:

$$\text{Labor} + \text{Capital} \rightarrow \text{Income}$$

If we ignore the return to capital (i.e., fail to include it in the base), we have a wage tax. Think of the payroll tax, which makes no attempt to tax savings.

A spending tax, on the other hand, exempts savings as a *use*, that is, on the right-hand side of the equation. This follows from a simple rearrangement of the basic definition. If

$$Income = Consumption + Savings,$$

then

$$Consumption = Income - Savings.$$

Think of a common sales tax, which does not apply to money saved in a bank account.

Both wage and spending taxes are, in other words, single taxes on household income, whether saved or spent.

A Simple Numeric Example

For readers who think well using numbers, a simple example helps to see the equivalence of wage and spending taxes. Consider Ant, the iconic saver from storybooks. Suppose Ant earns $200, the tax rate is 50% (for simplicity) and interest on savings is 10%. Ant will save her earnings and spend after two years.

Consider first a wage tax. Ant's $200 is reduced to $100, right away, by the wage tax. She saves this. In Year 1, her $100 grows to $110, at the 10% interest rate. In Year Two, she earns another $11, leaving her with $121 to spend at the end of the year.

Now consider a spending tax. Ant's $200 stays at $200 in her savings account, because she did not spend it. It grows to $220 after one year at 10% interest. In Year Two, Ant earns $22 on her savings, bring her balance to $242. Then she goes to spend this and faces the 50% spending tax, which reduces her amount available for consumption to $121, just as with the wage tax.

There is nothing magic about this example. The equivalence between wage and spending taxes holds with any constant tax rate and normal rates of return, for any length of time. And both are preferable, to a saver like Ant, to an income tax, which would be taxing both the initial receipt of earnings, Ant's $200, *and* the interest she receives on the savings, leaving her worse off, in a real economic sense, than her spendthrift friend Grasshopper.

✷ 1.5 A Common View: The Income Tax as a "Hybrid"

An important reason to consider the alternative tax bases of wage and spending (or what some experts call "prepaid" and "postpaid" consumption taxes, referring to when, in the flow of funds, the tax gets paid: as value enters (wage) or leaves (spending) a household, respectively), is that they are both present *in the current income tax*. The so-called income tax, Title 26 of the U.S. Code, has often been called a "hybrid," because it has elements of a consumption tax within it. It turns out that it has significant elements of *both* types of consumption tax, wage and spending.

Consider traditional Individual Retirement Accounts (IRAs) (IRC Section 408). These work along a spending tax model. You start with your income, say $50,000. If you contribute $4,000 to a qualified IRA, you get to *subtract* this amount from taxable income. You pay tax, now, on $50,000 minus $4,000, or $46,000. This follows the form of Income – Savings = Consumption. The money in the IRA, meanwhile, sits there, growing tax-free, until you withdraw it, when tax is due. This is single-tax, consumption, spending tax treatment: you pay tax later, not now, and just once. It is like Ant in the second part of the prior example.

Next consider the more modern "Roth-style IRAs" (IRC Section 408A), now the most common template for pro-savings plans in the Code. You get no deduction for the contribution to the IRA, but as long as the ever-present rules and requirements are met you never pay tax again. You do not pay tax on the increase in value of the account, even on withdrawal. This is wage tax treatment: pay tax now, not later, and just once. It is like Ant in the first part of the prior example.

These two routes lead to the same place, given constant tax rates and normal investment returns.

Why, then has Congress been favoring the Roth-style approach, adding more and more provisions—for retirement, health, and educational savings accounts—along these lines? Never forget in learning about tax that the government is a player in all that is done. Under Roth-style accounts, the government gets its one tax *now*, which is better, in an age of budget deficits, fiscal constraints, and ten year "budget windows," than later—better, that is, for the government.

An income tax, in contrast to either form of consumption tax, taxes savings both when the initial earnings come into the household and when the nonconsumed wealth—which is what savings is—generates an additional yield. If you earn $50,000 and save $4,000, there is no deduction for the $4,000 under a pure income tax. It is part of what you are taxed on. If the $4,000 generates interest of $400, at a 10% rate, you pay income tax on that, as well.

One more turn of the screw: the kind of hybrid tax that simply mixes and matches wages, spending, and income tax bases makes little sense, and leads to a great deal of complexity without obvious good effect, as we will see shortly.

ℳ 1.6 The Real Story: The Income Tax as a Wage Tax

Ready for another surprise?

What you thought was an income tax when you picked up this book, and what you have just read described as a hybrid income-consumption tax is, in fact, largely a *wage* tax!

This is because the failure to include the yield to capital in the "income" tax base is quite systematic. And in what may come as yet one more surprise, the conscious, deliberate pro-savings policies mentioned above, like IRAs, are but a part—and a small part—of the story. The real story goes back to Tax Planning 101, and to the deep structural aspects of the Tax Code that make it easy for those with financial capital to avoid paying all tax.

Let us consider all this in turn.

1.6.1 Tax Planning 101

Three features built deeply into the fabric of the income tax—and rarely seriously questioned by legislators—conspire to make the tax into a virtual wage tax, where any taxation on capital is largely voluntary. These features are outlined as the following steps.

Step One of tax planning, the realization requirement from, among other sources, the celebrated 1920 U.S. Supreme Court case of *Eisner v. Macomber*, 252 U.S. 189, holds that the change in value of an existing asset is not income until and unless the gain is realized through a sale or other disposition.

This is a big deal. Professor William Andrews of Harvard Law School has famously called the realization requirement the "Achilles' heel" of the income tax. As a former classicist, I can remind you that Achilles died because of his mother's failure to protect his heel. You need not take my word for it, or listen to any academic sort at all. You can hear it straight from Robert Kiyosaki's huge best-seller, *Rich Dad/Poor Dad*:

> You must know the difference between an asset and a liability, and buy assets. If you want to be rich, this is all you need to know. It is rule no. 1, it is the only rule . . . It sure beats saving $100 a month, which actually starts off as $150 because it's after-tax income, for 40 years at 5 percent, and again you're taxed on the 5 percent. That is not too intelligent. It may be safe, but it's not smart.[5]

There are two pieces of critically important advice here.

The first is to buy assets rather than getting paid wages: that is, to get on the capital side of the capital-labor divide. This is because

---

5. Robert Kiyosaki (with Sharon Lechter), Rich Dad/Poor Dad: *What the Rich Teach Their Kids about Money—That the Poor and Middle Class Do Not!*, Warner (1997).

wages are taxed. In Rich Dad's example, the $150 of earnings was reduced to $100 under a 33 percent tax rate.

The second is to save in a form that avoids current taxation. "Ordinary" savings, such as those kept in a simple bank account, fall smack into the double-tax sting of the income tax. By *buying assets that rise in value without triggering taxable gains*—real estate works pretty well here—one gets to grow wealthy without taxation. This is Rich Dad's "rule no. 1," the "only rule." It leads people to invest in, and the economy to provide, non-cash-producing assets, such as real estate and Internet stocks: two asset classes prone to spectacular bubbles. The somewhat obscure debate over "carried interest" by hedge fund managers and private equity investors is all about the attempt by these highly compensated individuals to argue that their remuneration is "capital"—taxed at favorable capital gains rates when it is taxed at all.

You might be thinking that this is all fine and good, but how does one eat the kind of unrealized appreciation that following Step One generates? This question points to one of many ways in which the realization requirement seems intuitive, and even fair. How can people pay tax without a sale to generate cash with which to pay the tax? The answer, to Rich Dad, is easy. Here comes Step Two of Tax Planning 101: borrow.

Debt or borrowing is not income under the basic definition of income. When you borrow, there is no change in your net worth, no income, no "change in value of the store of property rights": the cash borrowed is offset by the liability to repay the debt. Under today's income tax, you can borrow against your unrealized appreciation from an asset and spend away, tax-free. This gets us to the real, deep problem that Tax Planning 101 poses today: *consumption financed by debt is income-tax free.*

This feature of tax factors into many recent financial crises. The U.S. tax system gives a large incentive to borrow and build up high degrees of leverage. Combine high debt levels with non-cash-producing assets and throw in any kind of fall in values, and it is easy to attain financial meltdown on a global scale. We have seen this with the Internet bubble of the 1990s, and the housing and credit crises of more recent vintage. Behind many great financial disasters lies a tax story.

You may be saying, fair enough, I will buy and borrow, but do I not have to pay tax eventually? Not so fast. Here is the final step, Step Three, in Tax Planning 101: die. The built-in gain, or the difference between the fair market value of an asset and its tax *basis*, which had been allowed to grow untaxed under the realization requirement of Step One, disappears on death, Step Three. "Basis" is an important word in the U.S. income tax, and we will encounter it often in the pages ahead. For now, consider that basis is initially the cost of an asset. If Ant bought stock for $1,000, and could not deduct that amount, she would have basis in the stock of $1,000. As the stock rose in value, to say $5,000, Ant's basis would stay at $1,000. The difference between the fair market value, $5,000, and Ant's basis, $1,000 – that is, $4,000 – would not be taxable, under the realization requirement, until and unless Ant sold or otherwise disposed of the stock. Ant would be holding the stock with a *built-in* gain, what I colloquially call a "tax time bomb," of $4,000. The point of Step Three, die, in buy/borrow/die is that this built-in gain *goes away on death*. The heirs take an asset with a "stepped-up" basis equal to its fair market value; Ant's children would get stock worth $5,000 with a basis of $5,000. The kids can inherit your asset, sell it, and pay off your debts—all tax-free. The circle is complete.[6]

---

6. Under the strange political tale of the gift and estate tax, there was, briefly, no estate tax and a carryover basis regime in place for the single year, 2010. The carryover basis component of this law was especially unpopular. When Congress and President Obama finally decided to clarify the situation for at least the two years 2011–2012, they gave taxpayers an option, retroactively, to use stepped-up basis for 2010. This parallels a story from Jimmy Carter's presidency in the 1970s. Congress voted to replace stepped-up basis with carryover basis on death, but the law never took effect, and was retroactively repealed under President Reagan. Stepped-up basis on death, like the other planks in Tax Planning 101—and like the home mortgage interest and other personal deductions discussed—appears to have attained the status of a "sacred cow" in tax.

These three features of the income tax together form *Tax Planning 101*. This is my own coinage, the simple tax planning doctrine that I teach tax students on the first day of a course in basic federal income taxation, and which I have explained in a few short pages here:

- Buy
- Borrow
- Die

That is it. By buying capital assets that appreciate without producing taxable dividends, borrowing to finance present consumption, and continuing the game straight onto death, the rich can avoid all federal taxes. Rich Dad, Warren Buffet, Bill Gates, and countless others among the rich and famous have figured this all out, perfectly well.

Tax Planning 101 avoids *all federal taxes*. It avoids the income tax because of the three doctrines just noted. It avoids the increasingly important social security or payroll tax system by the simple expedient of never actually working. It avoids the estate tax because that is a net tax, on assets minus liabilities held at death. If Tax Planning 101 is taken to its limits, there is no net estate. Tax Planning 101 means no taxes, notwithstanding a comfortable lifestyle for those with the assets in hand to play it. Those, that is, who live on the capital side of the capital-labor divide.

1.6.2 Beyond Tax Planning 101

I cannot tell you how many rich Americans take Tax Planning 101 to its limit, paying no taxes. I can tell you that the advice is widely available, as from Rich Dad, and that I know from my time as a real-world tax lawyer that many wealthy individuals and families follow this blueprint. Yet because the rich are few and secretive, putting a number on the bottom-line consequences of Tax Planning

101 is elusive. But this is not my point, or the idea to get across in this short introduction. There can be no doubt about the analytic facts of the matter, that is, about the legal steps in Tax Planning 101's buy/borrow/die advice. This is basic tax. Any real-world tax lawyer or accountant who does not understand the simple steps in buy/borrow/die would be committing malpractice every day of her professional life. The very existence of the legal structure raises troubling questions of both fairness and efficiency.

The mere facts of Tax Planning 101—*not* the breadth of its actual incidence—constrain important matters of practical tax design. Features such as low capital gains tax rates on realization, the subject of Chapter 6, follow from the current regime. There is simply no good way, under the current income tax, heavily to burden capital, given that people can avoid all taxation by not selling their assets and playing Tax Planning 101. If taxpayers are not flocking to advisers to avoid a 15 percent capital gains tax (which is what we have as I write), would they not do so at a 40 or 50 percent level? Evidence that some taxpayers pay some capital gains taxes at the favorable rates that persist today does not contradict the fact that these are, indeed, favorable capital gains rates. The present structure of tax haunts the possibilities for its better future.

Low capital gains rates are not the only feature of tax that follows from the realization requirement and the mere possibilities of Tax Planning 101. Many aspects of tax do. For example, consider residential housing. When you buy a house, and it goes up in value—as we normally expect that it will and as, for the most part, it has—you do not pay tax on that "mere appreciation." Houses, like many assets, become holdings with large built-in gain. This discourages people from selling their houses and moving into bigger houses, or into a different geographic area to follow a good job prospect. What to do? For many years, the law allowed people who sold a home and bought another to "roll over" the gain into the new house. Good enough, but what happens when the kids leave the nest, and mom and dad want to retire to a smaller home in a sunnier clime? OK, thought Congress, we will allow a one-time exemption from taxing gain in a residence for taxpayers older than 55. More complexity followed. Finally, under President Clinton, Congress said let us more or less forget the whole thing, and allow up to $500,000 of gain to be tax-free pretty much anytime a couple sells a house. IRC Section 121. Within a few years, a major residential real estate bubble had ballooned out and then popped. *Sic transit gloria mundi.*

I could go on and on—I have gone on, in more scholarly treatments elsewhere, in fact—pointing out aspects of the status quo that follow from the possibilities of Tax Planning 101. I am keeping things simple here. And the simple point is this: once you have made it very easy for a great deal of capital appreciation to escape tax, as via Tax Planning 101, it is both difficult and questionable policy to keep *any* capital in the tax base directly, at all. Thus we see a very light hand on the capital side of the capital-labor divide. And then once you have *that*, if you are a government that needs vast sums to feed itself—and what government these days does not?— you had better be very mindful about maintaining a *heavy* hand on the labor side of the divide, or you have nothing left to tax. This is what we see in tax today.

1.6.3 The Income Tax, Take Two: Ad Hoc Deviations

Tax Planning 101 consists of three deep structural features of the so-called income tax. Running side-by-side with these features are deliberate pro-savings provisions, such as pension plans and IRAs. These have been features of the income tax since the 1950s. Such pro-savings mechanisms result from a deliberate rejection of the income-tax model. Policymakers want to encourage savings, want to avoid Mill's double-tax sting. These pro-savings policies are at once interesting and paradoxical.

They are interesting because they point to conflicting principles about taxing savings, a theme I shall pick up later in Part III. They show, in short, that "we" the people do not want to double-tax savings, all the time, as a pure income tax would.

The ad hoc pro-savings features are problematic because, in short, they do not work under an income tax with a realization requirement. Neither wage- nor spending-based pro-savings provisions give any reason at all to suggest that they will be helpful in generating *new* savings, and certainly are unlikely to do so among the middle classes at whom they seem to be aimed.

An income tax is *designed* to double-tax savings. Trying to exempt savings while keeping an income tax thus makes little if any sense. Most damaging, for example, is the fact that because one can borrow tax-free under an income tax, there is no logical assurance that savings will in fact increase with any nominal pro-savings provision within such a tax—and there is good evidence that savings has not increased with the panoply of nominal pro-savings provisions in the Code. A taxpayer can open up a traditional IRA, on the spending tax model, with $4,000, using one hand, and borrow $4,000 on a credit card, using the other. There is no savings in such a situation, but the taxpayer has gotten a tax savings, today, on account of the deduction for the IRA.[7]

Retirement savings—which, along with home equity, are the major assets for most Americans who have any assets at all (and most Americans do not) are taxed primarily on the spending tax model; a taxpayer gets a deduction when she puts money into a tax-favored account, and she pays tax when she withdraws funds from the account. Because of the tax deduction on contribution, there is no tax basis in the accounts – no tax has been paid on the contribution. Withdrawals are fully taxable, at ordinary income rates.

---

7. Some people object that the interest paid on the debt, which will generally be non-deductible under IRC Section 163 and 262 (see Chapter Three), is a cost of this simple strategy. But one gets interest on the savings of $4,000 as well. If the two are equal, this is a "wash." Of course if the interest rate on the debt is higher than the return on savings, the taxpayer is losing real money over time. Why might anyone do such a thing? Perhaps because he is *myopic*, or short-sighted, and values the tax deduction today more highly than the tax owed, tomorrow. Note that in such a case the supposedly pro-savings tax provision has led to a *reduction* in savings, as the short-sighted taxpayer gets deeper in debt.

A growing trend in contemporary tax policy has been to allow an option for taxpayers to choose a retirement savings plan structured under a wage tax model, such as the Roth IRA. Under these variations, there is no tax deduction up front, and there is no back-ended tax on withdrawal. Such wage tax savings plans avoid the tax-planning problem just noted: there is no reason to borrow funds with one hand in order to save with the other, since there is no immediate tax benefit to savings (or to pretend savings). The policy problem with such accounts is that they provide no assistance to *new* savings. Taxpayers with existing stores of capital can simply open up Roth-style accounts, subject to certain ceilings and so forth, and need never worry about paying tax on their investment returns again. This means that those with capital no longer need fancy tools or advisers to help them play Tax Planning 101. But for those working and living paycheck to paycheck—those living on the labor side of the great divide—there is no immediate aid to their cash flow if they try to save today, because there is no up-front deduction for the savings.

Moving toward a wage tax model has a deeper cost. The single tax under a wage tax falls due at the time of labor market earnings, typically when a worker has peak income and hence is in her most highly taxable years. As such—because there is no way to escape the burden of wage taxation—Roth-style tax savings plans are in tension with highly sloping marginal tax rates.[8]

Rates in general have gone up from their lows in the 1980s: from a top marginal rate of 28 or 33 percent under Ronald Reagan, to 39.6 percent under Bill Clinton, and then down again, to 35 percent, under George W. Bush, where they have remained under Barack Obama as

---

8. In theory, an income tax could solve this problem by employing a system of "income averaging," whereby taxpayers paid tax in any given year based on some average income over many years. The income tax once had such a mechanism in it. But it is complex, and raises many questions. One appeal of a progressive spending tax, considered again in Part III, is that for most people spending is far smoother than income or earnings – people use borrowing and savings to smooth out their consumption over a lifetime.

I write. But these rates essentially *only apply to wages.* Taxes on capital, when they come due at all, have gone down: capital gains are now taxed at 15 percent, and corporate dividends have been added to this low-rate category. Payroll taxes do not even attempt to apply to financial transactions. Meanwhile, more and more tax-favored savings provisions have been set up along the wage tax model, making it even easier for those who do save to pay no taxes at all, while doing nothing to help those millions of wage earners living paycheck to paycheck, hand to mouth, to save in the first place.

🌺 1.7 Tax Rates

We have so far been considering the tax base. Once you have the base or "what" of taxation down, it is time to apply tax rates to come up with tax owed.

Tax rates form a function over the relevant range: income, wages, or spending, depending on the base. These rates can be progressive, meaning increasing; flat or proportionate; or regressive, meaning decreasing—and, indeed, can be all three of these shapes over differing ranges of the base.

There are two different meanings of "tax rates." The income tax in the United States and in most developed nations around the world depends on a system of *progressive marginal rates* that work like a step function. Thus, and to simplify, for a family of four, there might be a "0 bracket" reaching up to $20,000; a 15 percent bracket extending from $20,000 to $60,000; and a 30 percent bracket over $60,000, as presented in Table 1:

TABLE 1 Sample Marginal Rate Schedule

Income	Marginal Tax Rate
$0 - $20,000	0%
$20,000 - $60,000	15%
Over $60,000	30%

This means that the family's "first" $20,000 is not taxed, and their "next" $40,000—the income that takes them from $20,000 to $60,000—is taxed at 15 percent. It does not mean that all of the family's income is taxed at 15 percent. So, for example, a family making $40,000 would pay $3,000 in taxes under this simplified rate structure: 0 on their first $20,000, plus 15 percent of $40,000–$20,000.

Average or (equivalently) effective tax rates, in contrast, equal the total taxes paid by a taxpayer divided by her income or other base. Using the same simplified example from Table 1, above, a family of four would face an average tax rate of 0 on their first $20,000 of income. At $30,000 of income, the family would pay $1,500 in taxes (15 percent of $30,000–$20,000), for an average tax rate of 5 percent ($1,500/$30,000); at $40,000, the family would pay $3,000 in taxes, as calculated above, for an average tax of 7.5 percent ($3,000/$40,000).

⅙ 1.8 Following the Tax Form

Coming back down to earth, what we have just considered actually tracks the flow of a basic tax return form, such as the dreaded 1040. You begin on the front page with adding up all of your sources of "income"—wages, interest, rents, profits from a business, capital gains and so on. This follows IRC Section 61, matters considered in Chapter Two. You next subtract whatever *deductions* you are allowed to take, the subject of Chapter 3. This leaves you with a *net taxable income*, your personal tax base, what you are being taxed on. You next apply the rate structure to come up with a tax owed, then subtract out any *credits* to which you are entitled. You mail in a check or get a refund for the balance. Along the way, you have at least implicitly taken into account the rules on timing (Chapter Four), attribution or the "who" of tax (Chapter Five), and capital gains (Chapter Six). We will go back and take another look at the flow and logic of the basic 1040 form in Chapter Three, once we have some more details under our belts.

✺ 1.9 The Goals of Tax Planning

What we have learned will feature heavily in Part III, when we consider options for tax reform. We can imagine various strategies for mixing and matching wage, spending, and income taxes, crossing them with flat or progressive rates. Indeed, I shall argue, as I have elsewhere, that a progressive spending tax is the last best hope for progressivity in tax, for people who desire such a thing.

The basic conceptual apparatus will also feature prominently in Part II, as we seek to understand tax today.

There are two senses in which one can "understand" tax. The good student will want to take a stab at both. One is to comprehend the rules as a descriptive or static matter, looking backward as it were, at any particular moment in time: to be able to apply the law to preexistent, given facts, as in a typical law school "issue spotting" exam. A second sense is to understand tax as a *dynamic* matter, to be able to apply the rules to *developing* facts, as a tax planner does. You will not really comprehend tax unless you have some sense of the dynamic interplay between law and behavior. You will not be able to understand what taxpayers *did* do unless you can put yourselves into their shoes, and figure out what they *wanted* to do. You will also not make nearly as much money from your understanding of tax law without the ability to put what you have learned into a dynamic, planning context.

Fortunately, the basic goals of tax planning are pretty basic.

It all starts with the simple fact that almost all people like money. Tax is anti-money: it is money that you have some claim to, for some period of time, which the government comes and takes away. So most people do not like taxes, although all seem to like the civilization that taxes purchase. Forget this at your peril.

Given that, the best thing is for a taxpayer to *escape* tax altogether, forever. One easy way to escape taxes is never to make or spend any material resources or wealth in the first place. You could lie on the beach or live on an island. But that is not much fun, for most of us, or we lack the skills to make it fun, or, at the very least, those of us who are ready, willing, and able to soak up purely psychic income do not need this book or tax planners to help us do so.

Thus when I talk about the first goal of tax planning, to *escape* tax, I shall hereafter mean to gain *economic* income or value without paying tax: to have your cake and eat it, tax-free, too. That is the holy grail of tax planning. Tax Planning 101 is an important example of how to obtain it. We will see more in Chapters 2 and 3.

Escape is just one, albeit the best, game to play. If one does have to pay tax, it is also typically true that *later is better than sooner*. (The major exception to this rule is if you think tax rates are going to go up, because of a change either in the law or in your own personal financial circumstances, you may want to pay tax sooner under today's lower rates.) The second goal of tax planning is thus to *defer*, or put off the day of reckoning as long as possible. We will see that in Chapter 4.

If you do have to pay tax, and you have to pay it now, the game of tax planning is still not over. There is the question of *who* is going to pay tax. For the third goal of tax planning, you are going to want to *shift* the responsibility of paying tax to some person or entity at a lower tax rate than your own. Now we are in the realm of the typical "you" here, not some saint. You are going to want to shift the responsibility of paying tax without actually changing what you do with "your" wealth or income. After all, signing a vow of poverty and giving away all of your income, like lying about on the beach, is another way to avoid any and all taxes. But such people do not make for high-paying clients. The game in income-shifting is to use relatives or family businesses to move around income without changing the economics—just lowering the total tax paid. We will see this in Chapter 5.

Finally, for goal four of tax planning, if you have to pay tax, and pay it now, and it is you who are going to have to pay, you will still want to *recharacterize* your taxable income, to *convert* it so as to pay tax at the—much lower—capital gains rates, 15 percent as compared with 35 percent as I write. We will consider this in Chapter 6.

These, then, are the goals of tax planning:

- Escape,
- Defer,
- Shift,
- Recharacterize or Convert.

Note another surprise, and one of the fun things in tax: everything is turned on its head if you are dealing with an item of loss, that is, negative income. Then you will want to create, not escape; accelerate, not defer; shift to (or up) not away from (or down); and convert to a higher not lower rate, ordinary rather than capital.

And of course it should go without saying that the government or IRS is in the opposite position of taxpayers, yet again: they want to create or accelerate items of income, and escape or defer matters of loss, and so on.

ℳ 1.10 The Capital-Labor Divide, Redux

We are ready for the coup de grâce, the last surprise in what I hope was a chapter of surprises:

Everything we just learned about tax planning is easy if you have capital, or financial wealth, and increasingly difficult if you do not.

Most important, Tax Planning 101 is a strategy for escape. Rich Dad using this strategy needs not pay tax. Yet he has plenty of real economic income to enjoy.

Owning property also makes it very easy to defer tax. In Tax Planning 101, Rich Dad holds his assets until death and never pays tax. This is the limiting case. Holding for years and then selling is an easy and effective way to defer tax and hence lower the real effective tax burden.

It is also very easy for those with capital to shift, as by giving appreciated property to one's kids and letting them sell it.

Finally, selling property is the canonical example of a transaction entitling one to capital gains, with their lower tax rate.

All of this is hard and getting harder if you have wages, living on the labor side of the divide.

The law makes it difficult, outside of a few exceptions blessed by explicit statute (such as employer-provided health insurance), not to pay tax on income received from an employer. There is a practical component to this as well, as the employer will report to the government, on W-2 forms, exactly what your taxable wages are. There is not much room for cheating here. Why do employers do this? Aside from following the law, their own ability to deduct wages paid turns on their reporting them to the government. Self-interest is a powerful force in tax compliance as it is elsewhere in life.

Again, absent a clear statutory exception, as in the qualified pension plans, wage income cannot be deferred.

Wage income cannot be shifted, either.

And wages are the canonical example of *ordinary* income, taxable at maximum rates.

So there you have it, what Rich Dad already knew: People who work for wages pay taxes, and at fairly high rates; people with capital need not pay any tax, and pay at lower rates when they do pay. This stark capital-labor divide shall be with us throughout our short introduction.

⅏ 1.11 Summary

Here is what we have learned thus far:

- Any tax consists of a base, the "what" of taxation, times a rate structure, the "how much;"
- In addition to what and how much, "when" and "who" are important basic questions in designing a tax system;
- There are three principal choices for a comprehensive individual level tax base: wages, spending, and income;

- The basic definition of Income, the most commonly thought of tax base, tells us that Income = Consumption + Savings;
- We can expand this basic definition to consider the basic sources of income, giving us Capital + Labor → Income = Consumption + Savings;
- A pure income tax is a "double tax" on savings;
- The double-tax critique has led many to advocate consumption taxes of various sorts;
- One type of consumption tax is a wage tax, which simply does not include the yield to savings in the tax base;
- A second type of consumption tax is a spending tax, which operates along the lines of a simple rearrangement of the basic definition, as Consumption = Income − Savings. Such a spending tax features an unlimited deduction for savings;
- Wage and spending taxes are essentially equivalent, given constant tax rates and normal rates of investment returns;
- The actual so-called income tax contains elements of both wage taxes (such as Roth IRAs) and spending taxes (such as traditional IRAs), leading many to call it a "hybrid" tax. In fact, it is a pretty incoherent mess;
- Many people believe that the *reason* to have a consumption tax, of one or the other sort, is to avoid ever taxing savings. This leads to calls for wage taxes and *flat-rate* spending taxes, which in fact have been common proposals in the United States;
- Under the actual income tax, it is fairly easy to avoid paying additional tax on one's savings, most importantly via Tax Planning 101, the simple advice to Buy/Borrow/Die. Tax Planning 101 in turn opens up a Pandora's box, leading to the widespread ability to avoid or pay minimal taxes on the yield to capital. It is not just our say-so; Robert Kiyosaki's Rich Dad knows this, too;
- This makes the so-called income tax largely a wage tax. When added to the payroll tax system, we have a high wage tax and little effective taxation of capital in America. This explains the

Warren Buffet paradox, whereby his secretary pays tax at a higher rate than he does;

- The goals of tax planning are to:
    - escape,
    - defer,
    - shift, and
    - recharacterize or convert;
- All of these goals are easily obtained today for those with capital, but difficult or impossible to obtain for those living off labor returns;
- Tax is fun (remember?).

PART TWO

The Details

TWO

The "What" of Taxation, Part One
Inclusions in the Tax Base

WE NOW START in on the project of understanding the income tax the way it is, tracking the basic logic of tax, following the flow of a tax return form. We start with the tax base, or the "what" of taxation—which, in the case of the individual income tax, means getting a sense of what "income" means.

Income comes mainly from labor, capital, or both combined. We are learning that the so-called income tax is only really effective in getting at income from labor. The income tax does a poor job of getting at income from capital. It is thus critical to the government that the individual income tax include payments for labor as thoroughly as possible. Wages make up the major part of gross domestic product (GDP) on the sources side of the basic equation, Income = Consumption + Savings. If the government were to let wages slide out of the tax base, there would be virtually nothing left to tax. By parallel reasoning, when we turn to *subtractions* from income in Chapter Three, we will see that personal consumption must not be allowed out of the base or, again, there would be little left to tax, now looking to the uses or right-hand side of the basic equation.

And so, in a nutshell, while tax on the returns to financial capital can be easily avoided, taxes on wages are hard to avoid. The government seeks to tax compensation whether in cash or in noncash form, to do so currently, to the earner, at ordinary rates, and to shut down all attempts to "shelter" such labor income from tax. All of the goals of tax planning—escape, defer, shift, convert—are challenging, if not quite impossible, when it comes to ordinary wage income.

This chapter looks at the base of the income tax as a positive matter, that is, what gets *included* in it. This is a gross concept. Chapter Three considers what gets taken out, or subtracted, from the base. Together, these two chapters take us to the net concept of actually taxable income.

A Tip: Reading the Code. Spend some time with the Table of Contents to the Internal Revenue Code. You will find a surprising order. The good news is that, for learning basic tax, you do not need to consider many Code Sections, and the ones that you really must know cluster together in a logical pattern. In the Appendix, I have prepared a chart of what I take to be the one hundred most important Code Sections for learning tax, and, to further simplify, my personal Top Ten list. Others will disagree here and there. You may not get to all these Code Sections in a class on income taxation, and you may consider others. But a key point is that the very *order* of the Sections in the Code is a helpful guide to understanding tax. Tax rates are discussed beginning in Section 1, and the tax base beginning in Section 61, the key statutory definition of income.

🎐 2.1 Three Definitions of Income

We call what we have an "income tax." It would be nice to have a handy definition of "income."

Alas, we get no such luck. This Section looks at three *types* of definition of income, coming from the U.S. Constitution and statutes; judicial decisions; and the academy, respectively. At the end of it, we will still not exactly have a precise definition of "income." We will be left instead with more of a "we'll know it when we see it" approach. This is the sense that tax professionals carry about with them every day.

2.1.1 Constitutional and Statutory Definitions

The Sixteenth Amendment, ratified in 1913, gives Congress the power to tax "all incomes, from whatever source derived, without regard to apportionment among the several States." This was an important amendment, although for reasons that are now somewhat obscure.

The United States had an income tax in place briefly during the Civil War and then again in the progressive era of the 1890s. The Supreme Court struck down the latter tax, in the case of *Pollock v. Farmers Loan & Trust Co.*, 157 U.S. 429, affirmed on rehearing, 158 U.S. 601 (1895). The Court held that the inclusion of *capital* gains and interest, dividends, and the like violated the Constitution's prohibition on any "capitation or other direct tax" without "apportionment." U.S. Constitution Art. I, Section 9. This was an early sign of the capital-labor divide. Article I's constitutional provision was meant to ensure that a majority of states did not gang up on a minority, as by imposing a tax on Wall Street banks, dairy farms—or slaves—which would affect citizens of only some states and hence might easily garner a majority vote of the others.

Almost all scholars now think that the fuss over direct and indirect taxes was inapt. Congress can pretty much tax whatever it wants. Still, the constitutional background played a role in the seminal *Macomber* case, discussed above and below.

The trouble is that the Sixteenth Amendment hardly defines "income." In fact, it does not even try. It just states that Congress has the power to tax "incomes, from whatever source derived" and leaves it at that.

We turn next to the statute. IRC Section 61, one of the most commonly cited and important Code Sections, is the "definition" of gross income. "Gross" does not mean yucky, although things get messy enough in tax. It means the widest sense of income, before deductions that will lead us to a net taxable income concept, the subject of Chapter Three. Section 62 gives us adjusted gross income, basically gross income minus business expenses (along with other "above the line" deductions).[1] Section 63 gives us taxable income, or adjusted gross income minus further, mainly personal, deductions, and which is the actual base that gets taxed.

The trouble is, once again, that Section 61 hardly gives us a definition of "income." It begins as follows:

> Except as otherwise provided in this subtitle, gross income means all income from whatever source derived, including (but not limited to) the following items:

This opening language is then followed by a list, now including fifteen enumerated categories, of various items of "income." The most important of these items are, in the Code's wording and numbering:

(1) Compensation for services, including fees, commissions, fringe benefits, and similar items;
(2) Gross income derived from business;
(3) Gains derived from dealings in property;
(4) Interest;
(5) Rents;
(6) Royalties; and
(7) Dividends . . .

The list gives a good sense of the matter, the comprehensiveness with which the Code is trying to set out "income." It should come as no surprise both that the first listed item is "compensation for services"—the labor side of the great divide—and that this item is set forth expansively, as including "fees, commissions, fringe benefits, and similar items." This is a major theme, again: a solicitude for including *labor* compensation in all its possible forms as income.

---

1. "Above the line" refers to a line on the tax return, Form 1040. Once one has calculated adjusted gross income, or A.G.I, she faces a choice "below the line" to take the standard deduction or to "itemize" her deductions instead. This is all explained later.

Yet Section 61 is not a definition at all. The "flush" or introductory language states that "gross income means all income from whatever source derived." That is not a definition—it is a *circle*. Stripped of adjectives, modifiers, and phrases, it says simply that "income means income." Surely we know *that*, even without yet having mastered this short introduction.

What is going on? The keys to understanding Section 61 lie in two aspects: one, its deliberate *failure* to define "income," and, two, its sense of all-encompassing breadth. I have commented above on the former. As for the latter, note the very opening words, "except as otherwise provided." Congress is here laying out a *default*, the sense that anything that looks like income *is* income, unless *and only unless* there is a clear statutory exception (more on this anon).

Could it be any clearer that Congress means to give itself the power to tax anything that might conceivably be income? Actually, it can. Consider Treasury Regulation Section 1.61-1(a),[2] which states in full:

> *General Definition*—Gross income means all income from whatever source derived, unless excluded by law. Gross income includes income realized in any form, whether in money, property, or services. Income may be realized, therefore, in the form of services, meals, accommodations, stock, or other property, as well as in cash. Section 61 lists the more common items of gross income for purposes of illustration. For purposes of further illustration, Section 1.61-14 mentions

---

2. Treasury Regulations are generated by the administrative agency enforcing and interpreting the laws, namely the IRS and Treasury Department. After an initial digit, the next numbers follow the statute or Internal Revenue Code. Thus Treasury Regulation Section 1.61 falls under Section 61 of the IRC. Regulations can be "interpretive" or "legislative." Legislative regulations are those passed under an explicit statutory grant, as where the statute refers to regulations to be enacted to implement its meaning. Interpretive regulations, the older and more common form, are meant to explain and illustrate how the IRS views the statute. The Regulation quoted in the text is an interpretive one.

several miscellaneous items of gross income not listed specifically in section 61. *Gross income, however, is not limited to
the items so enumerated.* (emphasis supplied).

Got it? In this highly repetitious, belt-and-suspenders approach,
we see the government stressing, over and over again, that it has *not*
given a formal, exclusive definition of income. Regulation Section
1.61-14, referred to in Section 1.61-1, continues and underlines the
theme by noting several more items of "income," such as "treble
damages under the antitrust laws"—the subject of the *Glenshaw
Glass* case, to be discussed later—"illegal gains," and, my personal
favorite, "treasure trove, to the extent of its value in United States
currency."

The idea is clear. The law means to capture all "income," without
ever committing itself to a specific definition of what that means.

2.1.2 Judicial Definitions

Neither the Constitution nor the statute—by design—are very helpful in defining "income." We might expect judges to rush in to fill the
void. This is, indeed, what we got—with mixed results.

The most important early definition of "income" came from
Eisner v. Macomber, decided in 1920. No case is more important in
the history of tax.

Macomber produced a definition of income. It had to, or so
the Justices thought. They took the question—literally and narrowly, whether the IRS could tax a stock-on-stock dividend,[3] or the

---

3. A stock-on-stock dividend occurs when a company transfers additional shares
of stock to its current shareholders. In the typical case of a pro-rata distribution, this affects the numbers of shares one holds but not their combined value.
If Marge owned 10 shares of Z Corp, worth $100 each, her holdings would be
worth $1,000. If Z Corp distributed one share for each share held, Marge would
now have 20 shares of Z Corp stock. But, given that every other shareholder saw

antecedent gain in the stock at the time of the dividend—as being a question of "what is income." The question came down to whether the *change in value of an existing asset* could be "income." If "mere" appreciation were "income," Congress could tax it, under the Sixteenth Amendment; if it were not, we would be back to the need to apportion among the states, in the manner of the Constitution's Article I, Section 9.

The majority sought to define "income." They did so by first looking to dictionaries, then to prior case law. Finally they came up with the following:

> Income may be defined as the gain derived from capital or from labor or from both derived.

The *Macomber* definition is enormously interesting. We clearly see the capital-labor divide. The Court was obviously influenced by the constitutional and statutory language looking to "whatever source derived." Most important, the definition connects the *what* question with the *when* one, through the "derived from" language.

Derivation from is a temporal phenomenon, a matter of timing: there can be no gain, *yet*, until there is some "derivation from" capital or labor or both combined. Hence the *realization requirement* comes from *Macomber*: the rise in value of an existing asset is *not* income, until and unless there has been some "derivation from," some *realization* of the gain. This seemingly innocuous rule got Tax

---

a doubling of his or her number of shares, too, Marge's Z Corp holdings would still be worth $1,000—the stock-on-stock dividend cannot, in itself, create value in Z Corp. Each share of Z Corp stock would now be worth $5, one-half of what it was worth before the doubling of shares. When the government in arguing *Macomber* came to see this point, it switched gears and argued that it was not the stock dividend itself it was attempting to tax – it was simply using this event as a convenient time to tax. Then the focus turned to the appreciation of the stock since Mrs. Macomber first acquired it. This argument, too, ended badly for the government.

Planning 101 started. It has been called the Achilles' heel of the income tax.[4]

That can wait a spell. We are still trying to get a definition of income. In this regard, *Macomber*'s definition, like that of the Constitution and the statute, is lacking. First off, it puts the definition of "income" over to the word "gain," which is hardly a self-defining term. In fact, looking for "gain" leads to a significant conceptual confusion in tax, as we will see in a moment. Second, the *Macomber* definition draws attention to finding an ultimate source for every item of "income" in capital or labor, or both combined. This may be fine for us, in this short introduction; in fact we have as a primary theme that most taxable income comes from labor. *Macomber*'s statement would have made sense to Karl Marx and John Stuart Mill, looking at the great factors of production. But how does it play in the real world? What about manna from heaven, chance findings, and other miscellaneous matters that arguably come from something other than labor, capital, or both combined?

We got that answer, finally, in *Commissioner v. Glenshaw Glass*, 348 U.S. 426, decided by the Supreme Court in 1955. The case involved the two-third portion of an antitrust award. When one company is found to have violated the law, it must, in certain circumstances, pay three times the damages it caused. The first-third simply replaces the wronged company's lost profits, and thus is unquestionably taxable. What of the remaining two-thirds, added by Congress to deter antitrust violations?

We already know, from Regulation Section 1.61-14 just quoted, that this is, indeed, "income." But is it "gain derived from labor, from capital, or from both combined"? The one-third component of the damage award that simply replaced lost profits could be seen as "gain derived from labor." But the extra component came from Congress's

---

4. *See* William D. Andrews, "The Achilles' Heel of the Comprehensive Income Tax," in *New Directions for Federal Tax Policy for the 1980s*, 278, Charles E. Walker and Mark Bloomfield, editors, American Council for Capital Formation, at 280 (1980).

desire to punish the bad guys, not, necessarily, from any "labor or capital, or both combined" of the taxpayer. The taxpayer did not pay tax on this component, relying on *Macomber*'s definition of income.

And yet—here is the key point—who cares whence the value came? If "income," the most important word in getting income tax law down, is meant to do anything *principled*, surely it must be about trying to get at some compelling conception of how much individuals should pay in tax: some sense of what resources they have available to them, or, in a phrase often used by tax policy experts, what their *ability to pay* is.

The very question of classifying the source of a payment seems misguided. If Jack and Jill are otherwise equal, but Jack finds $100,000 on the hill, does not he have a greater ability to pay taxes than Jill? Does it matter whether or not we can successfully argue that Jack's good fortune comes from "labor or capital or both combined"? If one takes an approach to taxation that heavily considers economic matters of incentives and efficiency, there is a strong case to be made for rather *highly* taxing any unexpected windfalls, because there are minimal disincentives associated with taxing them. Jack is going to pick up the $100,000 he finds, taxable or not, but he might take a vacation rather than work extra hard to get a bonus that will be subject to tax at high rates.

Without explicitly overruling *Macomber, Glenshaw Glass* gave us a new and improved definition of income:

> Here we have an undeniable accession to wealth, clearly realized, and over which the taxpayer has dominion.

This definition is the best judicial one we have. You should use it. Gone from *Macomber*'s definition are the specific references to labor and capital. Instead we have a focus on an "accession to wealth," a *change* or *increase* in one net's worth. See the section below, on the balance sheet approach to "income."

Note well that we are still far from any crisp, all-encompassing definition of "income." We will not get *that* until we return to the

Haig-Simons definition or identity, looking outside the world of tax law, per se, to economic reality. The positive law, in the statute, *wants* to have an all-encompassing sense and definition of income—"all income, from whatever source derived." Courts, in their attempts to put words on this skeleton, keep adding in limitations and qualifications. This forms a theme of the dynamic aspects of tax law: a court, agency, or Congress tries to define something; sophisticated lawyers, accountants, and taxpayers work around the definition; eventually the IRS catches on and tries to close the "loophole"; there is a round of litigation with mixed results for the government and perhaps statutory changes as well; and on and on we go, returning to step one.

There are three elements of *Glenshaw Glass*'s definition that limit the plenary power of Congress to tax "all incomes, from whatever source derived," as the Constitution and Section 61 had hoped.

One, the "accession to wealth" must be "undeniable." It is as if the burden is on the government: dubious or "deniable" accessions fall out of the definition and base.

Two, the taxpayer must have "dominion" over the "accession." This relates to the issue of control that we will see again in Chapter 4, on timing, when we look at doctrines such as constructive receipt.

Three, and most important, we have the phrase "clearly realized." *Macomber*'s definition of "income" may have bitten the dust, but the realization requirement lives on in full force and effect. *The mere change in value of an existing asset is not "income" under the Glenshaw Glass definition.* We saw this, too, in the repeated use of the word "realized" in Regulation Section 1.61-1(a). Tax Planning 101 survived the move toward a basic definition of income.

The "Balance Sheet" Test

What are we left with as a definition of "income" under the law?

We have the idea of Congress's plenary power under Section 61 to tax "all income, from whatever source derived." We have a sense that the law is concerned not to limit this power in any way, by anything approaching a real definition. And we have *Glenshaw Glass*, with its key phrase, "an undeniable accession to wealth, clearly realized." That is, we have the concept of an "accession to wealth," of a change in one's material fortunes, *plus* the realization requirement. Realization will haunt us throughout—more than any other element of the law, it is key to the labor-capital divide. But what are we to make of the idea of an "undeniable accession to wealth"?

A helpful way to think of the accession concept, and hence of the word "income," is to look at a taxpayer's situation in *balance sheet* terms. A balance sheet is an accounting device, a so-called T account that lists *assets* on the left hand side and *liabilities* on the right. This allows for a simple visual to establish one's net worth: Assets minus Liabilities.

If Sally has $50,000 in a savings account, say, but $10,000 in credit card debt, her net worth is $40,000. Your net worth in financial terms could well be *negative*: in fact, it probably is, if you are a student reading this book to help learn basic tax. You may have student loans of $100,000 or more, against a few hundreds of dollars of cash on hand.

The idea of an *accession to wealth* is anything that *changes your net worth*. Suppose, as above, that Sally has a net worth of $40,000. She finds $10,000, or gets paid this amount by her employer, or receives it as a gift from Aunt Nellie. Sally's net worth has gone up, to $50,000. Under *Glenshaw Glass* she has income of $10,000. It really does not matter whether she got this extra wealth, this accession, from labor, a gift, found money, or capital. The simple balance sheets below illustrate Sally's situation.

Assets	Liabilities
Savings Account: 50,000	Credit Card Debt: 10,000
	Net worth: 40,000

Sally's Balance Sheet, 1

Assets	Liabilities
Savings Account: 50,000	Credit Card Debt: 10,000
Cash found 10,000	
	Net Worth 50,000

Sally's Balance Sheet, 2 (after finding money)

The other limitations come into play, however. That we are only looking at "undeniable" accessions to wealth that are "clearly realized" rules out mere expectancies, and, quite importantly, *changes in value of existing assets*—the classic "unrealized" appreciation. It is as if, under the balance sheet approach, there is no ongoing obligation to restate the value of assets one is holding: in financial lingo, there is no "mark to market" requirement. If instead of a savings account, Sally held corporate stock worth $50,000 the day that she bought it, in economic reality the value would go up and down every day the stock changed price. But the tax law would not consider these changes until and unless there was some definite realization event, so Sally's balance sheet would not change and she would have no "income." The evolving definition of income also rules out more abstract matters, such as the value of one's human capital. In fact, if we were to take into account the latter, students with debt might not really be in the "red." The value of your human capital or skills, as measured by the present value of potential earnings, can be quite high—no doubt is quite high if you are understanding this book.

I call this way of thinking about "income" the "balance sheet" approach. Take a snapshot of your net worth. Then consider an event or transaction. Does it change that net worth, in financial terms? If so, is it "undeniable"? Do you have "dominion"? And is it "clearly realized"? If the answer to all of these questions is "yes," you have "income" under Section 61 and *Glenshaw Glass*.

Debt

A benefit of the balance sheet approach is that it helps considerably when it comes to understanding the important, and often puzzling, subject matter of the income tax treatment of debt. There are three points in time to consider: when you first borrow, when you pay off the debt, and when, sometimes, the debt is forgiven or discharged. Neither of the first two events are "income"; the third one is.

When you first borrow money, there is no income because there is no "accession to wealth." This gave us Step Two in Tax Planning 101 (see Chapter One).

Suppose that Sally uses the found money in the running example to pay off her credit card debt. She still has a net worth of $50,000. Sally next borrows $10,000 as a student loan. Sally now has $60,000 of assets, with the new $10,000 of cash joining her left-hand assets in her savings account. But Sally also now has $10,000 of liabilities, with the new debt showing up on the right-hand side of her T account. Her net wealth stays at $50,000. There has been no change in her net worth; borrowing is not income under an income tax. The new balance sheets show the story.

Assets	Liabilities
Savings Account: 50,000	
	Net worth: 50,000

Sally's Balance Sheet, 3 (after paying off credit card debt)

Assets	Liabilities
Savings Account: 60,000	Student Loan: 10,000
	Net Worth 50,000

Sally's Balance Sheet, 4 (after borrowing student loan)

Suppose now that Sally turns around and pays off the debt. Again, there is no "income," because there is no change in her net worth. In the running example, $10,000 of an asset, from the savings account, goes off Sally's books on the left, but so does the liability of $10,000 go off the books on the right.

Assets	Liabilities
Savings Account: 50,000	Student Loan: 0
	Net worth: 50,000

Sally's Balance Sheet, 5 (after paying off student loan)

Forgiveness of debt, however, *is* income. When a lender writes off a debt, your net worth increases even if you remain negative or in the red. Suppose that Sally had borrowed the $10,000 from her parents. One day, out of pride, exasperation, or a fit of realism, Sally's parents tell her to forget about it and forgive that debt. Now Sally's net wealth has increased, because the $10,000 liability or "IOU" has disappeared from the right-hand side of her personal balance sheet. Sally's net worth *increases*, on account of the *forgiveness of debt*, even if she had already spent all of the money and was, at the start of the day, $10,000 in the red. Becoming less indebted means becoming wealthier.

Assets	Liabilities
Savings Account: 60,000	Student Loan: 0
	Net worth: 60,000

Sally's Balance Sheet, 6 (after forgiveness of debt instead of repayment)

The forgiveness or cancellation of debt is income, under Section 61 and *Glenshaw Glass*. But here is a final word for now to the wise: just because something is "income" under Section 61 and *Glenshaw Glass* does not yet mean that it is *taxable income*. That question depends on an analysis of the exceptions to tax for items of income, which happen to include gifts under IRC Section 102, certain qualified discharges of debt under Section 108, and more. Stay tuned.

The Trouble with "Gain"

One of the challenges of learning tax is that ordinary terms take on special, and often multiple, meanings—"capital" being a leading example of the latter.

Consider "gain," key to *Macomber's* definition of "income." In an administrative ruling following *Macomber*, *Solicitor's Opinion 132*, I-1 C.B. 92 (1922), the IRS looked at compensation for personal injuries, such as payments for the alienation of affection in a divorce proceeding. The IRS specifically reconsidered its earlier position and now held that these kinds of things were not income because there was no "gain." The government even resorted to impressively poetic language, reasoning that to hold payments for alienation taxable would be equivalent to treating the ex-wife who was emotionally harmed like "chattel," meaning personal property.

This rule is now embodied, to some extent, in IRC Section 104, excluding certain "recoveries for personal injuries" from being taxable income.

What is wrong with that, you ask? It seems right and even kindhearted. But, as a matter of tax logic, it is quite wrong indeed. The problem is that "gain" *for tax purposes* cannot mean what this eloquent statement would have it mean, which is gain *for economic purposes*.

"Gain" in tax has the meaning given to it by IRC Section 1001, one of the Top Ten tax statutes: the difference between the fair market value of what you get minus the *basis* of what you give up. This is very important, so I will set it out as a formula, using subscripts:

$$\text{Gain}_{tax} = \text{fmv}_{received} - \text{basis}_{given\ up}$$

This—and this alone—is taxable gain. You will save yourself a lot of trouble (and almost certainly some mistakes on a final examination in tax), if you note this, and note it well.

The point with regard to *Solicitor's Opinion 132* is that the question of "gain" for tax purposes depends, *not just on the value of what is received, but also on the basis of what is given up*. There can be no "gain" for tax purposes *only* if the basis of what is given up equals the fair market value of what is received. If Jane receives $100,000 in a settlement for the economic harms she has suffered, she is taxable on the difference between the $100,000 and the basis she has in her wounded psyche. Again, "basis" is an important tax law concept. It means whatever the government considers to be not subject to further taxation. If we accept that "personhood," or even "psychological harm" or "disutility," has a basis equal to its fair market value—such that Jane would have no taxable gain—then there would be no wage tax! Consider that when Jane goes to work for a law firm, say, and it pays her $100,000 a year, the law firm strongly believes that it is getting considerably more than $100,000 worth of services from Jane. Standing from afar, we can easily say that the psychic disutility of having to work long hours and constantly fill out billing timesheets and so on offsets Jane's salary. But Jane would raise this as an argument against paying tax at peril of going to jail: she has *no* basis in herself—she has not paid taxes on her human capital—such that every penny Jane's employer pays her will be taxed by Uncle Sam.

The different senses of "gain"—the difference between tax and economics—lead to many common confusions. Here is a simple example, getting away from the metaphysics of personhood, to understand the point.

Suppose that Dick bought a building for $250,000. That amount becomes his *basis* in the asset for tax purposes, under IRC 1011. Dick happily sees the value of his building go up over time, to $400,000. This "mere" appreciation is not taxed presently, under *Macomber* and *Glenshaw Glass*. Tragically, one night while Dick is asleep the building burns down. To add insult to injury, it turns out that Dick had not maintained current insurance, such that he gets paid just $300,000 from the insurance company. What do you think of that?

Economically, Dick has a loss. He went to bed with an asset worth $400,000, the building, and he woke up with an asset, cash, worth $300,000, from the insurance proceeds. That is a bad day, all around.

But—to add injury to the injury—Dick *also* has a taxable gain! Recall the formula for *tax* gain: the fair market value of what you get, which is $300,000 here, the cash, minus the *basis* of what you give up, which is $250,000 here, what Dick paid for the building (to keep the example simple, I have assumed no *depreciation*, a subject we consider later). So, *for tax purposes*, Dick has a $50,000 gain, $300,000 - $250,000, following the equation just noted above for determining gain under the income tax. Dick may be able to defer paying tax on this gain, under a special *nonrecognition rule*, as we will consider in Chapter Four, and it may be a capital gain, as we will consider more in Chapter Six, but a gain it is for tax purposes.

Solicitor's Opinion 132 got this all wrong. Payment for emotional distress can *only* lead to no taxable gain if there is a clear statute that says so (such as IRC Section 104, at times), *or* if one has basis in the emotions that were harmed. But the basic logic of tax cannot countenance such basis. The government simply made a mistake, which is why I make a point of having my tax students read and discuss this administrative ruling each year. It is an easy mistake to make. But it is a mistake nonetheless. Tax gain or loss is different from economic gain or loss.

2.1.3 Academic Definitions

Glenshaw Glass and Section 61 give practical *citations* for what is "income." But the statute never really gives us a *definition* of income, and the case law has obvious limitations such as the realization requirement. For many reasons, we want something more "real" than these verbal formulations.

For this we can turn, as policymakers often do, to the Haig-Simons definition, which we had shortened to:

$$Income = Consumption + Savings$$

This basic definition is hardly profound. But it is interesting and helpful. It gets us away from cash, or money, for example, as do Section 61 and the regulations thereunder. The definition also draws our attention to the simple fact that sources equal uses. Implicitly, from the Constitution and Section 61 to the cases, the law tends to look to the sources side of this fundamental equation. But you get to the same bottom line—often with a different understanding—by looking to the uses side. We will consider that insight further in Chapter Three.

The Haig-Simons definition gives us our widest sense of "income." We can use it both to critique the real-world income tax and to see planning opportunities under it.

ℳ 2.2 *Macomber* and Why It Matters

Let us combine what we have just learned, contrasting the expansive definition of income from Haig-Simons with the actual working definitions of income found in the Code and the case law, all of which have the realization requirement from *Macomber* built into them. Here lies the main fault line in the capital-labor divide.

2.2.1 Tax versus Economics

A handy way to think about much of *tax planning* is that it concerns transactions designed to exploit the gap between tax and economics. Recall the basic goals of tax planning: to escape, defer, shift, recharacterize or convert. There are simple enough ways to do all these things *economically*, with the tax consequences following suit. For example, you can *escape* tax by the simple expedient of not earning any income: my teenage daughters have mastered this art. You can *defer* tax by telling your employer to pay you later. You can *shift tax* by giving all your income away, as to charity.

But none of these techniques are any fun. Tax planning is about having your cake (real, economic income) and eating it, too, which means avoiding or minimizing tax on the cake. Surfers and ascetics do not need tax lawyers. Rich people do.

Yet once again, the handiest, surest, simplest way to have your cake and eat it, tax-free, too, is to take advantage of the gaps on the capital side of the capital-labor divide, like Rich Dad does. Tax Planning 101 is the paradigm. By buying an asset that goes up in value without producing cash, you get *economic* income or value without present tax: without present tax, for sure, under the realization requirement, and without tax, ever, under the full Tax Planning 101. *Capital appreciation is Haig-Simons (or "real") income but not taxable income.* The literal language referring to savings in the Haig-Simons definition is the "change in value of the store of assets between the beginning and end of the period in question": there is no realization requirement. If your stock portfolio was worth $500,000 on January 1 in any given year, and $650,000 on December 31 of that same year, you have $150,000 of Haig-Simons income that year on the change in value of your portfolio or "store of assets."

This is rich terrain for Rich Dad to explore: a gap between tax and economics, and an important one. Where is the means for financing fun? Here is where Step Two of Tax Planning 101 comes into play, when you borrow. Borrowing while holding appreciated assets is a way to defer tax, and avoid it altogether if you play the game out until death, while enjoying real economic income. You can have your cake and eat it, tax-free, too.

An income tax with a realization requirement is a strange beast. It works like a balance sheet that does not require assets to be "marked to market," that is, periodically restated to reflect their fair market value. An economist, or even the average wealth-holder, does not typically think this way. People who own homes, pension plans, IRAs, stock accounts, or mutual funds tend to know what their assets are worth *today*. They most likely forget what they paid for them, what their tax basis is. If you bought Microsoft stock in the early 1970s for a few hundred dollars, and it is now worth over $100,000, you do not think that it is still worth only a few hundred dollars because you have not yet "realized" the gain. You are happy—and can enjoy your happiness, as by borrowing against the appreciation and spending away—today.

This gap between tax and economics is important to keep in mind as you learn tax. Wherever any gap occurs, clever tax planners will try to exploit it. That is their job.

2.2.2 On Basis and "Tax Time Bombs"

Much of the income tax's logic and vocabulary grows out of the realization requirement. Because the rise in value of an asset—mere appreciation—is not *yet* income, there must be a way to measure "gain" when the asset is ultimately sold or otherwise disposed of. See IRC Section 1001 and the discussion of realization and recognition events in Chapter Four. When an asset like Mrs. Macomber's stock that was acquired for $20 is later sold for $100, Section 1001 and its basic equation—gain equals fair market value of what is received minus basis of what is given up—tells us to tax $100 minus $20, or $80, of gain.

Basis typically starts out being equal to cost. IRC Section 1011. Basis can often get adjusted, as by depreciation deductions, which we will look at in Chapters Three and Four. There are many situations where the basis of an asset carries over to another person, such as gifts (IRC Section 102/1015, discussed below), or where the basis of one asset becomes another asset's basis, as in the case of like-kind exchanges (IRC Section 1031, see Chapter Four).[5] It is best to think of basis as after-tax dollars. This means dollars accounted for by the tax system, ones that will not be subject to tax in the future.

Just as when you enter a club or an amusement park and you have your hand stamped so that you can leave and reenter without paying again, certain dollars get credited with having paid tax. This can happen even if no actual tax is paid. Thus, for example, tax-free interest from state and local municipal bonds under IRC Section 103 has a tax basis, not because tax was paid, but precisely because tax does not have to *ever* be paid. (Think of what would happen if

---

5. The first situation, where the basis stays in an asset while the asset changes hands, is technically known as *transferred* or *carryover* basis; the second situation, where the taxpayer keeps her old basis in a new asset, is technically known as *substituted basis*. Many tax experts simply say "carryover" for all situations where there is not a full "step up" in basis, as happens in the case of a fully taxable sale or exchange, IRC Section 1001, or on death, IRC Section 1014.

we said that such dollars had "zero" basis.) In fact, here is a handy rule: cash always has a basis equal to its value. This explains an important aspect of debt—you have basis in the dollars you have borrowed—which will continue to factor into our analysis.

You can think of the difference between the fair market value of an asset and its basis, what tax lawyers call built-in gain, as a "tax time bomb." This leads to a rule.

2.2.3 Rule: Sooner or Later, Part I: Tax Time Bombs Go Off

There is a logic to tax. Nowhere is it more evident than in the important rules about the taxation of transactions in appreciated property. The rules about "basis," despite sounding bizarre at times, actually follow a relentless logic.

The basic rule is that sooner or later, tax time bombs go off, with two important exceptions. This rule means that a taxpayer will pay tax on her gain, or the difference between the fair market value and the tax basis of her asset, at some point. The realization requirement is "merely" a matter of timing. The Court in *Macomber* was not saying that the taxpayer did not *ever* have income, just that she did not have it, for tax purposes, *now*–there was not yet any derivation from labor or capital or both combined. The purpose of "basis" in tax is not only to keep track of what has been taxed, but also to set the floor underneath the gain that has not yet been taxed, to make sure that this does not escape taxation altogether.

The big mistake of *Macomber* is that the Court did not fully understand that time is money. Paying a tax on the gain later is like an interest-free loan. It is deferral, the second most beneficial kind of tax planning, behind escape.

Students, just like the Justices in *Macomber*, often misunderstand the critical significance of this point. They think that because you eventually have to pay tax, the realization requirement does not matter – why not wait for a handy moment, when the taxpayer has cash, and the asset has been valued in some fair sale or exchange? Not so fast.

Suppose, for example, that Mrs. Macomber bought her stock for $100. In Year 1, the stock goes up to $300. Mrs. Macomber has $200 of Haig-Simons income in Year 1, but it is not taxable now, under the realization requirement: here is a gap between tax and economics, to be exploited. Suppose that the tax rate is 30 percent. Mrs. Macomber "owes," in a certain sense, $60 of tax on her Year 1 gain (30% of $200). But she will not pay that tax until the ultimate sale or exchange of the stock. In the meantime, *she has the $60 to use.* Deferral is like an interest-free loan from the government. Suppose that Mrs. Macomber does not sell her stock for ten years, until the start of Year 11. Then she will owe the $60. So ask yourself this: Would you rather pay $60 to the government today, or the same $60 to the government in ten years?

But, you think, by Year 11 the stock will be worth more than $300, so the tax will be higher than $60. So it most likely will be. But each year that the stock goes up in value, the same deferral takes place. So if, in Year 2, the stock went from $300 to $400, Mrs. Macomber has another $100 of gain. That "should" generate tax of $30 but that tax, too, gets postponed, until Year 11. And so on.

Of course, assets sometimes fall in value. The realization requirement defers losses, too, which could be a bad thing for a taxpayer. Yet taxpayers are generally free to sell assets that fall in value below their basis, leading to a beneficial tax loss. This forms an element of Tax Planning 102 that I will discuss later. Other practical arguments in favor of the realization requirement are that it is hard to value assets without a sale or other disposition, and that taxpayers lack the liquid funds to pay tax on mere appreciation. There are answers to these criticisms that need not concern us here: technical policy proposals, such as to wait for a realization event to tax gain, but then to do so in a manner that takes into account the time value of money, charging interest to the taxpayer to correct for the otherwise interest-free loan aspect of the realization requirement. These ideas are interesting in theory but complex and extremely unlikely to be seen in practice. The point for this short introduction is that the deferral allowed by the realization requirement is a good thing for taxpayers.

Of course, in the limiting case of death, no tax will ever be paid, given the stepped-up basis on death. IRC Section 1014. This is Tax Planning 101, which converts a game of deferral, the realization requirement, into one of escape.

The "sooner or later" rule is important, because, given the realization requirement, appreciated property abounds. The good tax student will always consider how a transaction would be taxed if appreciated property is used instead of cash.

Suppose, for example, that Sally paid Harry a salary of $10,000. If Sally were running a business, that salary ought to be deductible, under IRC Section 162, as we will consider in Chapter Three. Harry will have income under Section 61 as wages. Now suppose that Sally uses appreciated stock or other property to pay Harry instead of cash. Sally once again gets a deduction for wages paid. Harry still has income, of $10,000—the fair market value of the property other than money that he received. But note also that *Sally* now has *taxable gain*. She has received services worth $10,000, and given up property with a basis less than that. She will pay tax on the difference between $10,000 and the basis of her stock or other property. Sooner or later tax time bombs go off: when an appreciated asset moves out of a taxpayer's hands, it is time to tax her, unless there is an explicit *nonrecognition* rule, as we consider in Chapter Four, to protect her.

A corollary of the "sooner or later" rule is that there are two types of transactions in property, taxable and nontaxable. Taxable transactions, which are fully *realized* and *recognized*, follow the form of *pay tax/get basis*.

If you sell your appreciated property with a basis of $200 for $1,000, you have gain of $800, IRC Section 1001, which is bad news. But then having paid that tax, you now have $1,000 of basis.

On the other hand, if a transaction is nontaxable, for whatever reason—merely holding an asset, or making a gift under IRC Section 102/1015—you do not pay tax and you do not get additional basis. The tax time bomb stays intact.

Now for the two important exceptions to the "sooner or later" rule for tax time bombs' going off. One is for charitable giving: you get to deduct the fair market value of certain appreciated property given to certain charities under IRC Section 170. This means that you get a tax benefit, the fair market value deduction, without ever having paid tax on the built-in gain. It is a good thing, for taxpayers and for charities. This exception has its own exceptions, and we will explore it a bit in the next chapter, on deductions.

Exception number two is for assets held until death: the "stepped-up" basis rule of IRC Section 1014. This exception is huge. It completes Tax Planning 101, and makes the realization requirement's deferral into a game of escape, the ultimate holy grail for taxpayers and their advisers.

Other than dying or making qualified gifts to charity, however, any transaction involving appreciated property should either produce taxable gain (or loss) in accordance with IRC Section 1001, *or* keep basis – and hence the built-in gain or tax time bomb – intact.

⅌ 2.3 Four Conceptual Items of *Non*Income

As we consider what is income, you should learn to identify anything that is *not* income. This helps to understand what is income. You will also want to see if you can structure your own or your client's affairs to fit into any category of nonincome, or to argue that something that was already done falls into it.

There are various ways to be not income: statutory exceptions found in Sections 101 and following, expenses matched by deductions as we will consider in Chapter Three. We start by looking at four items that fall out of the conceptual definition of income we are evolving, using Section 61 and *Glenshaw Glass*.

2.3.1 Psychic Income

Nonmonetary joy, like watching a sunset, is not income. It just is not. This may sound silly, but the noninclusion of "psychic income," like any noninclusion of an item of value, creates a distortion. People who get pleasure from nonmonetary activities have an advantage. Keep that in mind: if what you want in life are things that money must buy, you will soon find yourself having to earn roughly twice your pleasures, because you will have to share your wage earnings with the government. Better to keep your tastes simple and in nonmonetary form. Enjoy that sunset.

2.3.2 Imputed Income

Perhaps more important than psychic income is *imputed* income. This is how economists refer to value that is present somehow in the economy but is not reflected in a cash stream. More specifically, it is value derived from self-supplied labor or capital, the two great factors of production. Once again, this may sound silly or overly abstract. It is not. Not only are there important policy implications that follow from the failure to tax imputed income, but there are also practical tools to address the disparity in its two most common forms. Let us consider them in turn.

Self-Supplied Labor

If you hire someone to paint your house and you are in the 50 percent tax bracket, you have to earn twice as much as you pay the painter, because you have to pay Uncle Sam first. (There is no deduction allowed for paying someone to paint your personal residence, under IRC Section 262, discussed in Chapter Three). If you paint your house yourself, you skip the step of paying tax. The value from self-supplied labor—"sweat equity" as it is sometimes called—never shows up in a cash-flow stream that the government can identify and tax.

This creates an important bias toward building up value inside your own company, or investing in and improving real estate—two of the most common techniques touted by Robert Kiyosaki in *Rich Dad/Poor Dad*. If one way to make money, earning a paycheck from an employer, is cut by a third or a half by taxes, and another way, of using your own labor to build up the value in a capital asset, is taxed at far lower capital gains rates, and after a long period, if at all—the second way has a big advantage.

Consider the case of self-supplied child care. We'll discuss this more in Chapter 5, when I summarize my first book, *Taxing Women*.[6] The main point is that working spouses, two-earner households, must typically earn twice the value of child care, because they have to pay tax before they pay the child-care provider—child-care deductions being very limited, as we will look at further in Chapter Three. There is a bias—some readers might think it is a good bias, on policy grounds, but it is a bias nonetheless—in favor of stay-at-home care.

Suppose that we believe that this bias whereby two-earner households are more heavily burdened by tax than are one-earner households is a policy problem. It is *not* the case that the only solution is to tax stay-at-home caregivers, including their imputed labor value in "income." The problem after all is that stay-at-home spouses are not taxed on the value of their self-provided child-care services, but working spouses are taxed on the value of paid third-party care. We could level the playing field by taxing both—*or by taxing neither*. A more generous child-care deduction for two-earner couples does the trick as well as an inclusion for imputed income for one-earner couples. With a deduction, we have a principle that child care is not taxed. This is a sensible way to respond to an imputed income bias effect, although not one that U.S. law has chosen. There is a very

---

6. Edward J. McCaffery, *Taxing Women*, University of Chicago Press (1997).

limited child-care credit, which we will look at briefly in Chapter 3, that does little to address the bias. Tax laws push married parents to have one spouse stay at home, and punish those households where both parents work for pay outside the home; among the poor or lower income, the bias pushes against marriage itself. Tax matters in a great many ways.

Self-Supplied Capital

Imputed income can also spring from self-supplied capital. An important example is home ownership. This is not a point about the mortgage interest deduction, which is a separate can of worms to be considered in the next chapter. Here the idea is about imputed rent.

If you own a home worth $500,000 outright (that is, without a mortgage), you have an important asset. You are also paying a price, in what economists call an opportunity cost, for the interest you *could* be earning on the money tied up in the house. Where does this value go? To yourself, as imputed landlord! You "pay" for owning the home by sacrificing the yield on your savings. But you do not pay tax on the invisible yield from your self-owned home. It is imputed income, again.

Compare renters. They must earn twice as much to pay for their housing, just like two-earner households using paid child care. Suppose that instead of buying a house for $500,000, Homer opened up a bank account paying 5 percent, or $25,000, a year, money he intends to use for rent. Since the interest on the bank account is taxable—review the "definition" of Section 61 again, and consider that simple bank accounts generate cash, not unrealized appreciation—at ordinary income rates, and rent is nondeductible, Homer's yield gets cut in half at a 50 percent tax rate. He will have only $12,500, after taxes, to pay his rent,

Once again a solution to the "problem" of the nontaxation of imputed rent for homeowners could be a renter's deduction, so that housing is not taxed.

2.3.3 Unrealized Income

Now come the big two categories of economic "income" outside of
the tax law definitions. The first is unrealized appreciation, as we
have just considered with *Macomber*: the change in value of an existing asset. *Glenshaw Glass* preserved the realization requirement and
thus kept unrealized income out of the tax base. This gives us the
first plank in Tax Planning 101—buy, meaning, as Rich Dad knows,
buy assets that appreciate in value without producing a discernible
cash flow. It should be clear by now that unrealized income is *economic* income—having your real estate holdings or stock portfolio
go up in value is a real thing, and a good one—and one that you can
convert into immediate fun via borrowing, Step Two in Tax Planning
101, discussed next. We have a major gap between tax and economics, central to any tax planning opportunity.

2.3.4 Borrowing

Finally, debt is not income under Section 61, *Glenshaw Glass*, or
even the Haig-Simons definition. Consider again the balance sheet
approach. Suppose you are worth, to make things simple (if depress-
ing), $0. Now you borrow $5,000. Your net worth is unchanged: the
new asset, $5,000 of cash, is offset by the new liability, the IOU for
$5,000. You may or may not get a deduction, or create basis in some
asset, depending on what you do with the loan proceeds. *But the
borrowing itself is not income.* Under Haig-Simons, whatever you do
with the money—consumption or savings—is offset by the *negative*
savings that debt is. To be perfectly clear, borrowing against an
appreciated asset, or borrowing given the fact that you have some
significant appreciation in your holdings, is *not* a "realization event"
under the current tax law, although we could imagine that it should
be. In any event, borrowing as a conceptual item of nonincome
works hand in glove with the prior item, unrealized appreciation, to
give us the first two planks in Tax Planning 101.

✳ 2.4 Tax Planning 101

Now that we have learned all of the basic principles that we need for Tax Planning 101, we can take a deeper look. These simple planning steps convert *Macomber* from a story of deferral into one of escape. We start by buying assets that rise in value without producing a taxable cash flow. As they go up in value, creating tax time bombs, we borrow instead of selling, borrowing being nontaxable under an income tax. We hold both the assets and the debt straight through to death, when our heirs get the assets, income-tax-free (see discussion of IRC Section 102, below), and with a basis equal to current fair market value—without any tax time bomb, that is. IRC Section 1014. The heirs can sell the assets, tax free, and pay off the debts. We can smile down on them, knowing that no tax was ever paid in the use of our wealth.

2.4.1 Note: Tax Planning 102

In part to show how fun tax is, here is a minor twist on Tax Planning 101: after buying your assets in Step One, you can sell your losers and hold your winners in a Step One-A. A "loser" is any asset that falls in value beneath its tax basis. Fair market value minus basis can lead to a negative number under Section 1001. This is a loss for tax purposes.

We see an important asymmetry in the realization requirement. Tax time bombs do not go off until there has been a sale or exchange under IRC Section 1001. We will consider, in Chapter 4, a series of involuntary dispositions that will have taxpayers complaining about forced realizations—and we will see that the law generally gives them relief in the form of a nonrecognition rule. But the simplest, paradigmatic case for a realization event is a fully voluntary sale. *And you generally get to pick what and when to sell.*

This may seem like a fairly small matter and, these days, it largely is, except for the wealthy capitalists who play Tax Planning 101 and all of its variations for sport. But it is worth noting that the features we have just learned, alone, could have doomed the entire income tax.

Suppose, for example, that Pam earns $50,000 a year, and has managed to save $100,000. Just to illustrate the point, imagine that Pam could find an investment that worked like a coin-flip: a fifty-fifty shot to double her money or lose it all. (In reality, this would involve more complex financial transactions, what financiers call a "straddle.") Pam takes her savings and buys two financial options for $50,000 each—one on heads, one on tails. The stock market does what it does, say it comes up heads, and Pam has one option worth $100,000 and the other worth $0. Now comes the twist: Pam gets to sell her loser and open up the tax loss of $50,000: $0, the amount received, minus $50,000, the basis of the losing tails position. This loss offsets Pam's salary, *and she pays no tax.* Yet by playing this game, Pam has incurred no real, economic loss: she still has $100,000 of savings, in the winning "heads" option. But she has managed to generate a $50,000 *tax* loss that she can use to offset her $50,000 salary. She can consume her wages away, tax free. And Pam can repeat the game every year, until kingdom come.

If this sounds too good to be true, it is, now. *Do not try this technique at home alone without a skilled tax adviser guiding you.* Once again, this is not a tax planning book. Congress eventually saw this problem, and passed IRC Section 1211, the capital loss offset rule, and later more complex rules attacking "straddles" and such. Under Section 1211, any "capital" loss, such as obtained from selling the "tails" position in the above example, can only be used to offset capital gains, plus a limited amount of "ordinary" income, that is, wages (the present amount is $3,000 per year). There are other complexities here, such as the "wash sale" rules of Section 1091, and so on. We are getting ahead of ourselves, touching on matters of capital gains and losses, ordinary income, and timing—matters for Chapters 4 and 6. And the "straddle" technique is an example of a tax shelter, which we will explore more in Chapter 7. It all shows what a tangled web tax can become, quickly enough, and underscores the challenge of keeping this short introduction short.

But the main point is that we can understand Tax Planning 102 now. It illustrates many deep themes. It shows how the seemingly innocuous *Macomber* decision quickly blossomed into an Achilles' heel. It shows how piecing together seemingly disparate rules and provisions can lead to highly effective tax planning. It illustrates how the tax system typically, eventually, responds to problems and closes "loopholes," without necessarily rethinking first principles— note that what IRC Section 1211 changed was the ability to take a loss currently, not the realization requirement itself. Tax Planning 101 stayed intact. Most of all, Tax Planning 102 shows the capital-labor divide once more, in all its glory. Pam needed to do something to shelter her wage income from current taxation. And so she looked to the capital side, and played a basic heads-and-tails game with financial instruments. The law had to act to stop this, as it did, or the gaps on the capital side would swallow up all wage income, and the government would be left with nothing to tax.

Section 1211, a principal tool to stop any bleeding from Tax Planning 102 onto the wage side of the great divide, is a first look at what I call a *netting rule*: It in essence creates "baskets" of income, with different properties, within the single income tax. Here the "baskets" are capital and labor (ordinary income). *Losses generated on the capital side cannot be used to offset income from labor.* That will be a key theme of Chapter 7, when we look more extensively at tax shelters. The tax system eventually comes around to plug up the loopholes on the *labor side* of the great divide, but it generally leaves in place all of the deep structural features that allow tax to be avoided on the capital side. Tax Planning 101 lives.

In the real world there are other complexities in playing out a Tax Planning 101 strategy. Some people might be uncomfortable with the high debt levels that the game leads to in the end. Others might be squeamish about holding undiversified positions, putting too many of their eggs in a handful of appreciated baskets. There are financial vehicles to help mitigate these worries, but these lie beyond the scope of this short introduction. See your tax or financial adviser for details. The point for now is that, to avoid paying any and all taxes, it is generally worth it to take on some legal and financial complexity. The game is there to be played—if and only if you have financial capital to get a seat at the table.

✎ 2.5 Statutory Exclusions

There are multiple ways to avoid something of economic value being taxed as "income." The conceptual means we have just explored are deep and important. Congress can also step in and decide not to tax something that it could, under Section 61, the Constitution, and *Glenshaw Glass*, undeniably tax. Recall that Section 61 had begun with the clause "except as otherwise provided in this subtitle," meaning that Congress could provide that certain items of "income" are not taxable because it, Congress, does not want to tax them. These statutory exceptions are generally set out in IRC Section 101 and following—again, there is a logical order to the Code. It is worth looking over the major items on the list.

Section 101 excludes the proceeds from (most) life insurance policies. The parentheses are in order because as almost always, there are exceptions to the exceptions, involving such matters as life insurance policies that have been sold or owned by an employer.

Section 102 excludes "gifts, bequests and devises," putting enormous pressure on the definition of these words. We will explore that below. Section 102 applies to both *inter vivos* gifts, that is, among the living, and testamentary devises, what you inherit from a deceased relative or benefactor. This means that when Tax Planning 101 plays out to its last step, the heirs inherit the assets income-tax-free, under Section 102, and without a tax time bomb, because of the stepped-up basis rule of IRC Section 1014. They can sell the assets and pay off their benefactor's debts, keeping whatever is left over.[7]

---

7. The estate might be responsible for gift and estate taxes, if the cumulative amount of these transfers exceeds the relevant exemption level—$5 *million* per person as I write, $10 million for a married couple (with some planning).

Section 103 excludes the interest from (certain) state and local municipal bonds, so-called tax-exempt or "muni" bonds.

Section 104 excludes "personal injury recoveries." We talked about this Section in connection with *Solicitor's Opinion 132*. It has been much whittled down of late as part of Congress's halting efforts to effect *tort* reform, limiting the incentives for plaintiffs' lawyers to sue. As a general matter, tax-free recoveries must now be for *physical* injuries, ruling out purely psychological or emotional harms.

Sections 105 and 106 exclude employer provided health care, and the insurance payments or reimbursements from health insurance respectively. These sections represent an enormously important piece of social policy leading to the deep historic connection between health insurance and employment in this country, as further discussed later.

Section 108 allows for certain discharges of debt—which we now know should be generally taxable, under the basic definition of income—to be tax free. This Section serves to protect the U.S. bankruptcy laws. If court-approved discharges of debt were taxable income–we now know that they are income under the basic definition of income—then companies seeking to reorganize would get out of owing their regular creditors the full amount of their debts, only to find a new and more frightening creditor—Uncle Sam—at their doorsteps. IRC Section 108 prevents this result under certain circumstances.

I could go on, but you get the point, and we have mentioned the most important Sections. A few others will pop up as we continue our journey through tax's forest. Skim your Code to learn more. Next we explore one of the Sections, 102, at some greater length to get a sense of how things work.

The gift and estate tax is beyond the scope of this short introduction, which is focused on the individual income tax. But suffice it to say that it, too, is largely avoidable for those who plan ahead. *See* Edward J. McCaffery, *Fair not Flat*, University of Chicago Press (2002), Chapter Four.

ℳ 2.6 Gifts

Section 102 is a simple statute. It says that "gifts" are not taxable. But few things in tax stay simple, given the stakes involved—and bear in mind that income tax rates have been as high as 90 percent for significant stretches of U.S. history. Here, as often, the complexity comes in defining an important term.

Given Section 102, taxpayers want to argue that anything and everything they receive is a "gift." Where to draw the line? We will also see some twists when it comes to the giving of appreciated property. Always remember, given *Macomber* and the resulting income-with-realization tax, to consider what happens when a transaction—here a gift—involves appreciated property.

2.6.1 Definitions

First and most important, what is a "gift"? This is a critically important matter. The statute and its regulations are not very helpful, so we turn to the case law.

The major case, read by all students learning tax, is *Commissioner v. Duberstein*, 363 U.S. 278, decided by the Supreme Court in 1960.

Duberstein actually involved two cases combined together. One featured a cash payment made to an ex-employee on his termination; the other involved the purported "gift" of a car—a Cadillac, no less—to a business acquaintance who had given the purported "donor" valuable business referrals. The facts and holding of the case are complicated, muddled up by a multiplicity of separate opinions from the Justices. But students do not read *Duberstein* for its facts or its narrow holding. They read it for its definition of "gift" under Section 102.

Here then is a surprise, one common enough in tax: we do not actually get a definition. Recall that we never got a very good definition of "income," certainly not from the statute. In *Duberstein* we do not get a definition of "gift" at all. What we get instead is a list of factors and a clear mandate that what is a "gift" is generally a *factual* question, best left to the trier of fact—the judge or jury at the trial court level. Of the various factors to be considered, the most important, according to the Supreme Court, is the *subjective intent* of the donor, particular whether or not she made the transfer out of "detached and disinterested generosity"—that is, whether she was under any legal or other sense of obligation, or whether she received back any benefits, making it an exchange rather than a gift.

As an intuitive or a priori matter, this makes some sense: it is the kind of definition, or approach to a definition, that a smart person, unaware of the context of tax, might give. The problem is that *Duberstein* is a Supreme Court case purporting to set out a universal approach to the word "gift" under Section 102 of the tax code. Here, the key to understanding *Duberstein* is to see that it is nearly completely, perfectly *wrong* as a matter of tax policy. The tax system simply cannot leave a matter as important as the definition of "gift"—once gifts are made nontaxable under Section 102— to *either* trial courts *or* to the subjective intent of the donor. The problem is yet again a "loophole" that could swallow up the whole. Employers would restructure salaries such that more depended on "bonuses." Taxpayers well advised by tax practitioners would swear that their transfers were motivated by nothing more than "detached and disinterested generosity." The tax system would grind to a halt.

Interestingly, in reaching its opinion, the Court rejected—and even belittled—a series of government-proposed "tests." These included the ideas that corporations could not make gifts; that there could be no gifts in an employer-employee relationship; that claiming that a transfer was a gift was inconsistent with taking a tax deduction, the subject of Chapter 3, for the amount transferred. Each of these "tests" is in fact a quite sensible rule. All have more or less become the law without any court ever openly overruling *Duberstein*. Corporations cannot make gifts, at least if "gifts" mean something proceeding from detached and disinterested generosity, without any expectation of a return, because corporations are under a fiduciary duty to their shareholders to make a profit. The statute has now changed, in IRC Section 102(c), to prohibit employers from making "gifts" to their employees aside from minor items worth less than $25 (no more turkeys at holiday time). And there is something problematic with allowing a deduction to the maker of a "gift" while also allowing the recipient not to include the value in her taxable "income." The Court in *Duberstein*, in a well-meaning attempt to clarify the law and set the stage for judicial determinations of what is a "gift," actually made a mess of things by not giving a simpler definition. That would have to wait some time, as the law slouched toward a better sense of things.

Note: On Olk *and "Tokes"*

One of my favorite cases in teaching basic income tax follows *Duberstein*, *Olk v. United States*, 536 F.2d 876 (9th Cir.), cert. denied, 429 U.S. 920 (1976), decided by the Ninth Circuit Court of Appeals some sixteen years after *Duberstein*. The case concerned tips, or "tokes" (because they were given in the form of game tokens) given to blackjack dealers in Las Vegas. The dealers argued that these were "gifts," not taxable under Section 102. They had a powerful argument: not only were the donors or tippers under no obligation to leave the tips, but these donors *could not in fact legally get any benefits from giving the tokes*. A dealer who showed favoritism would lose his job and possibly face a prison term. This looks like "detached and disinterested generosity" under *Duberstein*. The lower court, being the trier of fact, agreed.

The Ninth Circuit reversed. It held that the fair market value of the "tokes" was taxable income to the dealers. Here we have an appeals court reversing a trial court, against the stated desires of the Supreme Court in *Duberstein* to leave matters to the trier of fact. What of the need for some showing of "detached and disinterested generosity"? The Ninth Circuit found this—as a matter of law (what appellate courts can decide on their own)—in the motivation of the donors to pay "tribute to the gods of fortune." But if paying tribute to gods takes something out of the realm of "detached and disinterested generosity," what does not do so? Any time someone makes a gift, we can search for and find some motivation. A mother making gifts to her son wants him to succeed and do well, maybe even wants an insurance policy if she later has needs. And so on. *Olk* was implicitly—not explicitly, being a lower court—changing the rules from *Duberstein.*

What did the Supreme Court do in *Olk*? They denied certiorari, meaning they let the Ninth Circuit opinion stand without further review.

Where Are We Left?

What, then, after *Duberstein*—still on the books as the definitive Supreme Court ruling on the matter—and *Olk* are we left with for the definition of "gift" under Section 102? In essence, as in many other areas of tax—recall again the definition of "income"—we have a "know it when we see it" standard. Tax practitioners develop instincts for these kinds of things; tax law and practice is as much art as science. This is one of the reasons why, when *Money* magazine runs an annual test, it finds that almost no two tax preparers come up with the same answers to a moderately complex hypothetical tax return situation.

In the case of gifts, our instincts are aided considerably by another core tax policy matter: the business-personal distinction. This will feature prominently in the next chapter, on deductions, where we will see the two important general rules that personal expenditures are not generally deductible and that business expenses are. For gifts, these are common in *personal* contexts but virtually nonexistent in *business* ones. This is what was going on in *Olk*: dealers were in essence being compensated in part by tips or tokes, and had to pay tax on that. The tokes look like *wages*. So, too, waiters must pay tax on their tips, and the IRS has developed means for approximating how much any particular waiter gets in tips, with reporting requirements on restaurant owners and so on. The "tests" that the Supreme Court rejected in *Duberstein* have in essence become the law. And this is not such a bad thing.

Note: On Two Tax Regimes

In lay terms, there are often objections to certain taxes being "double taxes"—this was Mill's criticism of the income tax's approach to savings. In general, the criticism is not compelling—the same *dollar* can be taxed many times in the flow of commerce. If you earn $1,000 in wages, you will pay both income and payroll taxes on this sum. If you pay someone to paint your house with what you have left over, the painter will pay tax, too (and you will get no deduction for this personal expense under IRC Section 262). If the painter buys a cup of coffee with some of his pay, he will pay sales tax. And so on.

Nonetheless, there are circumstances where, within a given tax, the system will try to avoid double-taxing. The tax concept of basis plays the important role of avoiding double-taxation of the same dollars to the same taxpayer on the capital side. When you purchase an asset with dollars that have already been taxed, and you get no deduction for the purchase, you have a basis in the asset equal to its cost. Then when you sell, under IRC Section 1001(a), you pay tax on the difference between the fair market value of what you get and the basis of what you give up—that is, you get to subtract out your basis, thus not paying tax again on those same dollars.

A similar logic applies to the typical passing of value between related parties.[8] There are two basic regimes, marking the personal or family side on the one hand and the business side on the other. When an employer pays you, she gets a deduction for wages paid, under Section 162, and you have an inclusion, for wages received,

---

8. When dealing with unrelated parties, there is a third regime: don't deduct/ include as income. This is what happens when you pay someone to paint your house: no deduction to you under IRC Section 262, inclusion to the painter under Section 61.

under Section 61. We can call this treatment, typical of the business world, "deduct/include." Section 102(c), picking up one of the government's arguments in *Duberstein*, effects this result for "gifts" from an employer—there are none. In contrast, on the personal or family side, there is generally no deduction for the amounts paid from parent to child—this is a personal expenditure blocked from deductibility by Section 262—and the amounts are not includible in income to the recipient under Section 102. We can call this regime the "don't deduct/don't include" one. It applies, not just to gifts, but also to child support, within a marriage or following a divorce—no deduction to the payor, no inclusion for the payee.

The result, then, is that, in both the typical business/employer and the personal/family contexts, money is taxed once as it moves between related parties. The difference is that, in the business context, the value is taxed at the recipient/employee's level. In the family context, it is taxed at the parent/donor's level.

Now we can make a policy argument for Section 102: *not* to allow gifts to be nontaxable would create a nightmare within families and other loving relationships. Transfers between parents and children would be double-taxed, both to parent and child, and hence discouraged. In the personal and family context, Section 102 makes sense. But it is not needed, and would create distortions of a different sort, in a business context. Allowing employees not to include payments that their employers had deducted would mean that the underlying value escaped tax altogether. The system cannot readily allow that, on the labor side of things.

One final twist: It may seem as if the entire scheme is beneficial to families. And so it is, looking at Section 102 alone. But if you are going to pay tax once, you would typically *rather* pay it at the recipient, child's level, because she is likely to be in a lower tax bracket than her parents. A deduction for mom and dad is more valuable to the family than an inclusion to son or daughter is harmful. We will pick up that theme again in Chapter 5, when we look at taxpayer attempts to shift income. Until then, the policy discussion helps us to get a sense of what is and is not a "gift," nontaxable under Section 102.

2.6.2 Gifts of Appreciated Property

Once more, a word to the increasingly wise: Always consider what happens under the income tax when you do something using appreciated property. What if, instead of giving cash to your child, you give her appreciated stock or real estate?

As this is in the personal context, and clearly is a gift (note, by the way, that you *can* have nongifts in the family context; you can buy things from a family member, or perform services for them, although the IRS will look at such circumstances with some suspicion) we are in the "no deduction/no inclusion" regime. You will not get a deduction for the gift, and your daughter will not have an inclusion under Section 102. But there are questions that arise because of the use of appreciated property: What happens to the built-in gain or tax time bomb? What basis does your daughter have in the property?

Suppose that the gift is of corporate stock that you bought many years ago for $2,000, and is now worth $10,000. There is built-in gain of $8,000 ($10,000 minus $2,000). If this were in the *business* regime—if, say, your employer had paid you for $10,000 worth of services with the stock—the tax time bomb would go off *in the employer's hands*. Looked at from his point of view, he exchanged an appreciated asset, the stock, for services worth $10,000. Under the basic equation for gain on sale or other disposition, IRC Section 1001(a), the employer has gain measured by the fair market value of what he received ($10,000 worth of services) minus the basis of what he gave up ($2,000 in the appreciated stock) or $8,000, total, here capital gain. (That this is capital is determined by the nature of what he gives up, the stock, typically "property" under IRC Section 1221. We will look at that more in Chapter 6.) To further complicate matters, the employer would also get a deduction for the value paid, $10,000, under Section 162. You the employee would have an inclusion for the fair market value of the property received as compensation, under Section 61. You would go forward with a basis in the stock equal to $10,000, because you showed taxable income of that amount: it is as if you were in fact paid in cash, paid tax on it, and then bought the stock. We can add "realization event" or "tax time bomb goes off" to the deduct/inclusion paradigm for business transfers where appreciated property is used.

Back to gifts: Perhaps again out of a spirit of not discouraging gifts, Congress decided that the moment of giving away appreciated property would *not* be a taxable one. This means that the donor does *not* see a tax time bomb explode in her hands. But recall our previous rule: sooner or later, tax time bombs go off. The only exceptions to this rule are certain charitable gifts and death. We do not have either exception here. What happens?

The answer is that your daughter, as gift recipient, takes a *carryover basis* under Section 1015. The basis "carries over" with the asset, so your daughter takes what had been your basis, that is, $2,000. The tax time bomb is preserved for a later day.

A taxpayer once complained of this situation, in the case of *Taft v. Bowers*, 278 U.S. 470, decided by the Supreme Court in 1929. The younger Ms. Bowers had received some stock from her mother as a gift. When she sold it, the IRS moved to tax her on the total gain from the initial purchase—that is, on the fair market value received minus her mother's old basis, under Section 1001. The younger Ms. Bowers complained that this was unfair, arguing that she was being made to pay a tax based on gain accrued while someone else—her mother—owned the stock. The Supreme Court rejected the argument and upheld the carryover basis rule of current Section 1015.

What is most interesting about *Taft v. Bowers*, aside from the fact that this very simple case made it all the way up to the Supreme Court, was that Ms. Bowers was complaining at all. Had she "won" the case, the appreciation in the hands of her mother would have disappeared. But surely Congress would have changed the rules to make giving itself a realization event. The tax time bomb would have gone off, in her mother's hands, at the time of the gift, just as it would for an employer paying wages using appreciated stock. This would almost always be *worse* for the taxpayer, both because the donor is apt to be in a higher tax bracket than the donee, and because one generally wants to *defer* taxes, to put them off as long as possible, as we know from our brief foray into the basic goals of tax planning. The younger Ms. Bowers should have been happy with the no tax/carryover basis rule.

Here again is a benefit of being on the capital side of the capital-labor divide. If you own financial capital, you can escape all tax, as we know, under Tax Planning 101. You are deferring taxes every day you do not sell or otherwise trigger a realization event on your assets. Now we have just seen how easy it is to *shift* the responsibility for the tax—just give the appreciated asset away before any sale.[9] If you are a wage earner, and only have cash to give away, you get no such luck. You have to pay taxes on your wages, first, and the cash you give away has no built-in gain to shift.

One final twist: the rule of Section 1015 and *Taft v. Bowers* means in essence that you can give away capital gains. Not so for losses. The precise rule of Section 1015 is that the donee's basis is the *lower* of the donor's basis or fair market value. This will usually mean donor's basis, the carryover rule just discussed, because most assets are worth more than their tax bases. In the case of assets that have gone down in value, however—that is, assets with built-in loss instead of built-in gain—the basis in the hands of the donee is the fair market value. This means that the loss has disappeared. Why such a wrinkle?

The basic gift regime encourages people to make gifts to those "beneath" them, in lower tax brackets, typically their children. Allowing *losses* to transfer over would give a perverse incentive to make gifts *upstream*, to people in higher tax brackets who would benefit more from the tax loss. Congress did not want to see that particular game. The lesser of basis or fair market value rule shuts this planning possibility down. What, then, should a parent with

---

9. The so-called kiddie tax, found in IRC Section 1(g), somewhat checks the ability to shift in this way, but only for children aged 14 or younger. You can still give appreciated property to your child to sell herself and pay for college, say. We will touch on the kiddie tax a bit more in Chapter 5.

a loss asset do? Simple: sell the asset, use the loss herself (subject to the capital loss offset rules of IRC Section 1211), and give the proceeds to the child. Or find some appreciated property to give to the kid instead.

⁂ 2.7 Beyond Cash

Let us return to the basic task for this chapter, trying to get a sense of what is included in "income" for tax purposes. We are developing instincts for tax. Perhaps no instinct is more important than that "income" can and does include items received in noncash form, measured at their objective fair market value—what a willing buyer would pay a willing seller in a transaction free of coercion or beneficence.

There is nothing really special about cash, except that it is easy to value, and it always works out to have basis equal to itself (the system could not live with cash having tax time bombs built into it). But the statute, in Section 61, the regulations, and abundant case law all make clear that items other than cash—property, services, "fringe" benefits, even the promise of future cash—can also be "income" under the law.

2.7.1 An Important Example

I like to begin my classes in basic tax with *Eisner v. Macomber*, a habit that few of my fellow tax teachers seem to follow these days. To me, almost all of the major themes in tax can be gleaned from *Macomber*: how hard it is to define "income"; the idea that the *what* and *when* questions in tax are centrally connected; the realization requirement and all that follows from it, such as Tax Planning 101. But *Macomber* is a hard and tricky case to read. Many students think that the realization requirement makes sense and is harmless enough—ironically, this is true under a consistent *spending* tax, a policy proposal toward which we are headed, but is quite wrong under an income tax. A more specific misunderstanding is that the realization requirement is all about cash—that nothing gets taxed until it is cashed out. This is most definitively not the case. It is critical to understand that the tax law concept of income is different from the *form* of value received—that there is nothing magic, that is, about cash.

To help clear up some misunderstandings, I like to have students read *United States v. Drescher*, 179 F.2d 863 (2nd Cir. 1950), cert. denied, 340 U.S. 821 (1950), next. In *Drescher*, decided by the Second Circuit of Appeals before *Glenshaw Glass*, a high-ranking officer at Bausch & Lomb received an annuity from his employer. In essence, the employer set aside $5,000, today, but Mr. Drescher could have no access to the money for years, until he retired—by which time the $5,000 would have grown in value, with interest and capital appreciation. The IRS argued, and the court agreed, that Drescher was taxable now. This is clearly the right answer, as a matter of the logic of an income tax, but my students, still perhaps confused over *Macomber*, generally fail to grasp it at first. Mr. Drescher has not yet realized the money, they think, so how can he be taxed now under *Macomber*?

The answer to the puzzle is that *Drescher* falls in the interplay between the realization requirement and the important principle that "income" can come in noncash form. Mr. Drescher got *something new*, something he did not have before—the annuity contract. *That contract* is "income," now, under Section 61 and *Glenshaw Glass*. Mr. Drescher had dominion over the contract, and his ownership of the contract is "clearly realized."

Further, Drescher's income came in the wage or labor context, where the law, as we are learning, needs to be especially solicitous to capture income. Think what would happen if we had a rule stating that wages in noncash form were not taxable. Employers would pay employees with food, shelter, clothes, cars, and so on, and no tax would ever get paid. If payments today into some fund payable to the employee in some future year were not taxable, employees would elect to get paid that way—and then borrow to make ends meet today. Again, no tax would be paid. Mr. Drescher must be taxed now, absent some statutory exclusion for the annuity contract.

In terms of the realization requirement, it is important to see that it is *not* about cash, at all. The realization requirement holds that the *change in value of an existing asset is not income, until and unless there is some sale or exchange.* Importantly, when that sale or disposition does arrive, under Section 1001(a), it need not be for cash. Trade one stock for another, and you will pay tax on the built-in gain on your initial holding (such a trade would not qualify for "like-kind" nonrecognition treatment under IRC Section 1031, as we will see in Chapter 4). Again, cash is but an example of a *form* of value that income can take on. Annuity contracts, discharge of debt, in-kind goods are others.

Finally, note that the realization requirement only comes up on the capital side of the great divide. Anything you get from your employer is taxable, now, at its objective fair market value, absent some statutory exception. Even the promise of a future payment, if undeniably received and clearly realized, is taxable now. (The rather tricky IRC Section 83, an important Code Section for employee compensation, deals with the situation of unsecured promises to pay, which, if properly structured—typically entailing some genuine economic risk—can avoid income tax today.) Realization only applies to existing stores of capital, managed under a "buy and hold" strategy picking up on Tax Planning 101.

2.7.2 Valuation Principles

When you have noncash income, there is a need to value it that does not arise with cash. Taxpayers can often play games, seeking to present a lower value to the IRS than is "real." This issue came up in *Drescher*.

Although the court held that the annuity contract was income, now, to Mr. Drescher, at its fair market value—holdings that follow from Section 61 and its regulations—it remanded the case back down to the trial court to determine what the contract's fair market value actually was. It could have skipped this step. Drescher's employer, Bausch & Lomb, had paid $5,000 for the contract. That should have decided the matter—it is what the contract cost on the open market. The court thought that because the annuity had various restrictions on it, such as when it could be converted into cash or assigned, its fair market value would be lower than its price. But that reasoning defies logic and introduces a wrinkle into tax that can lead to problems and contention.

As far as Drescher is concerned, suppose that he knew that the annuity contract would be taxable at its price. He could tell his employer to forget it, and take the $5,000 in cash, instead, or he could go ahead and receive the contract with its $5,000 cost and pay tax accordingly. By treating the cash and the contract as the same, for tax purposes, the choice would depend on Drescher's preferences, not some ability to cheat the IRS. If on the other hand the $5,000 in cash would be taxable but a $5,000 annuity contract would not be, Mr. Drescher would be comparing the annuity to his after-tax income which, in a 70 percent rate bracket, would be $1,500 (what would be left after he paid 70 percent of the $5,000, or $3,500, in tax). Waste could ensue: taxpayers would encourage their companies to buy annuities worth less to them than their cost. A similar problem haunts tax-free health insurance: high-bracket taxpayers have an incentive to get *overinsured* (think of no deductibles or copayments, coverage for elective procedures, and the like) because they compare taxable cash to nontaxable health insurance benefits.

A note on basis: Mr. Drescher will have basis in his annuity contract in the amount of taxable income with which he is charged today. Had he won the case, and paid no tax now, his basis would have been $0. If the IRS had won on both the timing and valuation fronts—as it should have—Drescher would get a basis of $5,000 in his annuity contract today, by virtue of having paid tax on that amount. In twenty-five years, if Drescher were to be paid a lump sum of $20,000, say, under the annuity contract, he would then be taxable on that amount minus his basis, $0 or $5,000, respectively. Thus note that the *Drescher* case is "only" about timing—it is only about the question for when Mr. Drescher pays tax on the $5,000. In both cases, he pays tax on at least $15,000 in Year 25 when he gets the $20,000. The question is does he pay tax on $5,000 now, and $15,000 later, or on the full $20,000 later. Mr. Drescher did not dispute this. The case is about timing, not escape. And yet— here is the take-home point—a case "only" about timing can be well worth litigating through the court system. Time really is money.

Further, in addition to getting deferral, the matter of timing— putting the tax off to a later date—Drescher was hoping to shift to *himself, at a later time*, when he would be in a lower tax bracket. If, as was likely, Mr. Drescher was in a 70 percent marginal rate bracket when he received the annuity during his peak earning years, but would be in a 30 percent bracket when it matured after his retirement, there would be additional savings of $2,000—40 percent, or the difference between 70 and 30 percent, of the $5,000—because of the annuity device. We can consider this shift as a matter of attribution— of the "who" that pays taxes—which we will get to in Chapter 5. The shift is between Mr. Drescher today and Mr. Drescher tomorrow. Nice work if Mr. Drescher could have gotten it; taxpayers in fact can get these benefits, under the "qualified pension plans" discussed briefly below, as a clear statutory exclusion from "income." Mr. Drescher was trying a form of "self-help," going beyond what the statute allows a wage earner to do. This should not work, and generally does not.

✻ 2.8 "Fringe" or Noncash Benefits

By now we should know the basic law and be developing good instincts about taxable income. You should therefore be able to predict the essentials of fringe benefit taxation: "Fringe" or noncash benefits received from an employer *are* "income" within the meaning of Section 61, *Glenshaw Glass*, and even the Haig-Simons definition. They are taxable *now*, when the taxpayer/employee receives them (even if they are a contract for, or a promise of, future cash, as in *Drescher*), and at their objective fair market value. But such fringe benefits may not actually be *taxable* income, because—and *only because*—Congress, having the power to tax them, under the Constitution and Section 61, may not have chosen to tax them. Indeed, for the two largest and most important categories of non-cash benefits, employer-provided health care and pension plans, Congress has decided to do just that, not taxing them (at least not currently, in the case of pension plans), under IRC Sections 105-6 and 401 and following, respectively.

All this we know from general principles and the instincts we are developing. These instincts include the very sound one that Congress is quite serious about taxing matters on the labor side of the great divide.

2.8.1 Exclusions Matter

It is hard to underestimate how important the tax exclusion for employer-provided health care, IRC Sections 105-6 is. Professor Michael Graetz has written that "[p]lacing so much reliance on the tax law to provide adequate health insurance has been the Titanic of twentieth-century American Domestic policy."[10] Given the history of policy mistakes in that or any other century, that is saying quite a bit. What is the problem, exactly? High tax rates in the middle of the twentieth century gave an incentive for highly compensated employees to take some of their compensation in the

---

10. Michael J. Graetz, "100 Million Unnecessary Returns: A Fresh Start for the U.S. Tax System," 112 *Yale Law Journal* 261 (2002) at 275.

form of nontaxable health insurance; employers did not care because they got a deduction for the insurance premia. At a 70 percent tax rate (and some employees were in even higher rate brackets in the 1950s!), a rational employee would compare $3,000 in cash, what she would get after taxes on a $10,000 bonus, say, with $10,000 worth of additional high-quality health insurance. As a predictable result, health insurance became tied to the workplace; the un- and under-employed were left uninsured; and the well employed became *over*insured. Health-care costs soared even as millions of Americans had no health insurance. Many Presidents tried and failed to rectify these situations – to rein in health-care costs and widen the net of insurance coverage – until President Obama was at last able to get some legislation enacted. It is still too early to tell if the changes will cure all of the ails, which began with a poorly chosen idea of making employer provided health care tax favored. Titanics, like Achilles Heels, are not good.

2.8.2 Plugging Up the Leaks

Both the difficulties of taxing noncash items and the importance of trying to do so in the wage context are illustrated in the ever-unfolding story of IRC Section 132. The IRS had been letting many matters of workplace economics more or less slide; the area is intrinsically difficult to police, not unlike family finances. Section 132, first enacted in 1984, was meant to codify existing law and reaffirm the principle that fringe benefits are taxable. Initially, the Section listed just a few exceptions to taxability, such as for "working condition fringes" and "qualified employee discounts." Each exception became the subject of significant regulatory development. The Section has since ballooned and takes up multiple pages of the Code. It is a good example of what a tangled web we weave when we choose a tax that must look at noncash items as income.

ℳ 2.9 Other Oddities

There are plenty of more twists and turns—details—we could explore in discussing "what is income." But the purpose of this short introduction is to give you a sense of the big picture, the forest, the essential principles. We are getting these down. On the labor side, everything you receive should be income, now, measured at its objective fair market value. You need a clear statute, like Section 105 or 106, 132, or 401 et seq., to get out of paying the piper now. On the capital side, you have income when you sell or otherwise dispose of an asset triggering realization and recognition (discussed at length in Chapter 4)—again absent a statutory exception, the main examples of which we will consider later—but not otherwise. Buying and holding financial property avoids taxes. Tax Planning 101 is a roadmap to nontaxation for those with capital.

Consider a further twist, in part to illustrate the important point that words matter. "Illegal income" is income, under Section 61, *Glenshaw Glass*, and otherwise. It has to be. If you steal money or other property, you should pay tax on it. (In the recent movie, *The Tourist*, starring Johnny Depp and Angelina Jolie, this rule comes into play.) You have a greater ability to pay, and so on. Conversely, the victim of theft may get a deduction, under Section 165(c)(3), though it is limited in various technical ways that we will consider in Chapter 3.

So that is a rule, and you should be able to understand it readily enough. But as much as we can understand rules, rules are always stated in words, and words can be interpreted, as we saw previously in the case of "gifts." Hence *Gilbert v. Commissioner*, 552 F.2d 478 (2nd Cir. 1977).

Gilbert was a high-ranking executive of a company. He had taken a bunch of money and fled to South America. Gilbert was found and brought back to the United States. The IRS claimed that he owed back taxes on his theft. But the court found that Gilbert had not "stolen" the money after all; he had merely "borrowed" it. As we know, from Tax Planning 101, borrowing is not income and does not generate tax.

Why did the court hold as it did? Executives who borrow money do not typically go into hiding abroad. Think for a moment about who really won the case. If the court had found the money to be illegal income, the government would have been able to collect all of Mr. Gilbert's remaining assets, given his likely 70 percent tax bracket, penalties, and interest. If the appropriation was instead a "loan" gone bad, as the court found, Gilbert's *company* would get all of his money back. The case was not about *Mr. Gilbert*, who ends up penniless in either event, at all. It was a battle between Gilbert's company and its owners, the shareholders, and the government. The court presumably felt more sympathy for the former, a true victim. This is yet another example of how things are not always what they seem in tax; matters that start one way often end up in another altogether.

☄ 2.10 Debt and Its Discharge

Speaking of debt, there is another rule to get down. Borrowing, or the initial incurrence of debt, is not "income," under Section 61, *Glenshaw Glass*, or the Haig-Simons definition. Hence the second plank in Tax Planning 101, buy/borrow/die. By parallel reasoning, the paying off of debt is not a taxable matter, either—no inclusion, no deduction. But one *does* have income when debt is *forgiven*. Why? Because the moment of forgiveness is an "undeniable accession to wealth, clearly realized," in the language of *Glenshaw Glass*.

Return to the balance sheet approach to thinking about income. Suppose that you are a student, $20,000 in debt. Your balance sheet shows a net worth of –$20,000. If your lender now forgives that debt, you instantly have an increase in your net worth, to $0. You have gone up $20,000 in net worth. That increase in your "store of property rights" is "income."

Now for some twists, as usual. One, paying someone's taxes counts as income: taxes are a form of debt, to the government, and if someone, such as your employer, pays them, you are made wealthier. You have income. *Old Colony Trust Company v. Commissioner*, 279 U.S. 716 (1929).[11]

Two, remember that just because something is "income" does not necessarily mean that it is *taxable* income. We must consider the statutory exclusions. Forgiveness of debt can be a form of *gift*, nontaxable under Section 102. There is also Section 108, which says, very generally, that debt forgiven as part of an official bankruptcy proceeding does not generate taxable income. Why do we have that rule? Because, if we did not, the basic purpose of the bankruptcy laws would be thwarted. Debtors would get relieved from paying their existing creditors, only to owe huge sums to a new creditor— the U.S. government. In fact, when the government wants to, it can come first in a line of creditors, as it does when it comes to tax liens. If the government asserted its full powers to collect tax on forgiven debt in bankruptcy, then the bankrupt party would not get the "fresh start" promised by the bankruptcy system.

---

11. *Old Colony* concerned Mr. Wood, a highly paid executive who, during World War I, had his company pay his income taxes for him. The Court ruled, quite rightly, that this payment constituted income to Mr. Wood. The taxpayer objected that this meant he was paying "tax on a tax," because he would have income in the amount of the taxes paid for him, on which he would have to pay further tax. But there is no deduction for *federal income taxes* paid under the federal income tax. IRC Section 164. This means, in technical terms, that the income tax is a "tax inclusive" tax – that is, that the tax itself is part of the tax base. We could convert it to a *tax-exclusive* tax by a simple adjustment in rates. Suppose for example that the tax rate is 50%. If Mr. Wood earned $100,000, he would have to pay $50,000 in tax – 50% of 100,000. He gets no deduction for the 50,000 taxes paid. But if we wanted to give him the deduction, we could "simply" raise the tax-exclusive rate to 100%! Mr. Wood would earn $100,000, subtract the 50,000 in taxes paid from his taxable income, and pay 100% of what was left, or 50,000. The dollars-and-cents would be the same, but the "optics" of the tax rates would be considerably different. At a 90% tax rate, for example, as we reached during World War II, the tax-exclusive rate would have to be 900%: Mr Wood would earn 100,000, subtract 90,000 in taxes paid, and pay 900% of the $10,000 he would have in his pocket after taxes. Taxpayers would be even less happy. Working with a leading academic psychologist, I have studied how people perceive tax rates and other taxing matters. Edward J. McCaffery and Jonathon Baron, "Thinking About Tax," 12 *Psychology, Public Policy, and the Law* 106 (2006).

Finally, a twist that matters for tax shelters and other subjects to come. When you borrow, you have no "income," as we know. But you do have *basis* in the proceeds of the borrowing, the cash. If you borrow and invest, say in a building, you have basis that you can use to take depreciation deductions. This is a huge advantage enabling you to get a tax benefit now on sums that you have borrowed. We will consider the resulting games further in Chapter 7, when we look at tax shelters more formally.

𝕸 2.11 A Small Taste of Theory

We will return more fully to theory in Part III. There I will sketch out the case for a certain kind of consumption tax, a progressive spending tax. A point to note briefly now is that such a tax treats debt very differently than does an income tax.

Under a spending tax, borrowing *is* taxable, now, when money is borrowed and consumed. Think of buying goods using a credit card. You pay the sales tax at the moment of purchase, which is also the moment of borrowing. On the other hand, repayments of principal are *not* taxable under a spending tax. You do not pay sales tax, again, when you pay off your credit card balance. It may sound as if this treatment of debt is a disadvantage of a spending tax, but we will come to see it has its considerable virtues.

Thus, importantly, a consistent spending tax shuts down Tax Planning 101. It does not do so by attacking Step One: a consistent spending tax has no need to tax "mere" appreciation or otherwise to challenge the realization requirement directly. Assets that are held and allowed to rise in value do not generate current spending or consumption. Instead, a consistent spending tax attacks Step Two: borrowing. Borrowing is income under a spending tax, whether enabled by assets on hand or future earnings potential. Rich Dad can buy and hold assets to his heart's content, but when he goes to convert his holdings into "fun" by borrowing, he will pay tax for the privilege. A consistent spending tax also finesses Step

Three: dying to get a stepped up basis. There is no concept of "basis" under a spending tax, because savings are not taxed directly. To come full circle, then, a consistent and progressive spending tax views *borrowing* and not the realization requirement as the Achilles' heel of the tax system. Borrowing with unrealized assets in hand allows for consumption without taxation. And that is the big problem in tax today, or so I shall argue.

🕊 2.12 Other Taxes

The income tax is not the only game in town. In fact, for *most* Americans, it is not even the major tax—the payroll tax, or social security/Medicare "contribution" system, is. This tax falls on wages starting with the first dollar earned: there is no "zero bracket," no deductions for anything or accomodations for family size, etc., under the payroll tax. This is an important policy point worth stressing. When we move away from a narrow focus on the individual income tax to look at the wider picture, we see that America heavily taxes labor, and lightly (if at all) taxes capital. The taxes more specifically aimed at capital, such as the corporate income and the gift and estate tax, are both far smaller in their magnitude and highly porous in their applications. The capital-labor divide persists across the entire U.S. tax system.

🕊 2.13 Summary

In this chapter we have learned:

- There are several definitions of "income." The Sixteenth Amendment and Section 61 give us a sense of comprehensiveness, but not a clear definition;
- Macomber gives us a poor definition of income, as "the gain derived from labor or capital or both combined," but does

leave us seemingly forever with the realization requirement, key to Tax Planning 101 and the labor-capital divide;

- Glenshaw Glass gives us a better judicial definition, as "an undeniable accession to wealth, clearly realized, and over which the taxpayer has dominion," leading to a balance sheet perspective, while importantly preserving the realization requirement;

- The Haig-Simons definition, essentially that Income = Consumption + Savings, gives us our widest sense of income; when tax laws diverge from economic realities, we have the potential for inequity and distortions;

- There are four important categories of nonincome that follow from concepts and definitions: psychic income, imputed income, unrealized appreciation, and debt;

- Tax Planning 101, the simple advice to buy/borrow/die, takes the basic principles of these definitions and converts them into a roadmap for paying no tax on the capital side of the labor-capital divide;

- The tax law concept of "basis" plays a very important role throughout tax, keeping track of what dollars need not be taxed, again, and setting a floor beneath the "built-in gain" or "tax time bomb" allowed to grow without current taxation because of the realization requirement of *Macomber* and subsequent law;

- One should always consider what happens when a transaction uses appreciated property instead of cash: there are two paradigms, pay tax/get basis, when a sale or exchange triggers tax on the built-in gain under Section 1001, or don't pay tax/don't get basis, when no gain is taxable and thus the basis carries over, preserving the tax time bomb for a later day;

- Basis has a consistent logic; one handy rule is that "sooner or later tax time bombs go off." The two important exceptions are for certain charitable contributions of appreciated property, under IRC Section 170, and death, which leads to a stepped-up basis under IRC 1014;

- The law is very concerned to pick up all forms of compensation for labor, whether in cash or noncash form;
- Noncash or fringe benefits are generally taxable, now, at their objective fair market value;
- Congress has the power not to tax items that are "income" under the statute, and has liberally used this power, under Section 101 and following;
- Section 102 provides that "gifts" are not taxable to the recipient; after the Supreme Court stumbled in its approach to gifts in the *Duberstein* case, the law evolved such that gifts are generally found in the personal context (following the don't deduct/don't include paradigm) but not in the business context (following the deduct/include paradigm);
- The most important categories of fringe benefits that are not currently taxable are employer-provided health insurance and qualified pension plans;
- Borrowing is not income under an income tax: it falls outside of the Haig-Simons definition and all legal ones. Borrowing does lead to basis in the cash proceeds, however, and the repaying of debt is also ignored for tax purposes. *Forgiveness of debt*, however, is "income," although whether or not it is taxable depends on the *reason* for the forgiveness: it could be a gift, non-taxable under Section 102, or part of a qualified discharge of debt in bankruptcy, IRC 108, for two examples;
- A consistent spending tax, as we will explore further in Part III, does tax borrowing when incurred, and allows a deduction for repayments of principal. Such a tax implicitly accepts the realization requirement, but views borrowing, not the realization requirement, as the Achilles' heel of tax;
- Tax is fun (remember?).

The "What" of Taxation, Part Two
Deductions from the Tax Base

WE NOW LOOK AT THE LOGIC, language, law, and policy of *deductions*, or subtractions from the "income" base just built up in the previous chapter. As usual, we start with some sense of the deepest policies in play, the "big picture." The key to understanding deductions is a three-fold distinction between (1) personal, (2) business, and (3) mixed business-personal expenditures.

※ 3.1 General Principles

The fundamental theory of an income tax suggests that personal items should not be deducted absent clear statutory language. This is precisely what IRC Section 262(a) states:

> Except as otherwise expressly provided in this chapter, no deduction shall be allowed for personal, living, or family expenses.

The reason for the policy is simple: if we allowed deductions for living expenses, or "fun," as I tell my students, there would be nothing left in the tax base. Go back to the basic definition of Income:

$$Income = Consumption + Savings$$

Most people do not save, and the income tax does a poor job of picking up savings in any event. *This means that an income tax is largely a consumption tax.* And "consumption" mainly means what we pay for food, clothing, shelter, entertainment, and so on. Allow deductions for any or all of these items of personal consumption, and the tax base rapidly shrinks away.

We will consider the chief exceptions to the policy of disallowing personal deductions—extraordinary medical expenses, casualty losses, qualified pensions and IRAs, charitable contributions, and home mortgage interest—in due course, and discuss the law and economic effects of the exceptions. The key point is that just like we need a clear statute to except something from the sweeping definition of "income" in the Code, under Section 61—and we find such exceptions set out in Section 101 and following—so, too, do we need a clear statute allowing a deduction for a personal matter.

Things are precisely the opposite when it comes to business expenses, the second category in our triad. "Ordinary and necessary" *business* expenses *should* be deductible, as they are under Section 162, because the government, as a "partner in business," wants to encourage profit-maximizing expenditures. A company spends $1 in the reasonable expectation that it will earn more than $1, say $1.20. The government is happy enough to give a deduction for the $1—in essence, paying its share of the expense—because it will be there to collect tax on the $1.20, netting a profit for itself, the government.

Suppose that the tax rate is 30 percent. The company, in spending $1, is really spending 70 cents after taxes ($1 minus the 30 cents saved by deducting $1 from its taxable income in a 30% bracket) in order to make 84 cents after taxes (70 percent of the $1.20 gross value received, or, equivalently, the $1.20 received less the 36 cents of tax owed on that amount of income). The government for its part is giving up 30 cents of tax revenue up front to get 36 cents of tax on the back end. Both the company and the government are making a 20 percent return on their "investment": the company's 70 cents of after-tax expense becomes 84 cents of after-tax profit, the government's 30 cents in forgone taxes becomes 36 cents in taxes collected.

If in contrast the company is spending $1 without an expectation of making more than $1, either this is not a "business" expense at all—a matter addressed below—or the company will go bankrupt soon enough, replaced by a more profitable business.

This leaves two questions under the topic of business expenses. One, are they "really" business expenses, as opposed to disguised personal expenses? Two, when is the right *time* to take the deduction? The latter question opens up a brief and nontechnical discussion of depreciation and capitalization, with another trilogy: (1) take an immediate expense deduction, (2) capitalize and depreciate the expense, or (3) capitalize and do not depreciate the expense.

Finally, we will discuss the "mixed business-personal" cases, the third part of the triad, involving such matters as education, commuting expenses, child care, work-related clothing, and the like. Here we discover that some cases that might best be thought of as being about *timing*—the subject of the next chapter—sometimes get analyzed under the "mixed business-personal" rubric, setting up a later discussion of passive activity loss rules under IRC Section 469 and the like, and re-introducing the concept of "netting," as under Section 183.

The chapter concludes with a discussion of the deductibility of interest under Section 163, pointing out how this illustrates the tripartite division among business (Section 163(a), fully deductible); personal (Section 163(h), not generally deductible, with a major exception (mortgage interest and home equity indebtedness)); and mixed because of passive investment (Section 163(d)'s netting rule).

I have drawn up a simple diagram, Figure 1, that might help you see a roadmap through this stretch of tax's forest.

We will come to see what this all means as we move through this Chapter.

ℳ 3.2 The Mechanics of Deductions

Let us next get some basic vocabulary and concepts down.

Deductions work as subtractions from the tax base: they reduce gross (Section 61) or adjusted gross income (Section 62) to yield taxable income (Section 63). Deductions come in two varieties.

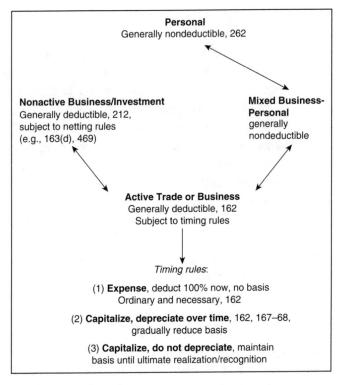

FIGURE 1   Diagram for Deductions

"Above the line" deductions move from gross to adjusted gross income. Generally, business expenses fall here. Itemized deductions move from adjusted gross to taxable income and require the taxpayer to fill out a separate schedule (Schedule A). Taxpayers have a choice of taking itemized deductions or a standard deduction, and will typically take whichever is larger. In 2011, the standard deduction for a married couple filing jointly is set to be $10,600; it is $5,800 for a single taxpayer. Most taxpayers—about 75 percent—do not itemize because this standard deduction is greater than their potential itemized ones. The standard deduction—plus personal dependency exemptions, discussed below—gives every household a basic amount immune from tax, and greatly simplifies record-keeping and form-completion chores.

It bears noting how much of the complexity and headaches of the income tax fall on a small percent of the population: about one-half of Americans pay no income tax, and only about one-quarter of those that do itemize. Most of the personal deductions that are allowed fall into the itemized category, as exceptions to the general policy just noted.

3.2.1 The Math of the Matter

The basic economics of deductions are simple enough to state but are a bit tricky to understand fully. Since a deduction is a subtraction from what would otherwise be taxable, *deductions save you money at your marginal rate.*

Suppose, for example, that you make $60,000, and, to keep things simple, are in a constant 30 percent rate bracket. You will pay $18,000, or 30 percent of $60,000, in tax. Now suppose that you have tax deductions of $10,000. These bring your taxable income down to $50,000, and your total tax down to $15,000, or 30 percent of $50,000. This means that the $10,000 deduction has saved you $3,000 in taxes; 30 percent of the amount deducted.

Tax policy types keep track of the money that the government gives up by allowing deductions that are inconsistent with the fundamental definition of income, calling them "tax expenditures." The idea is because Congress does not *have* to allow these deductions – unlike most business expenses, which likely must be allowed in calculating a fair and Constitutional sense of "income" – the government is spending money by not collecting the related tax. Allowing a $10,000 home mortgage interest deduction to a taxpayer in the 30% bracket, for example, "costs" the government $3,000 – money that it would have collected if it did not allow the deduction, but all other matters, such as the taxpayer's total income, stayed the same.

The aggregate dollars spent on such tax expenditures are very salient to Congress and others in this time of mounting government deficits and hence revenue needs. Personal deductions – where almost all tax expenditures fall – are thus constantly at risk of being repealed or limited. Employer-provided health care (because of the exclusion from gross income allowed by Sections 105-06),[1] home mortgage interest (Section 163(h)), and retirement savings provisions (pension plans and IRAs, Sections 401 and following) especially stand out. Many tax policy reform discussions of late have centered on eliminating tax expenditures or at least limiting their benefit, as we pick up in Part III. The alternative minimum tax (AMT) that we consider briefly below has this policy behind it, of limiting the benefit of deductions.

The mathematics of deductions mean that *deductions are regressive in a progressive marginal rate system.* That is, a $10,000 deduction is more valuable to a higher bracket taxpayer than a lower bracket one: Tom, in the 50% bracket, saves $5,000 in taxes from a $10,000 deduction, whereas Jerry, in a 15% bracket, saves only $1500. In the limiting case, the working poor who pay no *income* tax—but may pay significant payroll and other taxes—get no benefit at all from income tax deductions. For this reason, Congress often chooses to enact *credits* instead of *deductions.*

Instead of working as a subtraction from taxable income, credits work as a subtraction from the tax owed.

3.2.2 Following the Form (Again)

It may help here to consider again the flow of a basic tax form, the dreaded 1040: we are in essence tracking this flow in this central part of the short introduction.

---

1. An exclusion from gross income leads to the same place as an inclusion followed by a deduction. Suppose that Bart earned $50,000 on his job, and his employer also paid for health insurance in an annual amount of $5,000. That $5,000 (assuming as always all other qualifications are met) will not be taxable income to Bart under IRC Section 106. But we *could* say that it was, bringing Bart's income to $55,000, and then allow a deduction for employer provided health care, bringing Bart's taxable income back down to $50,000. In other words, an exclusion or non-inclusion = an inclusion plus an offsetting deduction. It follows that the non-inclusion of employer-provided health care under Sections 105-06 can be seen as a "tax expenditure," just as much as any personal deduction could be.

First, you add up all of your sources of gross income: from wages, investments, businesses, and so on. This follows Section 61, and occurs on the first page of the 1040. Then you subtract the "above the line" deductions to get an adjusted gross income. From there, you face the fork in the road: take the standard deduction or itemize. Either way, now on the back page of the 1040 form and using Schedule A if you itemize, you arrive at taxable income. You then calculate, from the tax rate tables, your tax owed. (A step I have ignored along the way is the separate calculation and schedule for "capital gains," a subject we shall address in Chapter 6.)

You have now arrived at tax owed, and it is time for *credits*. Each credit subtracts from what you need to pay then and there to the government. The most common and obvious credit is for taxes already paid, as via withholding from your paycheck. Congress also uses credits to advance its policy goals, oftentimes to get away from the regressivity of deductions in a progressive marginal rate system.

3.2.3 An Important Case Study: The Earned Income Tax Credit

The most important credit from a public policy perspective is the earned income tax credit of IRC Section 32 (EITC). This credit was put in place under the Nixon administration in the 1970s as a way to offset the payroll taxes paid by the working poor. It created a genuine "zero bracket" across the two taxes. In essence, looking at the EITC alone, workers are paid by the government—they face a "negative" tax—for their first dollars earned.

The EITC was expanded under Bill Clinton: it is the "workfare" that replaced "welfare" as we know it. A couple with three or more children now get 45 percent of their first $12,780 of earnings—$5,750—back under the credit. (These numbers are constantly changing due to inflation adjustments and statutory changes.) Unlike most other policy-related credits, the EITC is *refundable*, meaning that if subtracting it from the tax otherwise owed generates a negative number, the government will mail the taxpayer a check (or even allow "negative withholding" in paychecks). The EITC is now the major means of providing financial assistance to the poor in America.

The EITC has its problems and its critics. One needs to fill out tax forms to get it, and many poor do not: undercompliance is a problem of social justice. Some noncitizens are even afraid to file tax returns. The nonworking poor do not qualify. And the EITC also comes at a price—a "phase out" range that adds to the burdens on the near working poor. I explore some of these problems in other writings.[2]

ℳ 3.3 Personal Expenditures

A deep policy of tax frowns on deductions for personal matters. The principle is captured in IRC Section 262(a) as noted above: "Except as otherwise provided, no deduction shall be allowed for personal, family, or living expenses." I tell my students, in shorthand, that there is "no deduction for fun"; fun must be had with after-tax dollars.

This is the way it has to be. If the Code started allowing deductions for food, clothing, shelter, and recreation, the tax base would shrink to naught. The idea of a standard deduction is that everyone gets a "zero bracket" for the basics. Above that, the piper must be paid.

We see this, too, in the Haig-Simons definition. Income = Consumption + Savings. Most Americans do not have any positive savings in any particular year. So income *is* consumption. Just as we

---

2. *See* Edward J. McCaffery, "The Burdens of Benefits", 44 *Villanova Law Review* 445 (1999); I also discuss the EITC, its burdens on the working poor, and its affects on marriage in *Taxing Women* (University of Chicago Press (1997). *See also* Anne L. Alstott, "The Earned Income Tax Credit and the Limitations of Tax-Based Welfare Reform", 108 *Harvard Law Review* 533 (1995).

have to try and capture all "income," on the sources side, especially from labor, so too must we try and tax all or most consumption on the uses side of the basic definition.

Of course there are exceptions. But it helps to understand that they are exceptions to a deep principle, hence their status as tax expenditures. Personal deductions are typically limited to itemizers, and even beyond that. Let us consider a few.

Extraordinary medical expenses are deductible as an itemized matter under IRC Section 213. But there are limits, getting at what is considered "extraordinary." The main limitation is that you only get to deduct your expenses to the extent they exceed 7.5 percent of your adjusted gross income. If you earn $100,000, for example, only qualified medical expenses above $7,500 can get any tax benefit. You can think of this provision if you want as a strange form of insurance, with a high deductible (7.5 percent of your adjusted gross income) and a significant co-payment. What you have to pay is a percent of the expense set at 1 minus your tax rate; that is, if you are in the 30 percent tax bracket, any deduction saves you 30 percent, but you must pay 70 percent of the expense. If you spent $10,000 over the limit and are in the 30% bracket, the government will give you $3,000 off your taxes as compensation for the medical expense. You can also think of this as a small nod to the fact that people with large medical expenses may lack the ability of their healthier fellow citizens to pay taxes in addition to their medical expenses.

Generally speaking, *losses* for an individual taxpayer are only deductible if they come from an active trade or business, IRC Section 165(c)(1), or from an investment that is not part of an active trade or business, like a stock or mutual fund, 165(c)(2). But there is some ability to take purely personal losses if they arise from a "casualty" loss under Section 165(c)(3). Here the limits are severe. For one thing, your deduction is limited to the basis, not the fair market value, of your loss. Each loss must be at least $100. And you only benefit from all the losses over $100, combined, to the extent that they exceed 10 percent of your adjusted gross income.

Qualified employer-provided pension plans, under Section 401 et seq., are excluded from taxable income, a subject matter of the prior chapter. This reminds us of a basic point about the math of matters: it really does not matter *why* something is taken out of the taxable income basis—whether it is a conceptual noninclusion, a statutory exclusion, or a deduction. All roads lead to the same place: a smaller tax base, a lesser amount of income being taxed, and hence savings, compared to inclusion or nondeduction, at your marginal rate. A reason to bring up pension plans now is that there are other forms of pro-savings provisions, including traditional Individual Retirement Accounts (IRAs) under Section 408, that work as deductions. Other savings accounts work along the increasingly common "Roth-style" IRAs and savings plans, Section 408A, whereby there is no initial deduction for the contribution into the account, but no subsequent inclusion of any investment gains. We will discuss these various approaches to taxing savings in Part III, when we consider tax reform options more systematically.

The home mortgage interest deduction, under IRC Section 163(h), is perhaps the most popular of the personal deductions. We will discuss this at greater length later in this chapter, when we look at Section 163 and the subject of interest deductions more generally.

State and local income and property taxes, and, in some cases, sales taxes, are deductible, even if incurred in the personal context, under IRC Section 164.[3] A major limitation on this deduction, important for high earners in high-tax states such as New York and California, is that it gets put back into the alternative minimum tax as an "adjustment" under IRC Section 56. We will get to the AMT in a bit as well.

---

3. Recall from the discussion of *Old Colony* in the prior chapter that there is no deduction for federal income taxes within the federal income tax: the tax is a "tax inclusive" one, meaning that the tax paid is part of the base subject to tax.

Finally, individuals get deductions for their charitable contributions, under Section 170, if they itemize. These deductions, too, are
subject to various rules, regulations, and limits (for example, charitable contribution deductions can only be taken in any given year up
to one-half (50 percent) of one's adjusted gross income). Charitable
contributions also form an exception to the "sooner or later" rule for
tax time bombs, because one can get a fair market value deduction
for gifts of appreciated property—getting a tax benefit for the appreciation without ever paying tax on the built-in gain.

Suppose that Lisa had purchased some stock for $1,000, which
has appreciated without current taxation to being worth $10,000. If
Lisa gives this stock to her favorite charity – assuming all other con-
ditions met – she will be able to deduct the fair market value of
$10,000, although she has not yet paid tax on $9,000 of the gain. If
Lisa is in the 30% bracket, this deduction will save her $3,000 in
taxes. Like all deductions, this fair market value deduction used to
mean more with higher marginal tax rates. In a 90% bracket, for
example as we saw from the mid 1940s through to 1963, Lisa would
save $9,000 in taxes – netting more by giving than she would by sell-
ing and paying capital gains tax on the gain.

In any event, this benefit for appreciated property without triggering a tax time bomb is an exception to the "sooner or later, tax
time bombs go off"–the other exception, again, being death, IRC
Section 1014 and Step Three of Tax Planning 101 – and thus there
are predictably enough exceptions to it. One does not get a fair
market value deduction for giving "ordinary income property," such
as inventory, to a charity, or for contributions of "tangible personal
property" that are not used by the charity in furthering its exempt
function. IRC Section 170(e)(1)(B). Why this latter rule? There is a
lobbying story here, about a clever representative of the art museum
world, getting a law enacted designed to keep art in art museums.
Donors only get to deduct the fair market value of contributed tangible personal property—which includes, importantly, art—if the charitable recipient "uses" the art as part of its essential charitable purpose.
Of course art museums fit the bill. Many schools and hospitals,

however, have art prominently displayed on their walls (until they decide to sell it)—once again, a tax story lurks behind everyday reality.

These are all personal matters allowed as deductions because of a clear statute. Otherwise the rule of Section 262 blocks such deductions.

3.3.1 Note on Standard Deduction and Personal Dependency Exemptions

Personal dependency deductions are granted by Section 151; dependents are defined in Section 152. The amount of the deduction is indexed for inflation, set for $3,750 per dependent in 2011.

A taxpayer gets to claim herself as a dependent for this purpose; married couples filing jointly have two exemptions, and each child or other qualified dependent adds to the mix. When added to the standard deduction, which in 2011 is set at $10,600 for a married couple, the personal dependency exemptions form a "zero bracket" of tax: $18,100 for a married couple without children ($10,600 plus two times $3750). The structure of the dependency exemption widens this bracket for larger families—it is $25,600 for a married couple with two children, for example—making a nod toward seeing the family as the appropriate taxpaying unit, a subject matter we return to in Chapter 5.

A taxpayer gets the dependency exemptions whether she itemizes or not, so this is also a concession to the fact that some unquestionably "personal" expenditures should bear no net tax. But note that the dependency exemptions are "preferences" for purposes of the alternative minimum tax (AMT), discussed below. As a general matter, any accommodation for personal expenditures in the Code is fragile: Congress will not touch the business expense deductions, needed for the economy. But in an age of tight budget needs, all personal deductions stand at some risk.

3.3.2 Note on "Phase-outs" and Itemized Deductions

Continuing one of the above themes, namely the vulnerability of all personal deductions, exclusions, and accomodations in an age of budget stringency, Congress has shown a preference for rules that "phase out" itemized deductions as one's income rises. These phaseouts work like a hidden tax rate or bubble, because when one is in the range of losing the benefit, she is paying a tax both at her regular rate and via the loss of a benefit she would otherwise get. This technique, a general aspect of the Tax Reform Act of 1986 and of the EITC, has been applied to itemized deductions rather broadly, under Section 68. That provision is in limbo as I write, but it would hardly shock observers of tax policy of late to see its return at some point.

✎ 3.4 Business Expenditures (With Notes on Timing)

Everything is turned 180 degrees when we move to business expenses. Just as there is a deep policy of the law to disallow personal expenses, there is an equally deep policy to *allow* business expense deductions, such as salaries paid to employees, rent, interest, the cost of goods sold, and the like. IRC Section 162.

Why is the business expense deduction so sweeping? Because the tax system makes the government a silent partner in business, and business knows best.

There is not even much room for the IRS to regulate, on "public policy" grounds, business expense deductions. The handful of exceptions to business expense deductibility is set out in the statute, forming the bulk of the detail of Section 162's subparts. See *Stephens v. Commissioner*, 905 F.2d 667 (2d Cir. 1990), discussing the general limits on asserting policy grounds for disallowing a business-related expense.

This leaves two questions. One, is an expense, even if paid by a business, "really" a business one? There is a fair amount of outright fraud here: individuals paying for cars and condominiums primarily or exclusively for personal use on the corporate books. There are also genuinely close, hard cases, like travel, meals and entertainment. These types of items, some of which we will discuss below under the "mixed business personal" category, are increasingly subject to limitations and precise, detailed rules. See for example IRC Section 274, the so-called substantiation rules for the records one must keep to qualify for these types of deductions. Once again, we stray onto matters too detailed for this short introduction: the short form memorandum/piece of advice to all who might be affected is to save your receipts.

Two, even if an expense is deductible, *when* is it? To some considerable extent, this gets into matters for the next chapter, on timing: here is yet another place where the *what* and *when* of tax are vitally connected. Recall from the planning notes in Chapter 1 that everything in tax is turned on its head when we are looking at losses or subtractions instead of gains or additions. Thus, taxpayers want to *accelerate* deductions just as they want to defer inclusions.

3.4.1 Rule: Sooner or Later, Part II: You Get Your (Business or Investment) Basis Back

Time for another rule: When you expend resources in a business, or in another profit-seeking venture, like a stock market or real estate investment, "sooner or later" you get that money back. I mean this in the specific—and limited—sense of your being entitled to a deduction from taxable income for the amount expended. The government will not mail you a check for the entire amount of your investment, but they will let you "write off" the dollars you have put into the matter. In other words, you get a business expense deduction.

The question—the only question, once we have decided that something really is a "business" expense—is when. If you spend $100, somehow, somewhere, sometime, a minus $100 shows up on some tax return or schedule. As we now know, deductions save you money at your marginal rate. So if you are in the 30 percent bracket, spending $100 on a bona fide business will, one day, save you $30 in taxes. Put another way, you do not have to pay tax again on the amount you invest in a business, just on what you earn from it. Once again, the tax law concept of "basis" will do the work of sorting this all out.

All roads lead to the key question of when. There are three possible answers, set out in Figure 1, above:

(1) **now, right away**, what tax professionals call *expensing*, as befits "ordinary" expenditures under IRC Section 162;

(2) **later, but over time**, ratably, as *depreciation deductions*, ordinary expenses under IRC Section 162 that are nonetheless depreciable under Sections 167–168; and

(3) **later—way later**—on ultimate sale or disposition of the asset, pursuant to IRC Section 1001.

Recall that when we are discussing deductions, taxpayers generally want things sooner rather than later – that is, they want to accelerate them. So these answers are in descending order of attraction to the typical taxpayer. Also note that the important tax concept of basis is once again going to do the work of keeping track of all this, as we shall continue to explore. If you get an immediate expense deduction, option 1, you have no basis; if you have to defer matters, you get basis which gradually reduces under option 2 and serves as an offset to taxable gain under option 3.

In order to sort business and investment expenditures into three categories, we need to answer two questions.

3.4.2 Question One: Now or Later (Ordinary or Capital)?

The first question is: Is it appropriate to take a deduction now, option 1, or should the expense be *capitalized* and taken later, options 2 or 3? Put in other, but equivalent, terms: Is the expense "ordinary" or "capital"? Note again the multiple uses of "capital" and its cognates such as "capitalization." A "capital" expense is one that is not properly deductible immediately, all at once. It does not get the favored option 1.

This is one of the trickier questions in tax. Courts have come up with various answers to it. In the celebrated Supreme Court case of *Welch v. Helvering*, 290 U.S. 111 (1933), it appeared that Justice Cardozo was addressing the question of whether an expense—specifically the payment by a former employee of his ex-company's debts, which had been discharged in bankruptcy (the employee was trying to start up his own related business, and clearly wanted to restore good will from the prior customers)—was deductible *at all*, as an "ordinary and necessary" business expense under Section 162. But in fact the only question before the Court was one of *timing*; even the IRS conceded that the payments were, indeed, business expenses. The government "simply" wanted the expenditures capitalized and added to basis. Since the Court found the payments to be for corporate "goodwill," or general reputation, and since goodwill is an asset with a long life, the Court agreed with the government that the expenses had to be kept on the books as an item with tax basis. Option 3 prevailed.

Welch is excellent proof of the point that timing matters. Both the government and taxpayer agreed that Welch's payments were business-related; no one was asserting a *Duberstein*-like argument that they were gifts, nondeductible under IRC Section 262. The only question was when, option 1 or 3. Yet the parties litigated this dispute all the way up to the Supreme Court. Why? Because time really is money. Having the expenses capitalized and added to goodwill meant that Mr. Welch would have to wait until the day he sold his business to get his basis back; if he died before selling his business, the basis would be swallowed up by the general stepped-up basis on death under Section 1014.

There are various judicial standards for when something needs to be capitalized in this sense. "Ordinary" expenses are those for a current, short-term period: think of wages paid, rent, utilities, interest, and the like. An expense must be capitalized when it is for an item with a long expected life, like a machine, building, or car. Some courts use a "separate asset" test, others a "benefits beyond a year" one. Richard Posner, in an interesting opinion in the case of *Encyclopaedia Brittanica v. Commissioner*, 685 F.2d 212 (7th Cir. 1982), discusses the idea of "temporal matching," which gets to the deeper theory of capitalization and depreciation deductions. The idea is that, if an expense is allowed now, today, but the corresponding benefits or profits are apt to come in the future, there can be a distortion leading to poor investment decisions.

Suppose that a business in the 30 percent bracket invests $100 today. If it gets its deduction now, it immediately saves $30 in taxes. But if it does not make its profit until years down the road, it will have gotten an interest-free loan for that $30. Imagine that the company makes $110 in two years. That $110 is all taxable—since, by stipulation, the business got to deduct the $100, now, it has no basis (see discussion below of tracking basis). The $110 includes $10 of profit, which the company shares, under the tax system, with the government, $7 and $3. But it also includes a recoupment of the $100 initial investment. The government gets its $30 back, but the company has had two years to use it, without having to pay interest. That is, or could be, a distortion.

3.4.3 Question Two: If Later, Does the Deduction Come over Time or "Way Later"?

The second question for the timing of business expense deductions comes up once we have decided that it is inappropriate to take an immediate deduction. We are between options 2 and 3. If we must capitalize, can we depreciate, meaning take the deductions ratably over time, option 2, or must the expense sit in the basis of the asset, waiting for ultimate sale or disposition under IRC Section 1001, option 3?

Here, at least, there is handy language to guide us, mapping up with the basic policy. Some capital expenses are for "wasting assets": items that decline in value over time, through wear and tear and the like. In the language of tax, this second question comes down to whether or not the asset has a "finite and readily ascertainable useful life." Machines and buildings do; land, "goodwill" as in the *Welch* case, and corporate stock do not. (If you want to be very precise in your language, and impress whomever there is to be impressed by this kind of thing, one *depreciates* tangible assets, such as buildings and machines, and *amortizes* intangible assets, such as contracts, long-term leaseholds, patents, and the like.)

The details of depreciation are indeed details, best left to accountants and longer tomes on tax. For our purposes, the main idea is that depreciation is a way of getting one's basis back over time. It is a middle answer. The shorter or more "accelerated" the depreciation schedule, the better, because you want your deductions sooner rather than later, all things being equal. If you spend $100 in a business and must depreciate it, doing so over five years in a "straight line" format means a deduction of $20 a year for five years; a ten-year schedule means $10 a year for ten years. At a 30 percent tax rate, again, this means having the government pay you, in the form of reduced taxes, $6 a year for five years, or $3 a year for ten. Note again the interest-free nature of tax deferral/acceleration. Given constant tax rates, sooner is better.

3.4.4 Tracking Basis

Recall our second "sooner or later" rule, for money spent in a profit-seeking form, in an active trade or business or for investment: sooner or later, you get it back, in the form of a deduction from taxes. We have seen that this "getting back" can be now, today, option 1; over time, option 2; or on ultimate sale or disposition, option 3. Figure 1, above, has a summary.

To make sure you are really understanding matters, note that a key element of the logic of tax is that *as you take depreciation deductions, your basis goes down*. Depreciation is a *means* of basis recovery. You only get your basis back—rule number two—once.[4]

To summarize, in each case of a $100 business or investment expense, you get to write off $100 on a tax form. In option 1, you do so right away, and you are left with no basis. In option 2, you do so over a period of years, and your basis reduces in step as you do so. If you are depreciating $100 over five years at $20 a year, at the end of Year 1 you will have basis of $80, $60 at the end of Year 2, and so on. In option 3, you wait until ultimate sale or disposition, and then the expense which has been capitalized but not depreciated gets to be subtracted under the formula of IRC Section 1001(a) in determining ultimate gain or loss.

ℳ 3.5 Business-Personal Expenditures

The rules we have considered in this chapter so far, though they have a fair amount of detail beneath the surface, might seem refreshingly black-and-white above the surface: personal expenditures are not generally deductible, Section 262; business ones are generally deductible, Section 162. Then it is just a matter of getting

---

4. I am using "you" here rather loosely. More accurately, *someone* will get the basis back. There are many situations – such as typical contributions to a corporation or partnership – where because of an explicit non-recognition rule, no gain is realized, and the basis carries over to a different taxpayer. In such cases, the transferee taxpayer will get the basis back. Of course if one holds an appreciated asset until death, completing Tax Planning 101, the transferee taxpayer will be an heir who gets *more* than the original basis back, because of the stepped-up basis rule of Section 1014.

the handful of exceptions to the personal deductions down, and mastering the tricky timing questions for business expenses. Right?

Not quite so fast. The problem is that life is not typically black-and-white. Much of what we do has *both* a business *and* a personal component: clothes we wear to work; food consumed on the job; commuting expenses; education. These items are, at one and the same time, business *and* personal, matters covered by both Section 162 and Section 262. How does the tax law treat them?

As a general matter, the nondeductibility of Section 262 trumps. Most of these items are not generally deductible. A more specific but handy rule of thumb is that expenses needed to get you *to* a job are not deductible, while expenses occurred while *on* the job are. This explains both the rule about education expenses, Treasury Regulation 1.162-5, and commuting.

For education, any expenses to educate yourself to get qualified for a job—virtually all undergraduate and most graduate and professional school degrees—are *not* generally deductible.[5] Think of this as reflecting your *personal* choice to enter a certain line of work; if you prefer, consider that a general tuition deduction would be quite large, indeed, and tax rates would have to go up to compensate for it. On the other hand, educational expenses to maintain or improve workplace skills—money spent on the job, as it were—*are* generally deductible.

---

5. There are very limited tax breaks for education, such as IRC Section 222's qualified tuition and related expenses deduction, or the Hope credit for higher education, IRC Section 25A. Typically, however, these provisions do little good, because students incurring the expenses have little income, and there are phase-outs making the deductions and credits worthless to most graduates. There is a theme, growing more common of late, where tax provisions ostensibly helping some group end up costing the government little because of their limitations – but nonetheless generate some good publicity, a kind of tax policy by sound bite. For benefits available for education more generally, see IRS Publication 970, *Tax Benefits for Education*, available, like a great many other resources, at the IRS Web site, www.irs.gov.

For commuting, again, the costs of getting to work are not deductible. Think of this as reflecting the *personal* choice of where you live in relation to your work; or, again, consider the cost and complexity of a general commuting expense deduction. On the other hand, travel on the job *is* generally deductible as a work-related expense under Section 162.

Clothing expenses are not generally deductible unless they are for some kind of uniform essentially required by the employer, and not used for personal purposes. And so on. The general idea is to attempt to winnow out pure business expenses, and deny deductions for most mixed matters.

Child-care expenses are also not generally deductible, under a questionable decades-old lower court case, *Smith v. Commissioner*, 40 B.T.A. 1038 (1939), affirmed without opinion, 113 F.2d 114 (2nd Cir. 1940). The highly limited child-care credit of IRC Section 21 provides some relief for working parents, but not much.[6]

Finally, homes themselves are things that can straddle the business-personal distinction, partaking of each of the two worlds. IRC Section 280A deals specifically with the situation of the business use of one's home, including, most importantly, the home-office deduction. While taxpayers who work at home can qualify for some tax breaks here, they had best be careful: the business use must be regular and exclusive, and must also be somehow central to the taxpayer's business. This is a frequent area for audits and litigation. Section 280A covers some other mixed business-personal uses of the home, too, such as renting out one's home for a few days, or entering into a lease or purchase agreement with a family member (where the general rule is, not surprisingly, that everything must be done on an arm's-length, fair market value basis, lest the parent/owner/landlord be denied any and all investment tax breaks because of the personal, gift-like nature of the transaction).

---

6. I criticize the *Smith* case in My books, *Taxing Women, supra*, at 111–14, and discuss the child-care credit and its limits at 114–19.

3.5.1 Two Senses of Mixed Matters

A further complexity is that there are two, not one, intermediate categories between 162's business/generally deductible and 262's personal/generally not deductible rules. Figure 1, above, attempts to illustrate this.

One category is the genuinely, existentially mixed matters that we have just been discussing—education, commuting, work-related clothing, child care, home offices, and the like. These are matters that have both business, or profit-seeking, and personal dimensions to them.

A second mixed mode exists between two kinds of for-profit activities. These are sometimes characterized as "active trade or business," the language of IRC Section 162, versus investment (see Section 212 or 163(d)), or as "active" versus "passive" activity income (see Section 469, discussed at greater length in Chapter 7). This illustrates another important theme in tax: within the single "income" tax, there are actually various types of "income," placed into different "baskets"—ordinary versus capital, active versus passive, and so on.

In one case, there is an active trade or business incurring regular, ordinary expenses and generating regular, ordinary profits. In the other case, someone has bought a stock or a parcel of real property as an investment. From an economics point of view, it is not clear that there is any meaningful distinction here: in both cases, the individual wants to make money. In the abstract, the tax laws should not tilt an individual toward one or the other approach. Sometimes running your own business is the best shot you have; other times, investing your money and letting someone else handle things is the better way to go. You should make that decision on strictly rational grounds.

The problem is that tax must mark a very sharp distinction between these two types of profit-seeking activities. The *reason* for this critical differentiation is a matter of timing, harking back to *Macomber* once again. *Macomber* led to the realization requirement, meaning that the mere appreciation of a capital asset was not income until and unless the built-in gain was somehow "realized" through sale or other disposition under IRC Section 1001. This means that a good deal of investment leads to little or no taxable income: you buy stocks and let your winners ride, a buy and hold strategy at the core of Tax Planning 101.

Back to expenses and deductions: if the law allows you to deduct your expenses from investing, but your gains are not included because of the realization requirement, the government would have a huge problem on its hands. This is just the kind of "temporal mis-matching" that concerned Judge Posner in the *Encyclopaedia Brittanica* case mentioned above. The deductible expenses would offset the one category of income still showing up on tax returns— wages from labor income—and there would be no tax at all! We will consider this further in Chapter 7 as we explore tax shelters in greater depth. The point arises now because it explains why we need to treat expenses associated with investment or "passive" activities differently from those occurring in an active trade or business.

Considering the problem and reluctant to repeal *Macomber* or to alter the realization requirement (which could lead to showing appreciation on annual tax returns), the law came up with another answer. It adopted various "netting" rules. The idea is to create "baskets" where expenses can only be deducted against visible income *from the same basket*. We saw this approach above briefly with the capital loss offset rules, IRC Section 1211–capital losses can essentially be deducted only against realized and recognized capital gains–and we will see the approach more thoroughly below, in considering the investment interest expense deduction, Section 163(d). Quite a bit more generally, the passive activity loss (PAL) rules of Section 469, Congress' most systematic response to indi-vidual tax shelters, the subject of Chapter 7, takes a netting approach.

The key point for now is that an item of expenditure can be out of Section 162's near automatic deduction rule (subject to matters of timing, of course), for one of two reasons. One, because it has elements of personal consumption within it, that is, it is a mixed business-personal expense also covered by Section 262. Two, because, while it is incurred in a for-profit activity, its nature as a "passive" "investment" or something else other than an active trade or business makes deductions allocable to it problematic—because of *Macomber* and the realization requirement.

3.5.2   A Note on Using the Wrong Tools

Nickerson v. Commissioner, 700 F.2d 402 (7th Cir. 1983) illustrates the problem and the importance of asking the right question. Mr. Nickerson was a middle-aged and decently compensated advertising executive in Chicago. He started a dairy farm in Wisconsin where he spent his weekends and hired out help during the week. The dairy business showed, on its tax forms, a steady stream of losses: interest, depreciation, salaries for the hired help, and so on. These losses offset Nickerson's salary as an executive on his annual tax return.

The IRS viewed the central legal question in Mr. Nickerson's case as being whether the dairy farming was "business" or "personal." Like commuting, education, and so on, an entire "activity" can fall on either side of the business/personal line. Stamp collecting, movie making, novel writing—all can be done purely for personal pleasure, or for profit, or both combined. The law must decide which category an activity falls in for a particular taxpayer. When an activity is primarily personal, or a "hobby," IRC Section 183 denies any net losses from being able to subtract from wages or other unrelated income. (Gains from the activity can be offset by expenses from the activity, so a stamp collector who occasionally sells a stamp is allowed to subtract his current stamp-collecting expenses from the particular gain from stamp collecting).

The IRS argued that that dairy farming was a personal indulgence for Mr. Nickerson, akin to stamp collecting or painting watercolors in most cases. The trouble with this argument should have been apparent even to the government: what is so fun about dairy farming? The court concluded that Nickerson's activities on the Wisconsin dairy farm were indeed motivated by profit, not fun, and Nickerson won the case.

Here is the payoff: the IRS was asking the *wrong question* altogether. It was looking at the wrong category outside of Section 162, using the wrong tool. Look at Figure 1, above, again. The problem was *not* that Nickerson was smuggling fun into his deductible expenses, such that dairy farming was really a personal indulgence for the man. The problem was one of *timing*. Nickerson was running the farm to make a profit—why not?—but the expenses were showing up, now, while the gain would only come later, when he sold the farm. In short, Nickerson was following Rich Dad's advice, to buy an asset, and he was building up sweat equity, free from current taxation. He was playing Tax Planning 101! Even better than that, he was generating immediate expenses that could offset his salary from his day job in Chicago and thereby reduce his taxes today.

Nickerson's activity is a wonderful example of a tax shelter, discussed more fully in Chapter 7. Section 183, aimed at the business-personal blend—denying net deductions to those engaged in hobbies for fun—was powerless to shut Nickerson down. This would have to await the Tax Reform Act of 1986, and its passive activity loss rules of Section 469—which, to finally leave things in a complex muddle—may or may not have stopped Nickerson in his tax-planning tracks.

✎ 3.6 The Tripartite Distinction in Action: Interest Deduction Rules

We can look at deductions for interest expense under Section 163, both as an important subject matter in itself and to illustrate the just discussed tripartite division, among (1) active business, (2) passive business or investment, and (3) personal matters.

Section 163(a) states the general rule that all interest expense is deductible. This was actually the principal rule on interest until 1986. This is shocking: As we shall see more fully in Chapter 7, an unlimited interest deduction—combined, yet again, with the realization requirement under *Macomber*—can easily lead to the death of the income tax. Achilles' heels are fatal.

Today, what 163(a) giveth, other provisions, added by the 1986 Act, taketh away. Section 163(a) has remained intact, seeming giving an interest deduction to all. But Section 163(d) provides a netting rule that *investment* interest expenses can only be deducted against *investment* income, for the nonactive business or investment category noted in Figure 1. This sounds simple and obvious enough, but the absence of this provision prior to 1986 generated a huge number of tax shelters. Sue could "simply" borrow money to buy corporate stock, allow the interest deduction to offset her salary, and then live by borrowing against the appreciation in her stock portfolio. Section 163(d) prevents this, because the interest expense can only be used to offset investment income – which Sue, as a good student of Tax Planning 101, has no interest (pun intended) in showing to the government.

Section 163(h) states the general rule for interest expense on personal loans: there is none.

So we see perfectly well illustrated the Sections 162–212–262 triad. An unlimited deduction for interest expenses incurred in an active trade or business (subject to capitalization, see IRC Section 263A), just like 162; a netting rule for interest expenses incurred in activities or investments made for profit but not within an active trade or business, akin to 212; and no deduction of personal interest expense, akin to 262.

But of course Congress with its great powers can always make exceptions to general rules. And so it has, in the case of Section 163(h)(3), allowing a deduction for interest on up to $1 million of principal "home acquisition indebtedness," and a further $100,000 worth of "home equity loans." These provisions for mortgage interest expenses have provided an incentive for great leverage in the personal residential sector, contributing to the occasional bubble or credit-market meltdown. For better or worse, they have also obtained the status of "sacred cows" in tax policy—the elected official who proposes reducing or eliminating the home mortgage interest deduction tax expenditure does so at her grave electoral peril.

3.6.1 Losses

You can also see the triad of deductible expenses under IRC Section 165(c) dealing with losses to individuals. A loss occurs when there has been a realization and recognition event—subject matter for the next chapter—and the calculation under Section 1001(a) leads to a negative number; the amount realized is less than the basis of the asset given up. If Bob bought some asset for $10,000, and sells it for $8,000, he generally has a $2,000 loss under Section 1001. Can he use this loss on a tax return?

Sections 165(c)(1) and (2) allow losses to be taken immediately when incurred in an active trade or business or in an investment. Why is there no netting for investments here? For one reason, because the taxpayer is "cashing out" of her investment, and showing, due to the realization and recognition and application of IRC Section 1001, the gains from the activity. But it is also true that the netting rules of Section 469 (passive activity loss rules) and Section 1211 (capital loss offset) stand in the background, such that not all losses will be allowed currently.

Section 165(c)(3) then says that an individual cannot tax a loss for a personal item, except in certain extraordinary circumstances of "casualty losses"—fire, storm, theft, and the like—and any deduction is limited to basis, must exceed 10% of the taxpayer's adjusted gross income, and so on.

To illustrate, if you buy a car for $25,000 for personal reasons, you get no deduction because of Section 262. If you sell the car years later for $10,000, you have a loss, calculated under IRC Section 1001(a), as $10,000 (the amount realized) minus $25,000 (basis of car) equals −$15,000. You will not be able to take that as a tax loss, however, under Section 165(c)(3), because it is a personal matter and your loss was not a casualty one. In essence, you have "spent" $15,000, through wear and tear on your car, but in a personal way, governed by Section 262.

Note, however, a fundamental asymmetry in the tax law: if you happen to sell your old car for a *gain*—somehow it became a collector's item—you will have income. If you sold the car you bought for $25,000 for $40,000, the Section 1001(a) calculation would show $15,000 in gain (40,000 minus 25,000). This would be income, under Section 61. There is no provision saying that "personal" matters cannot yield taxable income—just not deductions, as a general matter.

3.6.2 A Quick Note on Gambling Losses

While we are on this point, take a look at Section 165(d). It is a special provision saying that gambling losses are deductible, *but only* against gambling income in the same year. It is a netting rule, like the allowance of deductions against some income from an essentially "hobby" activity under IRC Section 183, considered above in the *Nickerson* case.

Why this provision for partial gambling loss deductions? Think of a typical night in Vegas. You start with maybe $1,000 in your pocket. You end up broke, of course. But along the way, you have had some winnings and many losses. Quite technically, each time you win a bet or hit a jackpot, you have income, under Section 61, *Glenshaw Glass*, and so on. But each time you *lose*, you have no deduction, because of the general rules of IRC Section 262 and Section 165(c)(3)—gambling losses are not casualty ones. Under the basic logic of tax, your night in Vegas should lead to a sizable increase in your taxable income while leaving you economically penniless. Section 165(d) prevents this harsh result by allowing you to wipe out the responsibility for paying tax on your interim gains with the losses. What happens in Vegas stays in Vegas, off the tax form.

By the way, if you have the chance you should watch the opening scene in a movie called *The Grifters*. Angelica Huston is a "runner" for some shady characters, placing bets at a race track. Things are fixed, such that she knows she will win. While at the track, her character scoops up piles of losing bet tickets left on the floor by frustrated gamblers. Why? She is creating receipts to offset the income from her win—adding a clever bit of tax fraud onto her other crimes and misdemeanors.

ℳ 3.7 A Note on the AMT

Right when you thought that it was getting easy, here comes yet another twist. Chapters 2 and 3 give us a good chunk of tax, moving through an imaginary basic tax form 1040. In Chapter 2, we built up the concept of income by adding things into the base; in this chapter, we have subtracted from that base to end up with net taxable income. Now we need only apply the rate structure to this base, factor in credits for taxes already paid and any other ones for which we qualify, and then mail in our form, with a check for taxes still owed or in joyful anticipation of a refund.

Alas, not so fast. The trouble is that the Code and Congress have given us multiple bases and rates within the same law. Before we are ready to send in Form 1040, we have to check to see if we are in fact governed by the alternative minimum tax, or AMT. The AMT was introduced in the 1970s as a way of making sure that all individuals, especially the wealthy, pay some tax. Today it lingers on as a shadow tax within the "regular" income tax system, haunting many upper-middle-income taxpayers whether they know it or not.

Fortunately, it should now be fairly easy to understand at least the basic operation of the AMT. It simply substitutes a new, wider, *base*, and a lower but flatter *rate schedule* for the "other," regular, income tax. The AMT (1) starts with the regular tax base, as just calculated, then (2) adds back in a series of "preferences" or other "adjustments" under IRC Sections 56-57, and then (3) subtracts a standard AMT exemption. Because the AMT is mainly about adding optional deductions back into the tax base, it makes sense to consider the AMT here and now: it is essentially a story about deductions foregone.

These disallowed deductions, not surprisingly, include some (but not all) of the personal expenditure deductions discussed above—the AMT, just like the regular income tax, has no conceptual problem with legitimate business expense deductions. The major add-ins under the AMT are the deduction for state and local taxes, Section 164, and personal dependency exemptions, Section 151. The AMT then subtracts a standard exemption, set at about $75,000 for married couples in 2011 (and scheduled to revert to $45,000 for 2012 as I write), and then applies a basically flat rate, 28 percent as I write, to the balance. IRC Section 55. (In actuality, nothing is ever as simple in tax as it at first seems: there is actually a 26% bracket in the AMT, up to $175,000 of AMT taxable income, and then the 28% rate applies.) You have to pay the greater of the regular tax or the AMT, making the latter the "minimum" tax.

The AMT has become a big deal of late, politically and economically. Why? Three major reasons stand out. One, the AMT exemption amount is not generally "indexed" for inflation, so in real terms it has been falling: officially, it is set at the $45,000 level for married couples filing jointly that is set to return in 2012, although Congress keeps increasing it on a short-term basis. Two, regular rates have come down dramatically since the AMT was born in the 1970s, At a top ordinary income tax rate of 35 percent as I write, with lower rate brackets leading up to that, it is easy to see how a relatively flat 28% AMT on a wider base could exceed the regular tax. Three. adjustment and preference items such as state and local taxes are rising. These factors create a perfect storm wherein the middle and upper-middle classes are at risk of being hit by the AMT, especially if they live in high-tax states such as New York and California.

Congress has responded to preempt the potential taxpayer unrest by enacting a series of "patches" that effectively raise the exemption level for a year or two at a time, without doing anything more fundamental. Once again, budgetary games lurk behind the confusion: by keeping the AMT on the books, and at a low exemption level, long term budget projections can *show* greater federal revenues. When push comes to shove, we will not see these dollars coming into the fisc—Congress will keep patching to prevent a significant middle class tax increase. But push only comes to shove tomorrow and, inside the Beltway, tomorrow never seems to come.

Here is another twist: the AMT was designed to make sure that the very rich pay at least some tax, by limiting the benefit of deductions and exclusions. It is in fact now threatening vast numbers of the upper-middle class, as just noted. Yet the AMT does *nothing* about the *real* rich, the Rich Dads, because it takes no stand on the capital side of the capital-labor divide. Tax Planning 101 is completely unaffected by the AMT—unrealized appreciation, borrowing, and stepped-up basis are *not* preferences under the AMT. Warren Buffet, Bill Gates, and Rich Dad need not worry. They can all still buy/borrow/die to their hearts' content, tax free.

𝕸 3.8 Summary

In this chapter we have considered subtractions from "income" on the way toward arriving at a net taxable amount. We learned:

- Deductions are subtractions from the tax base, they save you money at your marginal rate;
- In a progressive marginal rate system, deductions are essentially regressive;
- For this reason, the Code sometimes uses credits, which work as dollar-for-dollar reductions to the tax owed;

- The earned income tax credit (EITC) of IRC Section 32 is an especially important credit;
- The fundamental logic of an income tax suggests that personal expenses should not be deductible, Section 262, and that business expenses should be, Section 162;
- Some personal expenditures are deductible for itemizers because of a clear statute; we briefly considered extraordinary medical expenses, casualty losses, state and local taxes, charitable contributions, and home mortgage interest;
- Each of these allowable personal expense deductions can be thought of as a *tax expenditure* and each has been the subject of recent tax reform discussions aimed at reducing or eliminating them, to raise tax revenue;
- Most Americans do not itemize; they get a standard deduction;
- Personal dependency deductions under Sections 151–152 plus the standard deduction create a "zero bracket" exempt from tax;
- Business expenses are generally allowable as deductions, under Section 162, absent very clear statutory authority to the contrary;
- The major question with business expenses, aside from ascertaining that they really are business (and not disguised personal) expenses, is one of timing. Business expenses can be taken now, immediately, under 162, or may have to be capitalized; if capitalized, they can be depreciated over time, in the case of assets having a finite and readily ascertainable useful life, or the ultimate recovery of basis must await final sale or other disposition under Section 1001;
- There are a host of items that fall into a gray area between business and personal expenses, such as expenses for education, commuting, work-related child care and clothing, home offices, and the like; generally these items are not deductible, as Section 262 trumps Section 162; expenses incurred on the job, or to maintain or improve job-related skills, are deductible;

- Another triad arises because of timing issues with an income tax that has a realization requirement. Thus a distinction is drawn between "active" trades or businesses, under Section 162, and nonactive business or investments, where deductions are generally allowed, IRC Section 212, but there are a host of "netting" rules forcing losses or expenses from such investments to be deducted only against gains from the same category; see IRC Sections 163(d), 469, 1211 and others;

- An entire activity, like stamp collecting or dairy farming, can be seen as "personal" or "business," and, further, as an active trade or business or as a passive investment. In the *Nickerson* case the IRS attacked dairy farming as a personal acticity, with no net deduction allowed under IRC Section 183; the case is better seen as a problem of timing, because Mr. Nickerson was allowed to deduct losses from his dairy farming against his wage income today, while deferring tax on the gain in the farm's value. Ultimately IRC Section 469, the passive activity loss rules, is a better designed tool to attack the Nickersons of the world;

- Both interest expenses under IRC 163 and losses under 165 track the second triad. Interest and losses incurred in an active trade or business are deductible, as are losses from investment, subject to netting rules of Section 1211 and 469. Investment interest must be netted against investment income under Section 163(d). Personal interest and losses are not generally allowed, but there are exceptions to this rule, for mortgage interest expenses, Section 163(h), and casualty losses 165(c)(3);

- The AMT gives an alternative tax base and rate schedule, adding back in certain "preferences," that is, items allowed as personal deductions under the regular tax, the most important being state and local taxes under Section 164 and the personal dependency deductions, and then subtracting out an exemption amount, set for roughly $75,000 in 2011 for married couples filing jointly but scheduled to drop to $45,000 in 2012.

FOUR

The "When" of Taxation
Timing with a Capital and Lowercase T

WE NOW KNOW, I should hope, that timing matters a great deal in tax. In coming to understand the tax base, as we have done in the prior two chapters, we have encountered issues of timing coming and going. In terms of what is "income," Chapter 2, *Macomber* centrally connected the "what" and "when" questions. "Mere" appreciation in an existing asset is not income, now, or yet, until and unless there is some realization event. Under Tax Planning 101, that day of reckoning need never come. *Time is money*, such that deferring a tax is a meaningful way to increase one's own real income. And we have just seen, in Chapter 3, that the timing of business expense deductions is a vitally important matter, one that encourages taxpayers to plan and litigate questions of time alone, as in *Welch v. Helvering*. Getting a deduction sooner rather than later means real cash in a taxpayer's pocket, today, not tomorrow.

This chapter has two broad topics. What I call "Timing with a capital T" concerns the first set of questions, involving financial property: accounting for transactions on the capital side of the great labor-capital divide. When is it that one must pay tax on the built-in gain left untaxed by *Macomber*--when, that is, do tax time bombs go off? Here we deal with the perhaps confusingly similar terms of *realization* and *recognition*. "Timing with a small t" concerns various more mundane rules about when matters are reflected on tax returns: the choice of accounting method; installment sale rules; the "annual accounting rule" and its variants; and so on. These are more in the nature of details but devils – and dollars – often lurk in the details of tax.

We start with the bigger T.

𝍵 4.1 Realization, Vel Non

Macomber and various aspects of the Code, such as Sections 61, 1001, and their regulations, tell us that gain must be "realized" in order for it to be taxable now. This is no longer thought to be a *constitutional* requirement, as the Justices in *Macomber* considered it to be; the story of "zero coupon bonds" or "original issue discount," relegated here to a note, proves this.[1]

What, then, is a "realization" event? The answer is just about anything.

In *Helvering v. Bruun*, 309 U.S. 461 (1940), the Supreme Court faced a situation where a tenant defaulted on a lease after adding a building to the property. Why would anyone do such a thing? Because a severe economic downtown, the Great Depression, made it impossible for the tenant to pay the rent even with the new building. This was, for the landlord, a bad *economic* event. His tenant

---

1. The realization requirement creates an obvious incentive to buy assets that appreciate in value without producing cash: real estate, growth stocks, works of art, and so on. One problem is that these assets can be financially risky. Many taxpayers are averse to risk. No bother: the realization requirement also creates an incentive for Wall Street to *create* assets that appreciate without producing cash. Hence, the story of "zero coupon bonds" or "original issue discount." These are financial instruments that predictably increase in value without producing current cash, which would be taxed even under *Macomber*. A U.S.-backed savings bond is an example. The purchaser buys the bond today, for a fixed dollar amount. It goes up in value every year, but the holder gets no cash back until a certain number of years—5, 10, 12, 30, whatever—have passed. Then the taxpayer gets back a sum much larger than what she initially paid, representing both a return of principal and accumulated but previously unpaid interest. A savings bond that will pay $200 in 12 years might cost $100 today, depending on interest rates. Financiers were widely using such bonds in the 1970s, a time of high inflation and interest rates, to help taxpayers escape current taxation. Congress shut the game down with the "original issue discount" (OID) rules of IRC Sections 1271–1274 and other provisions. These are highly complex rules, which essentially impute annual income to holders of zero coupon bonds. The complexity has a simple effect: the bonds are no longer terribly attractive. The point for the text is that neither Congress nor the courts stumbled much over the constitutionality of the anti-OID rules. *Macomber* and the realization requirement are habits, not rules.

walked away. Tough times made it difficult to get another tenant in place. Nonetheless, the IRS argued, by getting his land back with a new building on it, the landlord had *realized* a taxable *gain*—the building being a *new* thing or asset. Recall the discussion above, in Chapter 2, about the difference between "gain" for tax and economic purposes—bad days can and often do lead to taxable gain. Recall also the distinction between *Drescher* and *Macomber*: getting something new, something that you do not already own, is fundamentally different under *Macomber* from a change in value of an existing asset. The Supreme Court, after considering that the building was, technically, moveable—not an intrinsic part of the land—agreed with the IRS. The landlord had to pay tax on the value of the building, standing alone.

Perhaps the most important and celebrated case on determining what constitutes a realization event is *United States v. Davis*, 370 U.S. 65 (1962). A couple was getting divorced. The soon to be ex-husband transferred appreciated DuPont stock to his soon to be ex-wife as part of the property settlement. He was a high-ranking DuPont executive and his company stock had a low basis: imagine a fair market value of $1 million, with a basis of $200,000. Thus Mr. Davis satisfied an obligation to his ex-wife valued at $1,000,000 by transferring property with a basis of $200,000. The *obvious* result, which the Supreme Court got right but the lower courts got wrong, was that the *husband* faced a realization event: an $800,000 tax time bomb went off in his hands. ($1,000,000 minus $200,000). Recall the importance of considering the tax consequences of using appreciated property to do one's bidding: we had explored paying an employee with appreciated stock, in Chapter 2, in contrast to the gift rule of *Taft v. Bowers* and Sections 102 and 1015. Here Mr. Davis was using appreciated property instead of cash, and he faced a tax time bomb's going off.

We analyze *Davis*, as all realization events, under the rule of 1001(a): gain equals the difference between the fair market value of the property received and the basis of the property given up. The details require a few extra words.

4.1.1 A Note on Valuation

In *Davis*, the lower courts stumbled over the fair market value of what the husband received—in essence, a release of his ex-wife's rights against him. What could these possibly be worth?

The Supreme Court had no such difficulty, nor should they have had. In any transaction where there is no obvious gift motive, what you get is presumed to be equal in its real economic fair market value to what you give up. The stock was worth, in our example, $1 million. *Therefore the marital rights released by the ex-wife were worth $1 million, too.* (You can get to the same place by understanding that the transfer of the $1,000,000 worth of stock was a discharge of an obligation or legally enforceable debt facing Mr. Davis.) There was certainly no gift motive attendant on the divorce settlement. The husband had gain of $800,000 (likely capital, see Chapter 6).

4.1.2 Looking at Both Sides

Davis illustrates an important rule of taxable transactions: *You have to analyze the two or more sides of a transaction independently.*

The husband in *Davis*, as we have just seen, had a taxable realization event, because he effected his side of the transaction using appreciated property. Had Mr. Davis paid his ex-wife cash, there would have been no built-in gain, and no tax time bomb would have gone off.

The now ex–*Mrs. Davis* has a taxable moment to consider, too, under 1001(a): she must pay tax on the difference between the fair market value of what she receives, here $1 million worth of stock, and the basis of what she gives up. The critical question then is what is her basis in her marital rights?

Here the answer, from *Solicitor's Opinion 132*, considered in Chapter 2, is the fair market value! The law considers that Mrs. Davis had basis in herself for purposes of the property settlement equal to the value of her inchoate marital rights—that is, in our example, $1 million. So *Mrs.* Davis has *no* gain, although she gets $1 million worth of DuPont stock; $1 million minus $1 million equals 0. *Mr.* Davis in contrast has $800,000 of gain on which to pay tax, although he gave up $1 million worth of stock and now has, economically, nothing—there being no way to sell his ex-wife's inchoate marital rights. Such is the inexorable logic of tax: *Davis* is an excellent illustration of the "sooner or later tax time bombs go off" rule, and of the complexity and counterintuitive results that follow from *Macomber*, yet again.

4.1.3 Strange Bedfellows, and a Note on Losses

A final case further illustrates the strangeness. *Cottage Savings Association v. Commissioner*, 499 U.S. 554 (1991) was set in the midst of the banking crisis of the 1980s. Many banks held mortgages that were no longer worth their face value, because the underlying properties had deteriorated in value and the borrowers were at risk of default. If a bank holds a typical nonrecourse mortgage (meaning that it, the bank, would have to foreclose on the property rather than go after the debtor personally) with a $500,000 principal amount, but the house that secures the mortgage is now worth only $400,000, the bank does not really have a $500,000 asset, because the home-owner/debtor could default at any time, leaving the bank with the house, not the mortgage. This meant that the mortgages, assets to the banks, had *losses* built into them: in our example, a basis of $500,000 (what the bank gave the debtor to get the mortgage) with a fair market value of $400,000. The banks would like to realize such losses for tax purposes.

This reminds us that everything is turned upside down when losses are involved—taxpayers want to accelerate losses, the government wants to defer them. Normally when someone has a loss asset, she simply sells it; recall Tax Planning 102. Why could not the banks in *Cottage Savings* just sell their bad loans? Because to do so would have led them to confront an unpleasant *economic* fact—namely that they, the savings and loan banks, were under water, too; they lacked the minimum capitalization to stay in business. Selling the loans would have opened up the tax losses, a good thing, but would have made manifest the actual *economic* losses, a bad thing. Instead of carrying a mortgage with a face amount of $500,000 on their books, they would have to show the $400,000 that someone paid them for that particular mortgage – its fair market value, given the decline in house prices. The fall in value of the banks' balance sheets would place many of them at risk of being shut down for lacking adequate funds to stay in business.

A federal regulator, of all people, came to the savings and loan banks' rescue. The Federal Savings and Loan Insurance Corporation (FSLIC) proposed that banks in this economic situation engage in "mortgage swaps." Financiers would package together bundles of economically equivalent mortgages, and banks could swap them—triggering a tax loss, under the realization requirement, but not requiring the banks to mark their loans to their fair market values, which would have involved shutting many of them down under the government's regulatory standards. Outraged by the audacity, the IRS in *Cottage Savings* argued that there was no realization event because of the economic equivalence of the swapped mortgage bundles.

The Supreme Court disagreed. The bundles had literally different loans in them. There was a "material" difference between what each bank gave up and what they received. Hence there was realization. The savings and loan crisis was deferred for a few years, as the influx of tax savings helped the underwater banks stay afloat for a bit.

4.1.4 A Note on Nothing

Cottage Savings perhaps best illustrates the point first made above, that a realization event is "anything other than nothing" that can happen to an asset. Another historic example involved corporations changing their place of business, triggering a realization of gain for their shareholders who were considered to own new and different stock (Standard Oil of Delaware rather than Standard Oil of Ohio, say).

Does this mean that *Macomber* is unimportant, or that Tax Planning 101 is a quirk, because almost anything other than nothing is a realization event? Not at all. Here I ask my students to consider the most common thing in their lives, what they do most of the time. This is of course—if they are anything like my teenage daughters—"nothing." Merely holding an asset that appreciates in value does not produce a realization event, under *Macomber* and all subsequent law, and this is a *very* common thing to do, for a very long time. Just ask Warren Buffet, Bill Gates, or Rich Dad. Tax Planning 101 is hugely important, precisely because nothing happens all the time.

4.2 Recognition, Vel Non

There is another reason why *Macomber* matters. Merely holding an appreciated asset does not generate current taxable income. But then doing almost anything else—anything other than nothing—is a realization event. Since taxpayers are typically triggering their own losses by selling or otherwise disposing of loss assets, under IRC Section 1001 and Tax Planning 102, this means that the cases on realization events tend to center on involuntary and unfortunate circumstances, like a tenant default, divorce, or an insured casualty loss. *Macomber* and the legacy of the realization requirement then generate an argument based on fairness: if a fire rages through the town, burning down some but not all the houses, why should the unlucky homeowners who lost their houses also have to pay tax on the "realization event" of getting the insurance proceeds? It seems that the tax law is adding injury to injury.

It turns out that realization is necessary but not sufficient for current taxation. Realization is the timing equivalent of the "what" question's "income." To be taxable, something needs to be income under Section 61, the Sixteenth Amendment, *Glenshaw Glass*. But not all "income" is *taxable* income, because Congress does not always live up to its full power to tax: gifts, for example, are not income under Section 102.

Similarly, to be taxable *now* there must be some realization event. But not all realization events trigger current tax, because Congress chooses not to tax all of them now. This is especially so because many realization events seem like unfair times to tax: the tenant default in *Bruun*, the divorce in *Davis*, or the running example of the burned down house covered by insurance proceeds. There is nothing in the realization doctrine that says things must be voluntary, as the landlord in *Bruun* figured out. But it seems harsh to tax the house that burns down, not the one across the street that escaped the path of the fire and is rising in value immune from any realization.

In a perhaps unfortunate word choice, though it is a clear concept, the Code and tax practitioners use the language of *rexcognition* and *nonrecognition* to deal with the question of whether or not a *realized* gain will be taxable, now. Nonrecognition is the timing equivalent of "nontaxable." To be taxable now, a gain must be *both* realized *and* recognized. If it is not both, then no tax gets paid, and no adjustment to basis follows, under the general pay tax/get basis, do not pay tax/do not get basis rule.

Nonrecognition statutes are important because, as we have been considering, many realization events are, economically and equitably, unfortunate. There is another problem with the realization requirement, a more narrowly economic one: It generates a "lock-in" effect under which taxpayers are reluctant to sell assets with built-in gain, thereby triggering a tax time bomb going off. This lock-in effect has serious social and economic costs, as taxpayers are reluctant to sell their asset for fear of p[aying tax, and instead cling on to them until death – as Tax Planning 101 teaches them to do. But this means that assets do not flow to their highest and best use and users, and the economy suffers.

Most of the Code's nonrecognition provisions cluster around Section 1031, dealing with "like-kind exchanges," and an important provision for real estate owners and practitioners, discussed below. Section 1033 exempts "involuntary" conversions, involving insurance proceeds, from current taxation, covering our running hypothetical of the under-insured, low-basis house that burns down. Section 1041 provides a nonrecognition rule for transfers between spouses during marriage or incident to divorce—it is the anti-*Davis* rule. Gifts are also subject to a nonrecognition rule, under Sections 102 and 1015, as discussed above in the context of *Taft v. Bowers*. *Bruun* was also overruled by statute, in Section 109 (tenant improvements not income) and Section 1019 (no adjustment to basis after tenant default). Congress would later learn that it could combine the no income or gain/no basis adjustment components into a single statute, hence Section 1031 and following, compared to the 102/1015, 109/1019 two-step approaches of earlier law.

All of these nonrecognition rules have their own complexities and twists. The main points to get across in this short introduction are that they exist, and that the basic logic of tax dictates that, if no tax is paid now, there is no adjustment to basis now, either, while if tax is paid basis goes up.

4.2.1 Note on Davis, Section 1041, and Divorce

To illustrate the basic logic, consider Section 1041. This Section overrules the holding of the *Davis* case and makes transfers between spouses, during marriage or incident to divorce, nonrecognition events. This means that in the facts of *Davis* as we presented them, the $800,000 built-in gain tax time bomb would *not* go off today when Mr. Davis transfers the stock to his soon to be ex-wife. But, on the other hand—as part of the inexorable logic of tax—the ex–Mrs. Davis must take the stock with a carryover basis, of $200,000, to preserve the gain for a later day—divorce is *not* an exception to the "sooner or later" rule. If the tax time bomb does not go off today, it must be preserved for a later time.

Some of my students think that this is unfair to Mrs. Davis, or to any spouse, typically the wife, receiving appreciated property in a divorce settlement. This is wrong. Having the tax time bomb go off now means that Mr. Davis must pay tax this year, and likely at a higher tax rate than his ex-wife would pay. These results—acceleration of gain and a shifting up of the tax burden—are bad for the *community*, Mr. and Mrs. Davis combined. Under the law as it existed in *Davis*, Mr. Davis had to pay a large capital gains tax in the midst of the divorce proceeding. This meant less wealth to share, and hence less wealth that could be transferred to the now ex–Mrs. Davis. Under Section 1041, that tax gets deferred – perhaps forever, under Tax Planning 101 – and likely would get paid in a lower rate bracket. Those tax savings should mean more value at the time of divorce for *both* Mr. and Mrs. Davis, since their common Uncle Sam need not be paid at the moment of divorce.

Suppose for example that Mrs. Davis was getting one-half of the couple's net wealth. Properly advised, this half would be determined *after taxes*. If Mr. Davis had to pay $250,000 to the IRS, under the capital gains rates in place at the time, there would be less to give to Mrs. Davis. The couple may have decided to part ways in life, but, as taxpayers, they are still joined together—against the IRS.

🎞 4.3 A Case Study: *Starker* and Like-Kind Exchanges, with a Note on Boot

The saga of like-kind exchanges illustrates several important themes and gives a good case study of nonrecognition rules and their logic.

Something like the current Section 1031 has long been a part of the law.[2] The Section holds that if one exchanges an asset "solely"

---

2. For an interesting discussion, see Marjorie E. Kornhauser, "Section 1031: We Don't Need Another Hero", 60 *Southern California Law Review* 397 (1987).

for a "like-kind" asset, there is no recognition of gain: the tax time bomb does not go off. The initial Code provision was motivated by some senators thinking of swapping horses, and how silly it would be for either to pay tax. Over time, the IRS successfully argued that many things were not "like-kind"—girl and boy cows, for example— and the statute itself excluded many kinds of property, importantly including stocks and other financial securities. In essence, the law settled down to being about real estate, where longstanding doc-trine holds, in essence, that all real estate is like-kind to all other real estate. (Property used for personal purposes is out of the stat-ute, however, and now foreign real estate is, too).

The basic operation of Section 1031 is easy enough to state, and should be largely review by now. Suppose that Harry owns Blue-acre, worth $1 million, with a basis of $400,000. He wants to trade with Sally, who owns Green-acre, also worth $1 million, with a basis to Sally of $700,000. Section 1031 provides that—if all the i's are dotted and all the t's are crossed (warning: do not try this yourself at home alone)—Harry and Sally can swap properties, tax-free. Harry will now own Green-acre, with a *substituted basis* of $400,000, which is *Harry's* former basis in Blue-acre. Sally will own Blue-acre with her substituted basis of $700,000, her former basis in Green-acre. No tax is paid, now, and each person keeps his or her basis and hence his or her "tax time bomb" for a later day: Harry had and still has $600,000 of built-in gain, Sally had and still has $300,000. Only the identity of their real estate holdings has changed.

Good enough, but the problem is that Harry and Sally were lucky to find each other, each happening to own a parcel of real estate that the other wanted with precisely the same fair market value. This is the kind of thing that happens only in classrooms (or movies).

Suppose more realistically that Harry has found a buyer for Blue-acre, willing to pay $1 million in cash, but owning no other property that Harry wants. In *Starker v. United States*, 602 F.2d 1341 (9th Cir. 1979), the Harry figure was played by Mr. Starker. He set things up such that the $1 million was placed in a trust under a third party's control. Mr. Starker then went out shopping, and, when he found property worth $1 million, he directed the trustee of the trust to buy it and transfer it to him, so that his exchange would be "solely like kind." Crazy and clever as it seems, this bit of planning worked, and today "three-party *Starker* deferred like-kind exchanges" are an essential part of the real estate landscape.

There is also the matter of *boot*. This is non-like-kind property added into an exchange to make the real economic values match.

Suppose that Sally's Green-acre was only worth $900,000. In trading this to Harry for Blue-acre, worth $1 million, Sally would have to add in $100,000 "to boot" to make the values come out even. The rule on boot is simple enough to state: the recipient of boot, here Harry, pays tax on the boot up to the amount of his built-in gain. Since Harry has $600,000 of built-in gain (the $1 million value minus his $400,000 basis), he would pay tax, likely capital gains (see Chapter 6) on the $100,000 of boot. He would have basis in the cash received of $100,000, and a remaining built-in gain of $500,000. Green-acre, worth $900,000, would have a substituted basis of $400,000. Sally would have basis in Blue-acre equal to her former basis in Green-acre, say $700,000 *plus* $100,000 for the "boot" she put into the deal.

The story gets more complex in the case of boot that exceeds gain, or using appreciated property in lieu of cash as boot, or where there are mortgages and liabilities involved. But enough for now. The important point to see in this short introduction is once again that there is a logic here, and that problems can be solved—tax time bombs either go off, and tax gets paid on gain, or the gain remains built-in, awaiting another day. We are dealing, here, with matters of timing, not escape. But time is money. These games are worth playing. Just ask Mr. Starker or his rather clever lawyers.

∰ 4.4 Small t Timing: Matters of Accounting

We are about to get into smaller print, more minutia. We are turning from "Timing with a capital T," concerning the important subject matter of when tax time bombs go off on transactions involving property—something squarely on the capital side of the great divide, and important for the Rich Dads and others playing Tax Planning 101 to understand—to "timing with a small t."

Here we address the narrow but common question of when, exactly, are we supposed to put something down on a tax form. There are many rules and subrules here, and they get complex, and can easily take us away from a big picture view of tax's forest. Yet once again, time is money, and hence there is interest in the details.

⅍ 4.5 Methods of Accounting, Including Installment Sales and Inventory

In the real world, events do not follow neat time schedules, wrapping up by December 31 every year. The history of tax is replete with games taxpayers play with different *methods of accounting*, rules for determining when an item of income or expense occurs with enough finality to mark down on a tax return. There are four basic ones to consider: *cash*, *accrual*, *installment sales*, and *inventory*.

Fortunately for the understanding of basic tax, all individuals as individuals are now mandated to be on the cash method of accounting. (An individual operating a business as a sole proprietor might well be on the accrual method). Under the cash method, you have income when you are paid cash and you get a deduction when you pay cash. As per usual, however, things cannot be quite so simple. Recall from Chapter 2 the important principle that noncash items must be income, or we would be well on our way to a barter system. *Drescher*. This leads to the subjects covered in the next section— when, despite not literally receiving cash, is a taxpayer on the cash method nonetheless responsible for paying tax currently? These are matters of *constructive receipt*, *cash equivalence*, and *economic benefit*.

Many businesses are on the *accrual method of accounting*. Here the tax result follows the economic reality rather than cash flow per se. You have income or a deduction when all events have transpired that entitle you to the receipt of the item of income or obligate you for the payment of the item of expense. Depreciation, considered briefly in the prior chapter, works like a form of forced accrual: the tax deduction follows an economic reality, not a cash flow. (Expensing, or the immediate deduction of a business expense (option 1 from the last chapter, or Figure 1), is an instance of cash method.) When you buy a machine for $10,000 and the tax law requires you to capitalize the expense and take depreciation deductions over the life of the machine, the idea is to follow the *economic* reality—the gradual fall in value of the machine—rather than the cash outlay of $10,000 alone. Allowing an immediate deduction for the cash paid in purchasing a long-lived asset would overstate the immediate expense, given that the asset is on the books as a positive matter.

Inventory is a special case that need not concern most readers; there are actually different methods of keeping track of matters of expense when a business produces things on a regular basis. "FIFO" stands for first in, first out, meaning that the earliest item manufactured is considered the first one sold; "LIFO" stands for last in, first out, meaning that the item being sold is considered to be the last one made. The so-called uniform capitalization rules of IRC Section 263A force many manufacturers into a kind of inventory method of accounting for many goods, including the construction of residential housing.

Installment sales, now governed by IRC Section 453, show the interface between timing with a capital T and timing with a small t. Suppose that you sold an asset with built-in gain and got paid over time, getting back an installment note. Section 453 provides that as you receive payments, they will be divided between taxable gain and nontaxable recovery of basis.

Imagine a $1 million building, with a basis of $200,000, and an installment agreement to pay you $100,000 a year (plus interest) over ten years. Under the basic rule of IRC Section 1001, you pay tax on the fair market value of what is received minus the basis of what is given up. But when? And which comes first, the gain or the tax-free recovery of basis? A strong argument can be made that the full amount of $1 million is realized *now*, at the moment you exchange the asset for the installment sale contract. The contract itself looks like a noncash benefit, like the annuity contract in *Drescher*, valued at its face amount. This is the so-called *closed method* of accounting for installment sales, which the government prefers.

Taxpayers, in contrast, argue for an *open method*, whereby the first dollars are allocated to basis recovery, and tax is paid later. This would mean no tax at all for the first two years, as you receive $200,000 in payments, equal to your total basis in the asset sold. The taxpayer actually got the Supreme Court to agree to this approach in the particular case of *Burnet v. Logan*, 283 U.S. 404 (1931).

IRC Section 453 splits the difference. It treats each payment received—interest aside (and calculating interest in the case it is not stated is a complex matter that the law requires)—as part gain, part basis recovery, in proportion to the expected final whole. In the running example, each $100,000 principal payment gets treated as $80,000 of gain, $20,000 of tax-free basis recovery. If you are follow-ing the rules and logic of tax, you will know that each time there is some basis recovery, basis gets reduced, so it will be down to $180,000 after one year, $160,000 after two, and so on. At the end of the day, you will pay capital gains on $800,000 of gain, receive $200,000 of tax free basis recovery, and pay tax at ordinary rates on any interest received. It is all quite logical – if complex and stated in an alien tongue. Such is tax.

ℳ 4.6 Constructive Receipt, Cash Equivalence, Economic Benefit

There is a tension among the cash method, the realization require-ment, and the practical needs of tax. Generally, when you get something that is not nothing—that is not a "mere" change in value of an existing asset—you have income. We saw this in *Drescher*. *When* you have income is the question at hand.

Recall *Glenshaw Glass*, a huge improvement over *Macomber*'s definition of income, and still the best judicial definition we have today: "an undeniable accession to wealth, clearly realized, and over which the taxpayer has dominion." When is something other than cash "clearly realized"? When does a taxpayer obtain "dominion"? Many cases, like *Drescher*, involve cash that is deferred or placed in an account nominally beyond the taxpayer's reach. One trick is to see that it is not necessarily the *cash* that is the "income"—once again, if cash and only cash were income, we would be well on our way back to a barter economy. A taxpayer like Mr. Drescher can clearly realize and have dominion over a *contract*, and this becomes income at its objective fair market value, now.

Thus the policy of these various "common law," or judicially created doctrines we look at in this section. "Constructive" in law generally means "not" but treated "as if." "Constructive receipt" means that you do not actually have receipt but the law will treat you as if you do. If your employer mails you a check in December, you cannot avoid paying taxes on it in this year simply by not cashing it, or staying away from your mailbox. The law will say that you had constructive receipt even if you did not literally get or cash the check.

"Cash equivalence" means some noncash item that will be taxed as if it is cash, like Mr. Drescher's annuity contract.

"Economic benefit" is a wider phrase meaning that you got some economic benefit from the receipt of something other than cash, or from some action of a third party, and you are responsible for paying tax on the benefit. Suppose that your employer paid off your credit card balances rather than paying you directly. You would pay tax on that value, for which you received an economic benefit. Mr. Davis got an economic benefit, for another example, from his former wife's release of her inchoate claims against him.

All these verbal roads lead to the same place: income, now. In *Drescher*, for example, the court could have said that the taxpayer had constructive receipt of the money used to buy the annuity contract; or that the annuity contract itself was a cash equivalent; or that Mr. Drescher got an economic benefit from the annuity contract. In any and all events, he would be taxable now, at the objective fair market value of the contract.

None of that is to say that these doctrines and subdoctrines are not confusing, or that they are applied consistently. I have never denied that the real-world of tax is mindlessly complex. But the outline of the forest, at least, can and does make basic sense. Getting you to see the questions that have to be answered is a big part of the ambition of this short introduction.

⅏ 4.7 Annual Accounting Rule

Among the inevitable questions of tax is the choice of *accounting period*. This is different from the topic we have been considering, of accounting *method*, which deals with what real-world facts lead to putting something down on a tax return. The question of accounting period deals with what unit of time the return itself covers.

It is neither obvious nor necessary that the accounting period should be one year. Payroll and sales taxes, for two prominent examples, are collected and remitted to the government much more frequently than that. Nonetheless, the income tax chooses an annual period to settle things up. Its accounting period is one year.

Life and economic transactions do not, however, always follow a precise yearly schedule. Each year, typically around April when you are toting things up for the prior calendar year (individuals now have to be on calendar years; some businesses can choose *fiscal years* that do not begin on January 1 or end on December 31), you do the best you can. What if things change? What if an item you put down for income in one year has to get repaid in a later year? Or a transaction you thought would be profitable goes sour and you have a net loss over time? Or a charity returns a gift for which you had taken a tax deduction?

A core part of the answer to all of these questions is that if things have changed, you do *not* amend your earlier return. Amended returns are for mistakes you knew or should have known as of the end of that year—you discover a small item of income you neglected to mark down, say, or you added up your charitable contributions incorrectly. When things *change*, the *annual accounting rule* holds that you take this change into account later, in the year in which the change happened.

Why does this matter? Time for one thing—deferral or acceleration of items of income or expense mean real money to taxpayers and the government alike. But the doctrines also matter because of potentially varying tax rates.

Consider the seminal Supreme Court case of *Burnet v. Sanford & Brooks*, 282 U.S. 359 (1931). The taxpayer was a business performing work for the government. It expended sums in each of several years. The government later reneged on the contract, and, after a dispute, the company got its investment back. Imagine that the company had invested and deducted $100,000 a year for three years, and then got $300,000 back in the fourth. The taxpayer wanted to say it had no profit. Trouble was, the taxpayer had also deducted the $300,000, and so had no basis to offset the $300,000 receipt in Year 4. The taxpayer then wanted to go back and amend its returns to show no gain or loss in any year—just forget about the whole thing. The annual accounting rule prevented this; here was a change, in a later year, not a mistake in the year the losses were taken. The Court held that it was fitting and proper to tax the full $300,000 as income in Year 4.

What was the harm, you ask? The fourth year, when the company received back its $300,000 in our example, happened to be in the midst of World War I, with a top marginal tax rate of 70 percent. The tax rates in the earlier years had been trivial; imagine 20 percent. Because of the difference in rates, to illustrate, the taxpayer saved $60,000 from the deductions (20 percent times $300,000) in Years 1 through 3, and then had to pay tax of $210,000 (70 percent times $300,000) in Year 4. A real-world business transaction with no net economic gain led to net taxes of $150,000! The Supreme Court in *Sanford & Brooks* said, in essence, "tough luck."[3]

Such is the sometimes arbitrariness of applying a tax system with strong practical needs to a real world that does not always follow any standard clock.

✳ 4.8 Claim of Right and Tax Benefit Rules

Suppose that you include something as income in one year, and it turns out you have to pay it back in a later year. What do you do for tax purposes?

The answer is that you include the item of income now, deduct it later, and do not amend your return under the annual accounting rule. The Supreme Court upheld this result in the case of *United States v. Lewis*, 340 U.S. 590 (1951).

The problem, as we saw above, arises when tax rates are higher, in general or for you in particular, in the earlier year of inclusion. Thus in *Lewis* the taxpayer received a $20,000 bonus in Year 1, which he had to repay for legal reasons in a later year. Because he was in a high tax bracket when he got the bonus (it was World War II, this time), once again there was a net tax paid. Imagine that Mr. Lewis was in a 70 percent bracket when he got the bonus, and a 20 percent one when he had to pay it back. He would end up paying $10,000 in net taxes ($14,000 on the receipt of $20,000 subject to a 70 percent rate, minus $4,000 for the value of the deduction at a 20 percent rate) notwithstanding the economic "wash" of getting and later giving back the same amount of money.

---

3. In the event that the company had shown an actual net loss for the earlier years, it might have qualified for a net operating loss deduction under what is now Section 172. This is a complex provision, generally more available for corporations than individuals. For those interested, see IRS Publication 536, Net Operating Losses (NOLs) for Individuals, Estates and Trusts, available on the IRS Web site, www.irs.gov.

IRC Section 1341 now fixes this problem, in the case of these so-called *claim of right* matters, where the inclusion in the prior year is dictated by the fact that the taxpayer has a "claim of right" to the funds. In essence, the statute gives you a choice of taking the deduction at this year's or the prior year's rates—meaning, as a bottom line, that a taxpayer could make money from this transaction (if the deduction is worth more than the inclusion cost), but cannot lose money in taxes as Mr. Lewis himself did.

The statute is not parallel on the deduction side. Here the problem comes up if you have taken a deduction in one year, and something happens in a later year to render the deduction, in hindsight, inappropriate.

Once more, under the annual accounting rule, an amended return is not the remedy. Instead, you have an inclusion in the later year, in the amount of the prior deduction—the item of "income" is the unraveling of the prior deduction, to the extent it conferred a "tax benefit." See *Alice Phelan Sullivan Corp. v. United States*, 381 F. 2d 399 (Ct. Cl., 1967), finding income in the amount of a prior deduction (not, interestingly, in the amount of the then fair market value of the returned property) when a charity returned a gift to a donor. IRC Section 111 codifies this result.

The Supreme Court, in the case of *Hillsboro National Bank v. Commissioner*, 460 U.S. 370 (1983) (consolidated with a related case, *Bliss Dairy, Inc.*), complicated the matter somewhat by holding that an actual "recovery" was not necessary for an application of the tax benefit rule. Rather anything "fundamentally inconsistent" with the reason for the earlier deduction triggers the later inclusion. Thus a company that had taken a deduction for cattle feed and then liquidated was found to have income in the amount of the previously taken deduction, because it did not use the cattle feed in the course of its active trade or business under IRC Section 162—its use as part of the liquidation proceeds was "fundamentally inconsistent" with the deduction for business reasons. The logic of tax can be relentless.

🎜 4.9 Note on Depreciation and Capitalization

We considered the topics of capitalization and depreciation in Chapter 3 when discussing the "sooner or later" rule that you get your monies expended in business or investment back. Clearly these are also matters of timing.

In essence depreciation is a form of forced accrual accounting, making the tax deductions track the economic reality of the deterioration—the wear and tear of an asset—and not just the cash outflow. A legitimate business or investment expense must be *capitalized* when it creates an asset with a useful life beyond a year; it can then be *depreciated* if the asset has a finite and readily ascertainable useful life. If it does not—as in the case of raw land, paintings, corporate stock—the investment is capitalized and held in basis until ultimate sale or other disposition under Section 1001(a).

The precise details of depreciation schedules are detailed, ever-changing, and beyond the scope of this short introduction. We can more simply note that any depreciation schedule needs a length of time (the useful life), a rate (straight line, meaning an even amount per year, or something more "accelerated"), and a salvage value (what the asset is worth at the end of its useful life as scrap—which the law almost always deems to be zero). Calculators, computer programs, and/or accountants can do the rest.

🎜 4.10 Summary

In this chapter we considered matters of timing, which we have known since *Macomber* to be critically important to the income tax:

- Timing with a capital T concerns transactions in property, on the capital side of the great labor-capital divide;

- This starts with questions of the realization requirement, made pressing by *Macomber*, and kept relevant by *Glenshaw Glass*, Sections 61 and 1001, and the regulations thereunder;
- A realization event is basically something other than nothing: a sale or other disposition, any "material" change. *Cottage Savings*. Getting insurance proceeds after a loss, receiving property back from a tenant with an improvement on it, transferring property in a divorce settlement all count;
- Although almost anything counts as realization, nothing—"mere" appreciation in an existing asset—is common enough to make the realization requirement the Achilles' heel of the income tax, the key to Tax Planning 101 with its buy and hold strategy;
- It is not enough for a built-in gain to be realized; Congress must live up to its power to *recognize* the gain and trigger the tax time bomb;
- In fact, Congress has chosen to enact many important nonrecognition statutes, for like-kind exchanges (1031), involuntary conversions (insurance proceeds) (1033), exchanges between spouses or incident to divorce (1041), gifts (102 and 1015), tenant improvements (109 and 1019), and more;
- The logic of tax dictates that, if a gain is realized *and* recognized, basis increases (pay tax/get basis); if the gain is not realized or recognized, there is no basis increase, but some form of carryover basis instead that preserves the built-in gain or tax time bomb for a later day (don't pay tax/don't get basis);
- In addition to these large questions of timing attendant on appreciated property, there are many timing rules with a small t, affecting the filling out of annual tax returns;
- There are four basic methods of accounting: cash, accrual, installment sales, and inventory; individuals are now on the cash method;
- Although the cash method looks at cash, the income tax has a variety of common law or judicial doctrines to make sure that noncash benefits, especially noncash compensation, get taxed,

currently, as well: constructive receipt, cash equivalence, economic benefit are especially common;

- The annual accounting rule maintains that taxpayers are required to report their income as best they can on annual returns; if things change, they take the change into account in a later year and do not file amended returns; this can sometimes lead to a harsh result because of changing personal or statutory tax rates;

- The claim of right doctrine holds that a taxpayer has income when she receives something under a claim of right to keep it; if she loses it in a subsequent year, she reports a loss or deduction in that later year; Section 1341 operates to make sure that there is not a net tax paid because of the different years;

- The tax benefit rule, now codified in Section 111, holds that when an occurrence in a later year is "fundamentally inconsistent" with a deduction in an earlier year (*Hillsboro*), the taxpayer must report income in the later year in the amount of the no-longer-correct deduction of the earlier year;

- Capitalization and depreciation are subjects for the treatment of business and investment expenses, considered in Chapter 3, though of course also matters of timing; tax is a seamless web.

FIVE

The "Who" of Taxation
Questions of Attribution and the Appropriate Filing Unit

THE PERSON OR ENTITY responsible for paying taxes matters primarily because of progressive marginal rates. The subject of "who" must fill out the form and pay taxes on any particular item of income or expense was thus once considerably more important, when there was a greater gap between the top and bottom marginal tax rates. With a top marginal rate of 35 percent, the stakes in the income-shifting arena have lowered. Nonetheless, games persist. This chapter briefly considers the classic cases and doctrines.

✺ 5.1 General Themes

Let us first get an understanding of the math of the matter.

Under a system of progressive marginal rates, it matters who pays taxes because different individuals are in different rate brackets. You can see this even in the highly simplified rate schedule of Table 1, which we had used before to have a basic model before us.

Imagine Lear, a father, earning $100,000 of taxable income. The "last" $40,000 of this income will fall in the 30 percent bracket, generating $12,000 in tax.

Suppose that Lear could *shift* $20,000 to each of his two elder daughters, Regan and Goneril, as separate taxpayers without any other income. Each daughter's $20,000 of income would be exempt from tax, as falling within the zero bracket. Lear would appear to the IRS to be making $60,000. The $40,000 would have shifted from the 30 percent to the zero bracket, and the family would thereby save $12,000 in taxes.

TABLE 1 Sample Marginal Rate Schedule

Income	Marginal Tax Rate
$0—$20,000	0%
$20,000—$60,000	15%
Over $60,000	30%

Note by the way what is key to the example: the family has been able to shift where *taxable income* falls, or is seen by the government as falling, likely without changing where the *real economic income* went. If Lear and his daughters are anything like me and my family, surely each daughter would be *spending* (or costing, perhaps) $20,000 a year. The usual transfers from father to daughters would be ignored for tax purposes, under Sections 102 (no inclusion for daughters) and 262 (no deduction for dad). By making it appear as if the daughters have earned the $40,000 themselves, Lear's family changed its tax obligations without effecting any change in their daily lives or economic realities. This, again, is a feature of good tax planning: allowing the taxpayer to have his cake—doing what he wants to do—and eat it tax-free, too.

The current rate structure is not only relatively low, it is also relatively compressed or flat. The top marginal rate bracket as I write is 35 percent, and it kicks in at a historically low level of income. It is thus less beneficial than it once was to attempt the various income-shifting techniques we consider below. Recall that throughout much of history, the top marginal rate bracket was 70 percent or higher (it was at or over 90 percent from World War II until John F. Kennedy cut it to 70 percent in 1963), and you can see the stakes of times past. But income-shifting can still save taxes, as in the example of Lear and his daughters, which uses a simplified form of current rates.

It should come as no surprise that a bottom line for this chapter will be that it is difficult to shift wages or payment for *labor*. In the important early Supreme Court case of *Lucas v. Earl*, 281 U.S. 111, from 1930, Justice Oliver Wendell Holmes set forth what has come to be known as the "first rule of taxation," namely to "tax him who earns it." To this day, the government is solicitous to prevent shifting of labor income or wages. Because, however, it is easy enough to give away *capital* or *property*, it is also easy enough to shift the income from capital: in crude terms, all you have to do is give your kids the cash or property and they will be taxed on its yield. Thus the games have continued, with most of the fun coming on the capital side of the great divide.

𝒲 5.2 Husbands and Wives (With Some Historical Notes)

The questions of who pays taxes are inevitably wrapped up with issues about families. It is within the family that taxpayers can exploit tax rules without affecting economic realities. An early question the tax system had to address was what is the basic *taxable unit* given the fact that taxpayers tend to live in households, or, more particularly, how should the law tax husbands and wives?

The structural question of the appropriate taxable unit is integrally related to both the questions that arise and the nature of the tax-planning games and techniques that follow. If, for example, husbands and wives are treated as one, there is not much point in trying to shift some of your labor income to your spouse; if, on the other hand, husbands and wives are viewed as separate taxpayers, we can let the tax games between them begin.

The initial modern income tax, put in place in 1913, essentially treated husbands and wives as separate taxpayers, although an extra deduction was given to married men. The assumption was that wives would not work for income outside the home. This gave a tremendous incentive for married couples to attempt to shift income. Under even the simplified rate schedule of Table 1, above, two $60,000 incomes bear much less tax than a single $120,000 would (specifically $12,000 compared to $24,000; you can check the math.)

Couples tried various techniques to shift. In *Lucas v. Earl*, already cited, the device was a simple contract, holding that all earnings during marriage were to be shared equally. Mr. and Mrs. Earl filled out tax forms on the basis that each earned one-half the couple's whole income. Justice Holmes and his brethren on the Supreme Court, agreeing with the IRS, did not consider that to work, taxing Mr. Earl on 100 percent of his salary. But in a case decided in the very same year, *Poe v. Seaborn*, 282 U.S. 101 (1930), the Supreme Court held that state law could do the trick: community property states such as Washington, which gave the wife enough power and control over one-half of the "community" income, *did* effectively lead to split incomes by law. This led to a flurry of attempts by states all across the country to move toward community property, notwithstanding some nontax aversion to the concept.[1] Husbands also tried putting their wives on the payroll or incorporating themselves and giving half of the stock in the "company" to their spouses, and so on.

The games went on until after World War II, when much of the post-War "peace dividend" was spent in 1948 reforming the tax laws to allow husbands and wives to file jointly, at double the rate brackets for single persons. See Table 2.

This meant that all married couples were taxed *as if* they consisted of two persons each earning one-half the whole: all couples making $120,000, however divided, would pay $12,000 in taxes.

TABLE 2 Rate Structure with Joint Filing, 1948–1969

Income Single Persons	Marginal Tax Rate	Income Married Persons
$0—$20,000	0%	$0—$40,000
$20,000—$60,000	15%	$40,000—$120,000
Over $60,000	30%	Over $120,000

1. I discuss the history and law in *Taxing Women*, Chapter 2. *See also* Carolyn C. Jones, "Split Income and Separate Spheres: Tax Law and Gender Roles in the 1940s," 6 *Law and History Review* 259 (1988).

There was no longer any reason to shift—or pretend to shift—to your spouse. Those particular games, at least as played by spouses, dried up.

The 1948 *joint filing* solution gave a "marriage bonus" for high earners, almost always men, to marry low-earning spouses. A man making $120,000 could see his taxes cut in half by marrying a stay-at-home wife. But a marriage bonus is also a singles penalty—the same man would pay a price for *not* marrying, because his taxes would remain at the high singles-person level. Congress addressed this situation in 1969, the Summer of Love, by lowering the rate brackets for married couples by 20 percent. See Table 3.

Table 3 is constructed by multiplying the rate bracket levels of Table 2, above, by .8. Under it, married couples get the *benefits* of a *deemed* splitting of income, as if they were two persons each earning one-half of the whole, but also get the *burden* of having less favorable rate brackets (divide the married couple's column in half, you will see that it is less favorable, by 20 percent, than the separate persons' rate schedule on the left.)

This all means that some couples get a "marriage bonus," where one person earns most of the income and the benefits of income-splitting are significant; other couples see a "marriage penalty" if their incomes are already close to equal, such that they get little or no benefit from income-splitting but pay the price of the higher rates. The problem cannot be solved by taking advantage of the "married, filing separately" rate schedule, because this is set at one-half the "married, filing jointly" one—meaning you get the detriment of the higher rates (the brackets kick in 20 percent sooner than for single individuals) without the statutory benefit of income-splitting.

TABLE 3   Rate Structure with Joint Filing, 1969–Present

Income Single Persons	Marginal Tax Rate	Income Married Persons
$0—$20,000	0%	$0—$32,000
$20,000—$60,000	15%	$32,000—$96,000
Over $60,000	30%	Over $96,000

Very few married couples file separately: those that do are typically estranged and unable or unwilling to sign the same tax return form.

5.2.1 Marriage Penalties, Bonuses . . . and the Real Issue

The convoluted history of the taxation of married persons features prominently in my first book, *Taxing Women*, where I set out the history, law, and accounting realities at length. Ironically, the deep social problem turns out not to be marriage penalties or bonuses, which have attracted a great deal of popular and some legislative attention, at all. The problem instead is the *secondary-earner bias*, whereby two-earner households are discouraged.

Whether receiving a marriage penalty or a bonus, couples under joint filing face a certain inescapable marginal analysis. A "second" earner considering entering or staying in the workforce is in a marginal rate bracket dictated by the *primary* earner's salary. Typically, the spouse thinking of entering, reentering, or exiting the workforce is the wife, with young children at home. If her husband is a high enough earner, she will be in the 35 percent bracket on her *first* dollar of earned income. Add in state and local taxes, payroll taxes, and all of the costs of work and childcare for working mothers, which are generally nondeductible under Section 262(see discussion in Chapter 3),and the math of the secondary-earner bias is clear, and brutal, enough. And recall imputed income, a subject from Chapter 2: parents are not taxed on the very valuable services they perform for their children every day. Those parents who must work and pay others to help with child-care must earn roughly twice the cost of paying the sitters, because, yet again, their distant Uncle Sam must get paid first.

A bias against two-earner households cuts differently at different income levels. It leads to few marriages among the poor, stay-at-home wives among the rich, and a great deal of stress in the middle, where couples try and swim upstream and make every-thing work out. One simple fact stands out: the average working married mother in America sees more than two-thirds of her salary lost to taxes and work-related expenses. That is on average. Many women flat out *lose* money by working outside the home for pay. *Taxing Women* attempts to explain their story, and offers proposals for change—none of which have been adopted in the United States to date.[2]

5.2.2 Note on Head of Household Status

In addition to single persons and married persons, filing jointly or separately, IRC Section 1(b) has a rate schedule for heads of house-holds, essentially single parents. The rates are lower than they are for child less individuals. As roughly one-third of American children are now being raised by single parents, this is a good concession to social reality.

5.2.3 Note on Marriage for Federal Income Tax Purposes

The rules for married couples under the tax laws only apply to het-erosexual married couples. Under the federal Defense of Marriage Act (DOMA), the federal government does not (yet) recognize homosexual couples, even if legally married under state law. The feds get to set their own rules, under the Supremacy Clause of the

---

2. Overseas, there has been a much greater willingness to change and accommo-date two-earner households, whether for reasons of economics or justice. See Edward J. McCaffery, "Where's the Sex in Fiscal Sociology: Taxation and Gender in Comparative Perspective," in Isaac Martin, Ajay K. Mehrota, and Monica Prasad, *The New Fiscal Sociology: Taxation in Comparative and Historical Perspective*, Cambridge University Press (2009).

Constitution, so none of the tax breaks afforded married couples extend to same-sex couples, as of the moment I write this. The subject matter is in flux, however, as the Obama administration has announced its intent not to defend DOMA. The IRS has also agreed that same-sex couples entitled to community property rights, as for example registered domestic partners in California, can benefit from the income-splitting allowed by *Poe v. Seaborn*, above. Change in the direction of social justice can come slowly, indeed, in tax: stay tuned.

🎐 5.3 Kids

While the law went back and forth for married couples, and now moots any interspousal shifting games because of joint filing, a type of hybrid system continues to govern children and the wider family. For many purposes, the family is a single unit: children do not normally file their own tax returns, and each child entitles her parents to an additional dependency deduction under IRC Sections 151–152, considered above, in essence widening the zero bracket for families with children. There are also per child credits to be had, under IRC Section 24. Transfers between parents and their children are generally ignored, under the gift rules of Section 102 and 1015 and the nondeduction rule of Section 262. These features move toward making the household, kids included, the taxable unit.

Yet children *can* be their own separate taxpayers if and when they have their own income. IRC Section 73 expressly says as much, even in a case where the parent, as natural guardian or otherwise, receives the income on behalf of the child. This creates an incentive for high-income families, who no longer have any reason to play interspousal games, to try and shift income down to their children. Once again, the children are going to end up consuming a vast amount of the income, anyway; the tax planning game is about doing what one wants to do (get some income to the children) at a lower tax cost.

Lucas v. Earl still stands as the major barrier: one is not supposed to be able to shift wage income to anyone, including a child, under the "first principle of taxation," namely, to "tax him who earns it." There are still ways to shift, as by putting the child on the payroll, but these are limited by the truth and facts if performed legally.

But what the labor side denies, the capital side allows—and easily enough. There is nothing preventing a parent from giving money or other property to a child. The gift itself is a nontaxable event, under Sections 102 and 262, with carryover basis under Section 1015. Once the gift has been made, the *income from the property* has been effectively shifted. The child will collect and pay tax on the interest, rent, dividends, and so forth.

With clever enough planning, this can even help effect some shift of labor income. Consider the case of *Brooke v. United States*, 468 F.2d 1155 (9th Cir. 1972). A doctor engaged in solo practice owned his own medical office building. He gifted the building to his four children, tax-free of course, and then began paying rent to them as his landlords. The rent paid was a legitimate business deduction under Section 162, triggering income to his children under Section 61. There was no net amount of taxable income changed: every penny paid in rent by dad was picked up as income to his children on their tax returns. But the responsibility for paying tax on the rental amount had shifted—downstream—to the good doctor's children: it had exactly the same effect as our example of Lear and his daughters. The court reasoned that as long as fair market values were respected—note the perverse incentive the doctor faced to want to pay *excessive* rent—there was nothing to stop the clever plan. There would not be any impediment to Dr. Brooke's technique until the kiddie tax, discussed below, came along.

⅏ 5.4 Fruits and Trees

If that seems pretty simple—you cannot shift wage income directly, but you can give away capital and thereby change things—there are still twists to be had. Human nature being what it is, many parents feel uncomfortable giving capital outright to their children; perhaps they have actually read or watched *King Lear* and seen what happens when you give away the keys to the empire too early. Thus arises the classic "fruits and trees" distinction: property or capital on the one hand versus income from property or capital on the other. While trees or outright capital can be shifted easily enough, fruits or the income from property raise nettlesome issues.

Helvering v. Horst, 311 U.S. 112 (1940), arose in the days when bonds literally had coupons for the annual interest component that got "clipped" each year and taken to the bank (hence the origin of the phrase "coupon clippers," referring not to frugal shoppers clipping sales coupons to take to the grocery store but to the capitalist classes clipping coupons on their bond portfolios to take to the bank). A $10,000, ten-year bond, bearing 10 percent interest, might have ten $1,000 coupons—one for each year—representing the interest.

In *Horst*, the taxpayer father would clip the coupons and hand them to his son. The younger Horst boy would turn the coupons in at the bank—and report the $1,000 income (in our example) on his own tax return. The Supreme Court considered this an impermissible shift of income, although it came on the capital side. The reasoning is not crystal clear. It may be that the dad "controlled" the income, or that the income had already, in effect, accrued as of the moment dad clipped the coupon and gave it to his son—a matter of timing. But the most commonly thought-of explanation sounds in some naturalistic language often used by the Court: the dad had kept the tree, the bond itself with its obligation to restore principal, while attempting to shift away some of its "fruits," the annual interest payment.

The fruit-and-tree, property-versus-income-from-property distinction often confuses students, but the doctrine is pretty clear. In *Blair v. Commissioner*, 300 U.S. 5 (1937), the taxpayer had inherited a term of years, meaning that he would get income from a trust or other asset for, say, fifteen years, after which the trust principal or asset would pass to someone else. The dad assigned one-fourth of the income to each of his three children, keeping one-quarter for himself. The Court upheld this as a valid shift, taxing the children. What is the difference with *Horst*? The easiest way to see it is that the taxpayer in *Blair* gave away *all that he had*, in temporal terms. That is, he kept no *reversion*. It is true that each child only got one-fourth of the whole interest. But each fourth was given away forever, for as long as the father owned it. Again, there was no reversion. In *Horst*, in contrast, the taxpayer dad kept the main principal, or bond; he had a large reversionary interest. Whatever tree, sapling, or shrub existed in *Blair* was turned over to the kids.

The *Horst-Blair* distinction played itself out in a game involving trusts. Parents would set up trusts for their children, ideally on the day of their birth. They would allow the child to take the income from the trust for a period of time, say 18 years. Then the trust would revert back to them, the parents. Cases went back and forth, until the IRS issued relatively decisive rules after the case of *Helvering v. Clifford*, 309 U.S. 331 (1940), which held that a five-year trust set up for the benefit of a wife (this before the 1948 joint filing solution) was taxable to the husband. Now the matter is handled by statute, IRC Sections 671–679, where the key to an effective shift is that the value of the remainder or reversionary interest be no more than 5 percent of the whole.

5.4.1 A Note on Economics

All this brings up a point from the economics domain: there is, in economic reality, no large distinction between fruits and trees.

Economic interests that persist through time, like buildings paying rent, corporate stock, bonds and such are valued at their "capitalized income stream." If you divide an asset into different interests by time – giving the present income to one person, the future remainder to another – you do not create any additional value. The asset is still worth what the asset is worth. Suppose that Marge has $10,000 to invest. She buys a 30 year bond, which pays interest for 30 years and then gives Marge her principal, the $10,000, back. The bond – interest payments plus the promise to return principal in the future – is worth $10,000, what Marge paid for it, no more and no less. This means that the interest and principal components, *combined*, are worth $10,000; each component, standing alone, is worth less than that. The longer the time period for the interest or "fruits"component, the more it is worth, and the less the remainder or future component is worth.

In the case of Marge's thirty-year bond, for example, the right to get your principal back in the thirtieth year is worth pennies compared to the income interest over that time. Suppose you bought a thirty-year bond for $1,000. The bond is worth $1,000, what you paid for it. You would get interest for thirty years, and then your $1,000 back in Year 31. What would you pay, today, to get $1,000 in thirty years? That is what the remainder is worth. The rest of the value – the bulk of it – is in the income interest. Sometimes fruits can be worth much more than the tree.

Economists do not think or write this way. Yet the idea of a rigid distinction between fruits and trees, income from property and the property itself, runs deep in the tax law. We will see it again in the next chapter, on capital gains.

🕮 5.5 Note on Divorce

During a marriage, under the tax laws, families are essentially one, with joint filing and no separate deduction/inclusion for transfers from parent to child. A handy way to remember the rules for taxation on divorce is to recall the saying familiar to many families affected by divorce: parents divorce each other, not their children.

After divorce, the former husband and wife become separate taxpayers again. Hence, generally, alimony or spousal support is deductible by the payor and includible for the payee (IRC Sections 71 and 215, respectively)—the income really moves over to the recipient spouse. Both the economic and the tax realities shift. Couples can elect out of this treatment, which would be tax benefi-cial in the rare case that the recipient of spousal support is in a higher tax bracket than the payor. But child support payments are neither includible nor deductible: you have not divorced your chil-dren, and the support you are paying them now is like the support you were paying for them in marriage—nondeductible under Section 262.

✺ 5.6 A Statutory Response: The "Kiddie Tax"

The Tax Reform Act of 1986 (TRA 1986) systematically dealt with many tax-planning games, shutting down multiple loopholes on the labor side of the great divide. We will look at the Act at greater length in Chapter 7, when we consider tax shelters. It is, however, worth noting at this time the Act's response to income shifting within the family—meaning shifting to kids, joint filing having mooted the interspousal game.

TRA 1986 gave us the "kiddie tax," in IRC Section 1(g). Like other aspects of TRA 1986, the response to the perceived problem was thoughtful and systematic. The kiddie tax does not place the income tax system on a thorough household basis. It does not deny any of the shifting transactions, almost all involving capital or prop-erty, like Dr. Brooke's transfer of a medical office building to his chil-dren. Instead, the kiddie tax puts children in the *same rate bracket* as their parents. Thus the kiddie tax goes to the root of the problem, the motivation behind the shifting tax-planning games that taxpay-ers play: different rate brackets among interrelated individuals. After the kiddie tax, you can shift to your heart's content, within what the law allows (such as the Dr. Brooke trick), but you will not save any taxes on account of it.

Of course there are exceptions. The kiddie tax applies only to *unearned* income—a clear recognition that the principal games being played are on the property or capital side. Each child still has a "zero bracket" of her own, and then a limited 15 percent one; the present values, indexed for inflation, are approximately $700 each. So a parent *can* shift the responsibility for paying tax on unearned income, that is, income from property, up to $1,400 per child. Finally, the kiddie tax only applies to unearned income for children under the age of 14. Above that magic number, the games still apply. Many taxpayers plan to finance college by transferring appreciated stock—which they had been holding in a Tax Planning 101 kind of way—to their children and having them sell it prior to paying the college. Perhaps this is planning done by some members of Congress, because that particular game still works (although at a 15% capital gains rate, this game, too, may no longer be worth the candle – though transferring stock to one's children is a pretty inexpensive candle to use).

✹ 5.7 Shifting To and Through Entities

It is not just human beings who can play a role in income shifting. Entities such as corporations, partnerships, and trusts can, too. There are two ways that such legal fictions can play this role. One is as taxpaying entities themselves, to which the responsibility for tax can be shifted – this game can work for corporations and some trusts, not partnerships, because partnerships themselves do not pay tax but instead pass on tax liabilities to their individual partners. Two, entities can serve as conduits through which income can be shifted to others, such as family members. Partnerships can work here, if income earned by the partnership can be allocated to children or other persons in lower tax brackets than the primary taxpayer. There is a long and complex history of income-shifting transactions involving entities, and various rules and regulations for family corporations, partnerships, and trusts. But with the rate brackets historically compressed, and with individual income tax rates at or below those of corporations and trusts, the benefits are less than they have been.

5.7.1 Note on Shifting to a Later Self

A final note: One generally thinks of shifting to someone else, like a child, or something else, like a personal corporation. But one can also shift to *one's own self at a later time*. This is a large part of what Mr. Drescher was trying to do, in the case considered in Chapter 2, and what the tax-favored provisions for IRAs and qualified pension plans generally allow.

Not only is *Drescher* a good example of how the "what" and "when" questions in tax are connected—Drescher's attempt at deferral, getting paid an annuity contract with its promise of future instead of present cash, did not work—but it also illustrates an attempt to shift from one self, today, to the same self, tomorrow. Given that you can expect to be in a lower tax bracket when you retire, this can make a difference. At top marginal rates of 90 percent affecting your peak-earnings years, as Mr. Drescher faced, it can make a very large difference, indeed. And it does not run into the *King Lear* problem, because you are not passing on your hard-earned money to anyone other than yourself. Once again, standard and perfectly legal tax-favored retirement plans along the traditional IRA (or spending tax) model allow this result naturally. But the allure of this kind of shift is great enough that taxpayers like Mr. Drescher often resort to self-help to get more.

Lest anyone think that putting money into a deferred retirement account must effect a *real* shift in one's economic well-being or lifestyle, remember not to forget Tax Planning 101. There is nothing to prevent Mr. Drescher from borrowing, today, to enjoy the moment, knowing that he will have money, tomorrow, to pay off his debts – and the money will come taxed at a lower rate. Typically, Mr. Drescher cannot directly pledge his retirement accounts as security for any loan, but that need not stop him from running up consumer debt, as on credit cards. Even if he has to pay a high interest rate, the benefits of deferral and income-shifting to his lower-bracket future self create a cushion to make it worth his while to play this particular game. And the general myopia of human nature may have him borrowing today, in any event.

ℳ 5.8 Summary

The "who" question, of attribution or the appropriate taxable unit, matters. We have learned:

- Under a system of progressive marginal rates, who pays tax matters to the bottom line; simply put, two taxpayers making one-half the amount of a single third taxpayer pay less tax;
- This fact of the matter has led many taxpayers to attempt to shift income; as the game here is not to give money away to save taxes, but to attempt to have your cake and eat it, tax-free, too, the most common shifts occur within the family;
- The initial modern income tax treated husbands and wives as separate taxpayers, encouraging income shifting between spouses; beginning in 1948, the income tax has had a system of joint filing for married couples that moots these games;
- The choice to tax married couples as one has had effects, beyond mooting the income shifting games; it has led to a bias against second-earners that affects household composition and decisions about work and family;
- Income shifting remains possible between parents and their children, who can be separate taxpayers;
- As with other aspects of tax planning, income shifting is difficult when it comes to income from labor or wages; Lucas v. Earl stands for the basic proposition that wage income cannot be shifted;
- Capital or property, on the other hand, is easy to shift, via gifts, which are not includible in the recipient's income, under Section 102, nor deductible to the transferor, under 262. Once a gift has been made, the responsibility for paying income tax on the income from the property shifts to the recipient;
- The ability to shift capital and its yield can lead to some clever tax planning, as in the Brooke case, wherein a doctor dad, having gifted a medical office building to his children, paid them rent, giving himself a deduction (Section 162) offset by

an inclusion for the children (Section 61), producing a significant tax savings because of the different tax rates;

- The law generally attempts to maintain that, while property—and hence all of the future income from that property—can be shifted, "income from property" alone cannot be shifted, a distinction often analogized to "fruits and trees." The distinction is not all that principled, and clever taxpayers have found means to shift income from property notwithstanding it;

- The kiddie tax of IRC Section 1(g) was the TRA 1986's systematic response to the problem of income shifting within families, to children. It allows the shifts to go forward, but places the child in the same rate bracket as her parents, after an initial modest exemption and 15 percent bracket. This takes away the financial incentive to shift. But there are holes within the kiddie tax, including that it only applies to unearned income (that is, income from property), and, most important, does not apply to children age 14 or older;

- In addition to shifting to other persons within the family, shifts or attempted shifts can transpire to or through entities, such as corporations, partnerships, or trusts, or to the taxpayer himself at a later time, as Mr. Drescher attempted to do with his deferred compensation plan. There is nothing to stop Mr. Drescher from borrowing once he has "saved," a variant of Tax Planning 101 available for wage earners using qualified pension plans and other tax-favored retirement techniques.

SIX

The "How Much" of Taxation

Characterization of Ordinary Income and Capital Gains

WE ARE ALMOST DONE exploring the details of tax and pursuing our tax-planning goals: we have deliberately mingled describing the law and explaining how taxpayers can and did plan around it. Assume now that you have tried to escape taxes (Chapters 2 and 3); to defer them (Chapter 4); and to shift the responsibility for paying tax to some body, self, or entity in a lower tax bracket (Chapter 5). It is now time to pay tax. There is still one planning step left to consider: To characterize any gain as *capital*, allowing you to pay tax at a lower, preferential rate. Recall that if it is losses we are talking about, everything is inverted, so you will want the character of losses to be "ordinary." This chapter explores the attendant issues.

▓ 6.1 The Math of the Matter: A Question of Rates

The reason a taxpayer wants a realized and recognized gain classified as capital is that the capital gains tax rate is lower—much lower—than the ordinary income rate. Like income-shifting, this final issue used to matter more under higher marginal tax rates. Throughout most of the history of the income tax, the capital gains rate was set at 40 percent of the ordinary one. With a top rate of 90 percent on ordinary income during the 1940s and 50s, for example, we had a 36 percent capital gains rate; with a top rate of 70 percent ordinary income rate from 1963 until 1981, we had a 28 percent capital gains rate. For a brief period after the Tax Reform Act of

1986 there was *no* capital gains rate preference. It is back, with a top capital gains rate of 15 percent compared to 35 percent for ordinary income as I write. That is more than enough to create an incentive to play games.

✇ 6.2 The Policy (If Any) of It All

Why, you might be asking, on top of all of the other benefits afforded to capital, should we further bless that side of the divide with a significantly lower tax rate?

To begin, many *un*appealing answers have been offered.

One is that we need to counteract the effects of inflation.

If Jane bought stock for $1,000 many years ago, she would have a tax basis of $1,000 in the stock, as we know by now. Suppose that the stock is presently worth $5,000. It has a built-in gain of $4,000, taxable under Section 1001 on sale or other disposition. Yet surely some of this $4,000 "gain" in the stock's value is due to inflation, the simple rise in the price level without corresponding real economic gain or additional purchasing power.

But this inflation argument is hardly compelling. Simply giving a tax break of more than one-half the regular tax rate is a crude way to account for inflation. To qualify for long-term capital gains treatment, an asset must be held for a certain period of time, now, as typically, for more than one year. IRC Section 1222. Jane would pay the low 15% capital gains rate on the $4,000 of gain in her stock whether she held it for 13 months, 13 years, or more. This seems crude and inaccurate. It would be much better to *index* the basis for inflation, multiplying the historical basis by some factor based on the length of the holding period. (You can do this easily enough online, looking up various Consumer Price Index (CPI) websites that will tell you what some sum from the past is worth in real, inflation-adjusted terms, today.) Typically only a small amount of built-in gain would escape taxes if we properly indexed each asset's basis. Why give an across-the-board benefit to all capital assets, no matter how long held? Further, throughout most of the history of the income tax, the ordinary rate brackets were not indexed for inflation, meaning that wages or labor income were impacted by a rise in the price level. Why further favor capital, already multiply blessed by various rules including those constituting Tax Planning 101, by worrying about the effects of inflation on capital gains, alone? Further, ordinary savings, such as one gets from a regular bank savings account, is taxed at ordinary income tax rates—although all interest has a component of inflation-adjustment built into it. The general rate brackets are now indexed for inflation, after much delay in getting this result, so that wage earners and ordinary savers will not see their taxes go up due to inflation alone—but this has only been the case in the last couple of decades. Why did the solicitude for capital precede it?

Another bad answer to the policy puzzle of the capital gains preference is to point to the "bunching" effect: realized capital gains often come in small, concentrated bunches, it is argued.

Jane, a middle-class wage-earner, might suddenly show a large amount of income in a year when she sells a major capital asset. But there is little evidence that bunching is actually a big problem: most taxpayers who ever have capital gains show fairly regular levels of it. Further, self-help is available under the installment method considered in Chapter 4. Finally, as with the inflation argument, a more focused legislative solution could address bunching: we could allow taxpayers to average their capital gains and report them over several years, as a quick example. Again, simply giving all realized and recognized capital gains a 15 percent tax rate, less than one-half the ordinary one, seems overbroad.

Likewise, the argument that capital gains represent value that has already been taxed, that any capital gains tax falls on savings—John Stuart Mill's complaint—misses the mark. Once again, ordinary savings, such as in a bank savings account or a certificate of deposit, are not only taxed—they are taxed at ordinary rates. The interest that the average middle-class taxpayer gets on her savings account is taxed in full. Rich Dad mocked such savings accounts, which stray outside Tax Planning 101. The Rich Dads who buy assets that do not produce cash interest or dividends need never pay any tax. When they do pay, they do so at the lowest rates in town, 15 percent these days. It seems unfair, to say the least.

Yet another argument for some capital gains preference is that corporate shareholders face a double tax. The corporation itself is taxable on its income. But then when the corporation pays dividends to its shareholders, these payment are taxed again – and throughout most of history, at ordinary income rates. Corporate dividends are now entitled to the low 15% rate, too, under IRC Section 1(h). But the shareholder selling her shares, like Jane, can complain that she is paying tax on the rise in value of a corporation that has itself paid tax along the way. So stated, the objection here follows quickly: why extend a capital gains preference across the board, to all assets, not just corporate stock? And that objection is not even getting into all the ways that real corporations reduce their tax burdens, a subject matter outside the scope of this short introduction to the individual income tax.

Given all these rather poor arguments, why do we see the extent and persistence of a capital gains preference? Does not capital already get enough benefits?

The answer to these questions, paradoxically, is that we need a capital gains preference *because of* those other benefits afforded to capital.

It all starts yet again with *Macomber*, the realization requirement and the noncurrent taxation of "mere" appreciation—the Achilles' heel of the income tax. The fact of the matter is that taxpayers do not have to sell or dispose of any asset with a built-in gain: they can play Tax Planning 101 straight through death. The resulting "lock-in" of assets would mean an inefficient economy, in which assets failed to flow to their highest and best use and users.

Suppose that Harry holds a farm with a basis of $100,000. Sally offers $1,000,000 for it. If the farm is worth $800,000 to Harry, himself, he "ought" to sell out to Sally: she values it more highly. This is Economics 101, the fundamental lesson of Adam Smith and others: markets work, and allow assets to go to their highest and best use and user. But in the real world with taxes, on sale, Harry's tax time bomb of $900,000—the difference between Sally's offering price and Harry's basis—would go off in his hands. At a tax rate of 35 percent, Harry would pay just over $300,000 in taxes, netting him just under $700,000. It is not worth it for Harry to sell, given his $800,000 nontax value. The sale will not happen, and the farm will stay in Harry's less productive hands. Sally will keep looking for a lesser alternative.

In order to make sure that some capital gains get realized, to move assets along and keep the economy humming—to get Harry to sell to Sally—the tax system has little choice but to offer a lower capital gains rate. Tax is held hostage by its prior choices, however dimly made. Once we go down the route of favoring capital, it is hard to pull back in any noncomprehensive way. Some capital gains preference is all but certain to persist as long as we have an income-with-realization tax.

𝍖 6.3 Statutory Scheme

Now it is time to ask just what qualifies for this favorable capital gain treatment. We start with the statute.

Section 1(h) sets out the rate preference for capital gains. The key to understanding what is and is not "capital" rests with IRC Section 1221, the basic definition of a capital asset. This Section begins:

> For purposes of this subtitle, the term "capital asset" means property held by the taxpayer (whether or not connected with his trade or business), but does not include—
>
> (1) stock in trade of the taxpayer or other property of a kind which would properly be included in the inventory of the taxpayer if on hand at the close of the taxable year, or property held by the taxpayer primarily for sale to customers in the ordinary course of his trade or business....

IRC Section 1221 goes on to list other categories of "ordinary income property" that are specifically excluded from all other forms of "property" qualifying for the capital gains preference. We will return to Section 1221(1), the so-called stock-in-trade or inventory exception, soon. First let us continue our tour of the statute.

IRC Section 64 makes clear that any item which is not the sale of a "capital asset" or "property" is "ordinary."

Section 1221(2) deals with depreciable property used in one's trade or business. At first this seems like a major exception to capital gains treatment. But what Section 1221(2) seems to taketh away, Section 1231 giveth back. This latter Section makes clear that, if depreciable property is sold for a *loss*, that loss can be taken as an ordinary expense deduction under Section 162. If on the other hand the sale of depreciable business property results in a *gain*, that gain is capital.

This explicit asymmetry sounds like a large piece of favoritism for businesses—it gives them exactly what they want, ordinary losses and capital gains—and perhaps it is, in fact. But there is sound tax theory behind it. If depreciable property is sold for less than its basis, generating a loss, it appears in hindsight that the depreciation schedule was not quick or generous enough. The "excess" loss is indeed a legitimate business expense, a loss of value in an asset due to its use in a trade or business. If, on the other hand, depreciable property is sold for a gain, a value above basis, the law concludes that there has been some capital appreciation. The contrary position, that there has been excess depreciation which ought to be paid back in ordinary gain form, is not generally taken; the law has some provisions for "recapturing" depreciation deductions that seem over-generous in hindsight, but these are limited, typically tracking special "accelerated" depreciation schedules. See IRC Sections 1245 and 1250.

Note, by the way, that Section 1221(2) and Section 1231's asymmetry mirrors the treatment of gains and losses on personal assets: gains are includible, under Section 61, losses are not generally deductible, under Section 165(c)(3) and Section 262. Here, on the business side, we see that business losses are ordinary, gains capital.

Section 1221(3) carves out copyrights, artistic creations, patents, and the like—self-created assets, in the hands of the person who created them (or someone who got them in a transaction having carryover basis, to prevent the simple trick of gifting such assets to your children, for example). The theory of excluding such items from the general definition of property subject to capital gains rates is clear enough: gain in these kinds of assets represents *labor* income. Some people get paid, earn their wages, by creating property or selling inventory. Such property must be put on the other side of the great divide, with other forms of wages, subject to ordinary gains rates.

Section 1221(4) deals with accounts or notes receivable for inventory, the kind of property governed by Section 1221(1). The trick leading to this Section should be easy enough to guess: one cannot sell inventory and get capital gains treatment, under 1221(1), so taxpayers tried to sell the *contractual rights to buy the inventory* and then claimed that these paper contracts were "capital." Section 1221(4) shuts down that particular trick.

There are still more provisions in Section 1221, listing various forms of "property" that are *not* subject to the capital gains preference, but these are of lesser importance. Most of the cases over the definition of capital gains assets involve Section 1221(1), which we return to explore below.

The rate preference of Section 1(h) and the definition of Section 1221 are key to understanding the topic of capital gains. One also needs to meet a certain holding period—now and typically, more than one year, IRC Section 1222—for owning the asset to qualify for the favorable long-term capital gains rate. The law allows a taxpayer to tack the holding period from a prior owner where there has been a nontaxable transaction between them. If dad gifts stock that he has held for years to his daughter, who turns around to sell it to pay her college tuition (being older than 14 and out of the kiddie tax), the daughter is deemed to have held the stock for as long as her father, given the carryover basis rule of Section 1015.

Finally, a reminder of the capital loss offset rule of Section 1211, which allows capital losses to be taken only against realized and recognized capital gains, plus a small amount, currently $3,000, of ordinary income. Unused capital losses get to roll forward to future years indefinitely—until death moots the issue by giving a stepped-up basis under Section 1014.

ℳ 6.4 Two Big Examples of Section 1221(1): Real Estate and Securities

Most of the litigation over what is or is not "capital" for purposes of the capital gains preference concerns Section 1221(1), the "inventory" or "stock in trade" exception.

Disputes about such ordinary income property often involve real estate and securities. Both are assets that *can* be held for investment, as typical capital property, *or* as inventory for sale to customers in the ordinary course of one's trade or business. There are, after all, real estate and securities dealers.

In the case of real estate, taxpayers generally want capital gain; in the case of securities, taxpayers typically want ordinary treatment. Why? Because, as we recall from Tax Planning 102, the savvy taxpayer holding securities will be holding her winners and selling her losers: it is nice for her to get ordinary treatment for the losses. There are many cases and standards on this issue. Generally, tax practitioners know it when they see it. Securities dealers are typically short-term holders with large inventories and frequent sales; a taxpayer basically following a buy and hold strategy but attempting to sell his losers aggressively raises suspicions. Most real estate dealers build and develop properties and sell them often. Sometimes, the best way to get value for a large lot of land is to do just that. But a taxpayer who attempts to dispose of her real estate holdings by creating multiple lots runs the risk of slipping into becoming a dealer with inventory. She had best be careful, lest too far be seen by the IRS as being too far, and she would lose the benefits of the low capital gains rate.

ℳ 6.5 Playing with Definitions: *Corn Products* and *Arkansas Best*

Two Supreme Court cases deal with the question of what happens when a company engaged in an active trade or business uses various forms of financial transactions in its day-to-day business.

Corn Products Refining Co. v. Commissioner, 350 U.S. 46 (1955), concerned a company dealing in corn products, not surprisingly. To deal with the fluctuating price of corn, the company could have purchased large amounts when it considered the price low, and stored the actual corn, drawing down its reserves in times of higher prices. Instead, Corn Prooducts would buy futures or commodities options locking in a certain minimum price. For example, at a time when the price of corn was $20 a bushel, Corn Products might buy the right to purchase 1000 bushels of corn for $20 dollars at some future date. If by the appointed date the price of corn had gone up to $25 a bushel, Corn Product commodities option would be valuable. Specifically, Corn Products could get 1000 bushels of corn for $20,000, less than the $25,000 then going rate. Rather than take delivery on the corn itself—this only happens in movies, like *Trading Places* starring Eddie Murphy and Dan Aykroyd—Corn Products would simply sell its commodities option for $5,000, and then buy the corn for $25,000, using the $5,000 gain on its option to lower its real cost to $20,000.

Corn Products sought to pay capital gains rates on the gain, claiming that these commodities futures were "property" in their hands within the meaning of IRC Section 1221. The IRS argued, and the Supreme Court ultimately agreed, that the gain should be ordinary. The reasoning was not crystal clear, but it seemed to turn on the fact that the securities operations were an integral part of the taxpayer's trade or business, in that the corn futures were designed to deal with the fluctuating cost of real corn.[1]

---

1. My friend and colleague Ed Kleinbard has pointed out that here, as in many other places in this short introduction, I am simplifying matters. The *Corn*

It should come as no surprise that the next big related case to get to the Supreme Court concerned a similar fact pattern, except with *losses*. An interesting question in tax is whether or not the law should have explicitly asymmetric tests dealing with losses. *Cottage Savings*, considered in Chapter 4, in essence said "no." In that case, very minor deviations in mortgage holdings in the "mortgage swaps" triggered a realization and recognition of the savings and loans' losses. In reaching this result, the Supreme Court in large part relied on cases and *government* arguments taken from situations involving gain: the government was hoisted on its own petard, as the saying goes. Given that the taxpayer typically controls sales or other dispositions under IRC Section 1001(a)—the doctrinal fact that leads to Tax Planning 102 (the advice to sell your losers and hold your winners)—there is however something to be said for giving the government a break.

In any event, in *Arkansas Best Corporation v. Commissioner*, 485 U.S. 212 (1988), the taxpayer was a bank holding company, that is, it made investments in other companies. It kept putting money into one of its holdings, taking back securities, hoping to turn the subsidiary company around. It did not work, economically, and the subsidiary company became worthless. Arkansas Best, the taxpayer, then attempted to take ordinary losses under Section 165, citing to *Corn Products*.

The IRS and the Supreme Court once more disagreed with the taxpayer. The Court reanalyzed *Corn Products*, and came up with the reasoning that the earlier case was really about an "inventory substitute." Instead of holding corn, the taxpayer in *Corn Products* held financial instruments. Buying or selling the corn would fall into 1221(1)'s exclusion from "property" subject to a capital gains

---

Products doctrine that arose from the case was different than the facts of *Corn Products*, and there is much more to be said for the taxation of financial instruments such as options, hedges and straddles. *See* Edward D. Kleinbard and Suzanne F. Greenberg, "Business Hedges after Arkansas Best," 43 *Tax Law Review* 393 (1988) for more detail.

preference. The Court in *Arkansas Best* reasoned that the prior decision was about an expansive reading of the "inventory" exception,
Section 1221(1), not a narrow reading of the word "property" itself.
Arkansas Best did not deal with an inventory substitute, and the
stock held by the holding company looked like classic "property."
Hence the lower capital gains rate applied to the taxpayer's losses,
much to its chagrin. *Arkansas Best* and *Corn Products* illustrate a
theme in tax that has been at least implicit in our discussions, as of
"income" and "gift," all along: words matter. Where, as in the particular case of capital gains, any deeper theory seems to be wanting or
missing altogether, sometimes all we have to go on is words.

6.5.1 A Further Note on Capital Property

The word "property" matters in tax for more than just the capital
gains rate preference. It also matters for whether or not something
acquired from a decedent gets a stepped-up basis under Section
1014. This Section is titled "basis of property acquired from a decedent." What is "property"?

In *Miller v. Commissioner*, 299 F.2d 706 (2nd Cir.), cert. denied,
370 U.S. 923 (1962), the widow of Glen Miller—the bandleader, most
famous for "In the Mood," who died in a plane accident in the midst
of World War II—sold the rights to a movie, *The Glen Miller Story*, to
a studio. Mrs. Miller argued that she acquired the rights on death
from her late husband. If this argument prevailed, it would save her
all taxes, because she would have a stepped-up basis for property
acquired from a decedent under Section 1014. This is what is supposed to happen after the last step in Tax Planning 101, buy/
borrow/die.

Alas, Mrs. Miller lost. The court reasoned that not everything
that could not be classified as anything else would be "property":
property is not a general residual category. But it is a bit hard to see
what else the rights in Glen Miller's life story are, if not "property,"
and the case is at odds with *Arkansas Best*. Further, the holding is

inconsistent with the holding in cases involving Priscilla Presley, Elvis's widow, who *did* get stepped-up basis and capital gains treatment on Elvis's image. The distinction the courts made was that Elvis Presley had taken steps during his lifetime to commercialize his likeness, and thus was passing on an existing asset on death. I have my doubts, and cannot help giving my students another explanation for the discrepancy: Elvis lives.

ℳ 6.6 Anticipatory Income, or Fruits and Trees, Again

We saw the "fruits and trees" distinction, regarding property versus income from property, in the prior chapter. Taxpayers like Mr. Horst (*Helvering v. Horst*; see Chapter 5) tried to carve out a limited income interest to give to their children while keeping the principal or reversionary interest for themselves: that is, they kept the tree, and tried to shift away responsibility for paying tax on the fruits. Generally, this did not work, although we noted that the very distinction did not rest on sound economics.

The same issue recurs with capital gains. To bring yourself within the spirit of the metaphor, think of a tree as being capital. The tree yields fruit every year, just as capital yields gain, in the form of interest, dividends, royalties, rent and the like. Because the fruit or ordinary yield to capital is taxed at ordinary income rates, taxpayers often try to roll up future increments of ordinary income and sell the bundle today, as if it is property. Of course, in the event that the capital grows larger by "mere" appreciation, there is no current taxation, under *Macomber* and the realization requirement. Think of that as a non-fruit bearing tree that grows larger, the kind of tree that Rich Dad likes. But some trees bear fruit, and some uses of capital bear annual yields.

In *Commissioner v. P.G. Lake, Inc.*, 356 U.S. 260 (1958), the Supreme Court confronted a tax-planning technique prevalent at the time. Although the facts are considerably more complex, in essence a high-ranking executive of an oil company was given rights to future streams of oil. If this oil were to be drilled and brought into the company, it would be taxed as sold at ordinary income rates, as the yield to capital. Mr. Lake turned around and sold his rights to future oil back to his company, and claimed capital gains on the sale of the "property." In Mr. Lake's hands, the oil was not inventory or property held primarily for sale to customers in the ordinary course of a trade or business. Mr. Lake had no business of his own, except being a high-ranking employee. The statute would not help to shut this trick down in Section 1221(1).

Instead, the IRS relied on a common law doctrine or argument— that the oil "rights" were little more than an anticipatory grant of what would be ordinary income, and thus should be taxable as such. The Supreme Court, in a rare opinion by Justice Douglas upholding the government position in a tax case, agreed.[2]

P.G. Lake was an abusive case, pretty easy to spot and shut down. But the fruits and trees distinction is no more clear or compelling in the capital gains context than it is in the income-shifting one, notwithstanding the need for some doctrine to somehow stem the bleeding.

In *Hort v. Commissioner*, 313 U.S. 28 (1941) (not to be confused with *Horst*, above), the Supreme Court held that a lease acquired by a landlord's son on death was *not* property subject to a stepped-up basis under Section 1014 or capital gains treatment under Section 1221. Once again, the idea is that the owner of the lease normally sits there, getting rent payments, which are canonical examples of ordinary income under Section 61 and Section 64.

Push hard enough in your mind, however, and the distinction starts to blur. When Sam sells an apartment building, for example— imagine if you want that there are no preexisting leases—Sam

---

2. For an interesting study of Justice Douglas's tax jurisprudence, see Bernard Wolfman, Jonathan L. F. Silver, and Marjorie A. Silver, *Dissent Without Opinion: The Behavior of Justice William O. Douglas in Federal Tax Cases,* University of Pennsylvania Press (1975).

clearly gets capital gains treatment under Section 1221 unless he is a dealer in apartment buildings, subject to 1221(1). Yet why is an apartment building worth what it is worth, if not for the stream of rent payments that the landlord will receive over time? The buyer of Sam's apartment building likely performed an analysis of what net rents she would get over time, and compared buying the apartment building with some other investment. The building is worth the present value of the stream of net rents to be paid over time. Corporate stock is no different. The "p/e" ratio generally used to appraise a stock's value stands for its price/earnings ratio, meaning that the price (p) is some function of the anticipated future earnings (e). If you buy and hold stock, you get the benefits of its earnings over time, in the form of dividends or a rise in value of the shares themselves.

In all cases, in other words, a fruit-bearing tree is worth today the value of its fruits over time. The legal doctrine marking a sharp distinction between fruits and trees, property versus the income from property, needed to shore up aggressive taxpayer attempts at both income shifting and "conversion" to capital gains, rests on a deep misunderstanding. Such is life in the special and unique world of tax.

✳ 6.7 A Modern Day Issue: Carried Interest

Tax planning was not born yesterday. And it never ends.

Yesterday's oil and gas leases and interests, seen in *P.G. Lake*, have become today's "carried interest." This refers to the profit interest that managers have in various venture and "hedge" funds. Typically, in addition to an annual fee measured as a portion of the total assets invested (typically 2 percent), the manager of a hedge fund also gets a cut of the rise in value, typically 20 percent. Because this latter "carried interest" is a share in an ongoing financial partnership, the manager typically reports her gain—when and if she even realizes it—the same way other investors do, namely, as capital gains from the sale of property.

Hedge and venture fund managers made big news at the turn of the recent millennium, both for making huge amounts of money—hundreds of millions of dollars per year, for those most successful—and for paying the reduced capital gains rate when they realized their gains.[3]

The titillating news awoke Congress from its slumbers. Thus we have had legislative *proposals* to address the carried interest problem ever since 2007, and more from the Obama administration. Yet nothing has been enacted as of this writing.

Meanwhile, Rich Dad finds all of this amusing: Why should anyone even be complaining about a 15 percent tax rate on these incredibly well-compensated financiers, when the *really* rich dads need be paying no tax at all?

🎇 6.8 Summary

This chapter completes our tour through the basic elements of tax planning, adding *conversion* to capital gains to the list of escape, defer, and shift. We learned:

- Capital gains matter because of their lower rate, now a maximum of 15 percent compared to 35 percent for "ordinary" income; historically, the capital gains preference has been set at 40 percent of the top ordinary rate;
- There are several poor explanations for this capital gains preference, including accounting for inflation, dealing with the "bunching" problem, and avoiding the double-taxation of savings;
- The one truly compelling and enduring explanation for the capital gains preference is that we *have to have it*, given *Macomber* and the realization requirement. Because taxpayers

---

3. For a thorough discussion of the facts and related law, see Victor Fleischer, "Taxing Blackstone," 61 *Tax Law Review* 89 (2007-08).

need not sell any appreciated asset and pay tax—because they can easily play Tax Planning 101—there is a "lock-in" effect from the realization requirement, whereby taxpayers have incentives to hold onto appreciated assets until their death; This is bad for the economy, because assets fail to flow to their highest and best use and user. In order to unlock the gains to keep the economy moving—and to get *some* tax revenue from the capital side of the divide—the law must give taxpayers holding assets a lower tax rate;

- Section 1(h) sets out the rate preference. Section 1221 contains the principal definition of a capital asset, as all "property" except for certain enumerated, excluded categories of "ordinary income property," including most importantly inventory or stock in trade held primarily for sale to customers, 1221(1), and self-created assets, 1221(3). Section 64 confirms that anything not a "capital asset" or "property" is "ordinary;"

- Section 1221(2) purports to exclude depreciable business property from capital gains treatment, but, in fact, Section 1231 allows such property to get ordinary losses and capital gains, depending on the economics;

- In addition to the rate preference and the basic definition, one must also meet a minimum holding period to get the favorable rate; this is now set at one year as it typically has been. Taxpayers may tack together the holding period of prior owners where they have gotten the asset in a nontaxable transaction, such as a gift;

- Section 1211 limits one's ability to deduct capital losses currently to realized capital gains and $3,000 of ordinary income per year. Excess losses can carry forward to be used on future tax returns;

- There are many cases involving real estate and securities dealers versus investors under Section 1221(1). Taxpayers generally want real estate activities to be capital, and so try to avoid becoming "dealers" with inventory; other taxpayers try to look like securities dealers, because they are playing Tax Planning

102 and only recognizing their losses, which they want to be ordinary both for the rate preference and to offset their wages;

- *Corn Products* and *Arkansas Best* are two oft-cited Supreme Court cases dealing with financial securities held by businesses in their ordinary course of business. *Arkansas Best*, where the taxpayer was trying to get ordinary treatment, stands for the proposition that "property" in Section 1221 has a broad, common language meaning. *Arkansas Best* recast *Corn Products* as a case dealing with financial securities used as "inventory substitutes," and thus within the scope of 1221(1)'s exception;

- "Property" matters not just for capital gains treatment but also getting a stepped-up basis for assets acquired on death, under Section 1014; the widow of Glen Miller failed to get this treatment on Miller's life story, but Elvis's widow did get it for the late King's image;

- The fruits and trees/property versus income from property distinction, seen in Chapter 5 on income shifting, recurs with capital gains. The law holds that attempts to "anticipate" ordinary income by rolling it together into a present interest do not work; *P.G. Lake* looked at the then common situation of oil and gas "rights" or "interests." As before, the economics theory behind the distinction is weak or altogether lacking, leading to some inconsistent legal results and continued taxpayer attempts to push this particular envelope;

- Capital gains conversion games continue to be played out today, even with the fairly compressed 35/15 percent rates. A leading example is carried interest, the principal means by which financial managers of venture and hedge funds get compensated. The rich have gotten richer by treating these profit interests as property subject to capital gains rate, and Congress has done little more than show its outrage by *proposing* legislation to shut down the perceived abuse.

SEVEN

A Summary, of Sorts
Anatomy of a Tax Shelter

WE CONCLUDE PART II with a brief consideration of tax shelters past and present. There are several reasons for this placement of topics.

One, looking at tax shelters helps to review all of the main tools of tax planning: to escape, defer, shift, and/or convert.

Two, the subject of tax shelters generates an occasion to take a closer look at the critical role of debt, or "other people's money," in tax planning.

Three, even a brief consideration of tax shelters allows for an excellent look at the deepest theory in this short introduction, which we can see with our "big picture" view of tax's forest. Tax shelters are about hiding or "sheltering" income from the tax collector. Because there is little need to do this on the capital side, given what we now know, beginning with Tax Planning 101, tax shelters have always been principally about the labor side of the great divide, keeping wages away from current taxation. The central trick behind any good wage tax shelter is to use opportunities from the capital side to hide labor income. Because wage earners typically lack large stores of financial capital—or else they would quit their day jobs and play Tax Planning 101, like Rich Dad—debt becomes a key element in most tax shelters.

Finally, because wages are vital to the tax base, the law must shut down wage tax shelters. It has done so, most dramatically in the Tax Reform Act of 1986. But the law has made no serious attempt to shut down any of the planks in Tax Planning 101. This then leaves us with our most basic theme—the so-called income tax is in reality mainly a wage tax.

This chapter fills in the details of that story.

✎ 7.1 General Strategy of Tax Shelters

Much of the history of tax planning in the United States has concerned high wage earners and their search for "tax shelters." The
general strategy of a tax shelter (at least before 1986) is to get some
of the benefits that the capital classes have long enjoyed under the
basic structure of an income-with-realization tax as a wage earner:
to hide or "shelter" one's labor income from the tax collector.

Rich Dad and other capital owners do not need shelters, by and
large, because the realization requirement and the simple steps in
Tax Planning 101 that follow from it serve to keep their real income
from the tax collector perfectly, effectively, and legally. It is those
with large labor-market incomes who need help. Sometimes, too,
those with sudden and large capital gains find themselves search-
ing for shelters. This happened a lot in the 1990s, when the Internet
boom made for fast millionaires and even billionaires. When these
new-found rich individuals sold out, selling their stock or stock options to investors, they sought *capital loss generators* to offset their
gains. The particular shelters invoked typically involved entities and
complex provisions of corporate or partnership tax, far beyond the
scope of this short introduction. Ultimately, however, most if not all
were shut down by the use of old-fashioned common law tools,
especially the *economic substance* doctrine, discussed below.

Prior to the epochal Tax Reform Act of 1986 (TRA 1986), sheltering for wage earners had become almost as easy as avoiding taxes
for property owners: it was simple enough to play the game with
other people's money, or, indeed, with no money at all. The gaps in
tax opened up on the capital side had leaked over to the labor-market side as well, threatening the entire system as a revenue-raising
vehicle. Slowly, systematically, as marginal tax rates have come
down, and as the structural and ad hoc opportunities to avoid
"second" taxes on the yield to capital have expanded, the means for
sheltering *wage* income have dried up. This continues a central
theme that the so-called income tax system has morphed into an
effective wage tax.

To understand these points more fully, we first consider the shelter game, then and now.

🎐 7.2 Some Quick and Dirty Examples

Let us take a quick and simplified look at the way things were, prior to the 1986 Act, in order to understand where we are and where we are heading. Simply to make the point, take four fairly basic tricks of the ancient trade of tax sheltering, here given evocative names and hypothetical taxpayers to illustrate.

The interest dodge: Susie, who has no capital, is about to earn $100,000 a year as a tax and financial adviser. She borrows $1,000,000 at 10 percent interest. With an unlimited interest deduction under IRC Section 163, Susie offsets her $100,000 salary completely on her tax return by taking a $100,000 deduction for interest paid on her loan. With her $1,000,000 in cash, meanwhile, Susie plays Tax Planning 101. Susie buys capital-appreciating assets, such as growth stocks. When these go up by 10 percent, to $1,100,000, she borrows $100,000 against the appreciation to pay off her annual interest of $100,000, at 10%. (We shall see below, in the *Knetsch* case, a simple way to achieve these ends without actually having any risk – or real money.) Susie still has her $100,000 in wages, now tax-free because of the offsetting interest deduction, to consume. She has no net wealth, because her liability ($1,100,000) offsets her assets ($1,100,000). She consumes $100,000. She pays no income tax.

The simple straddle: Joe is in the same boat as Susie: about to make $100,000 a year as a tax practitioner, with no cash in his pocket. He borrows $200,000 and buys perfectly offsetting stock positions—in essence, he puts $100,000 on each side of a "heads or tails" coin flip. One position is guaranteed to double in value; the other to become worthless. Joe sells and then writes off the worthless one, claiming a $100,000 loss that, with unlimited loss offsets (that is, no IRC Section 1211), wipes out the entire tax liability on his salary on his tax return. Joe holds his $200,000 winner, which precisely offsets his loan balance of $200,000. Like Susie, Joe has no net assets. Also like Susie, he pays no income tax on his $100,000 salary. He, too, can consume away, tax-free.

The classic shelter. Sara is graduating from medical school, about to start earning $100,000 like her friends Susie and Joe, and also has no assets in hand. Sara buys an old hotel in Arizona for $3,000,000, giving the owner a nonrecourse note – meaning that the owner/ seller can *only* take the hotel back if Susie stops making payments on the note – for virtually the whole amount (no money down!). Sara then leases the hotel back to its owner, setting the rent she is owed on the hotel equal to the interest she owes to the prior owner on the $3,000,000 note, which has a balloon payment due and payable in thirty years (that is, the principal of $3,000,000 is all due at the end of the 30 year term; until then, the note is interest only). No real money ever changes hands because the "rent" that the "prior" owner pays Sara is equal to the "interest" that she pays him. Meanwhile, with a thirty-year depreciation schedule, Sara as the new "owner" of the hotel gets $100,000 in ordinary income deductions each year, having gotten basis when she "borrowed" the money to buy the hotel. Sara, too, like Susie and Joe, has no net assets; the $3,000,000 liability offsets the gross value of her holdings. Like her friends, she also pays no tax on her $100,000 salary. She will worry about what happens in Year 31 much later (and we will discuss this below in the next section). For now, she consumes away, tax-free.

The kiddie shift. Tom is about to become a doctor, earning $100,000. He has four young children. Tom decides to buy a small office building, perhaps using debt financing, which would generate a nice tax deduction to sweeten his basic plan, and then gifts fractional shares of the building to his children. Tom then pays each of his offspring rent. The rent is a business deduction for Tom under IRC Section 162, bringing his taxable income down, and just so happens to fall in each of his children's "zero bracket." Tom and kin pay no tax on the transferred amounts, which Tom directs his children to use for their basic food and clothing—indeed, he can do this himself, as their natural guardian.

More elaborate examples of the ancient sheltering art could be put forward, but these four simple tax-planning strategies serve to illustrate the point perfectly well. All were alive and flourishing, in one form or another, for long periods in American tax law. The interest dodge, the classic shelter, and the kiddie shift were in full flower up to the 1986 Act; either of the first two alone were sufficient, taken to their limits, to make the entire income tax voluntary, even for those without their own financial capital stakes to play Tax Planning 101.

✠ 7.3 *Crane, Tufts,* the Role of Debt, and a Deeper Look

Before getting to the systematic responses of the Tax Reform Act of 1986, let us take a deeper, more technical look at what I described above as the "classic" shelter.

The quick example mentioned above, with Sara and the old hotel, was based on the case of *Estate of Franklin*, 554 F.2d 1045 (9th Cir. 1976). Because of the presence of seller financing, a leaseback, and no attempt to pin down a real fair market value for the hotel or the rent—the rent was simply set equal to the interest on the note, by design—the government was successful in shutting down the taxpayers in that particular case as engaged in a "sham," one of the common law doctrines we will look at in a bit. But the classic shelter, turning on the use of debt, was alive and well in nonabusive forms.

This type of shelter essentially began with the case of *Crane v. Commissioner*, 331 U.S. 1 (1947), a Supreme Court decision that was actually a victory—a Pyrrhic victory, indeed—for the government. Mrs. Crane inherited a building subject to a nonrecourse debt. Such a loan, common in residential mortgages, once again means that the lender's *only* recourse in the event of a default is against the property: he could foreclose. Mrs. Crane herself had no personal liability, as she would with a recourse loan. The real economic risk of nonrecourse loans thus falls on the lender; if there is a fall in value of the secured asset, the borrower can walk away, and the lender is left holding the bag, so to speak.

Mrs. Crane took the asset subject to the nonrecourse debt. Let us say that the debt had a principal balance outstanding of $500,000, and, to keep matters simple, further assume that it was interest-only. Mrs. Crane gave herself a stepped-up basis to the fair market value of the property, for an asset acquired on death under IRC Section 1014. Assume that this value was $600,000. Mrs. Crane then began taking depreciation deductions which, as we know from above, served to reduce her tax basis in the property. After some years, when Mrs. Crane had taken perhaps $200,000 of depreciation deductions, bringing her basis down to $400,000, she transferred the building for an assumption of the loan – meaning that the buyer took on the responsibility for paying off the debt – plus $3,000. At first Mrs. Crane reported no gain whatsoever. But when the government challenged her, she reported a loss, because the building was worth less at the time of sale ($503,000) than it was on the date of her husband's death ($600,000). But the IRS argued, and the Court agreed, that the full amount of the debt that was discharged was an "amount realized" for purposes of Section 1001. This is clearly right, and we should know it by now: discharge of debt is income, as first noted in Chapter 2. Mrs. Crane had taxable (capital) gain, the difference between the $3,000 *plus the discharge of indebtedness*, or $500,000, less her remaining basis (after depreciation) in the building, of $400,000, all under IRC Section 1001(a). Her capital gain was $103,000: the fair market value of what was received ($3,000 plus the discharge of a $500,000 debt) minus her basis in what was given up, $400,000.

This all seems straightforward enough, but a footnote in *Crane* caused considerable confusion and doubt: it said that the case might be different if the value of the building was less than the amount of the debt, as opposed to the $3,000 of additional value or "equity" that Mrs. Crane had in the property. We will get to that in the next paragraph. Far more important is what *Crane* assumed: namely that one gets basis for debt, *even for nonrecourse debt*. This means that a taxpayer can borrow on a nonrecourse basis, with no real downside economic risk, and create tax basis to use for generating depreciation deductions. This is what the taxpayers were taking to abusive limits in *Estate of Franklin*. If we are dealing with nonrecourse debt and long-term loans with balloon payments, why not put a $3 million value on the hotel, as Sara did in our quick example of a classic shelter above.

The chickens came home to roost in the case of *Commissioner v. Tufts*, 461 U.S. 300 (1983), set in Texas during the savings and loans crisis of the 1980s. A group of investors—think doctors, dentists, lawyers—had gone in on a deal structured through a limited partnership. Slightly simplifying the math, the investors borrowed $1.8 million on a nonrecourse basis, putting almost no money down. They bought an office building in Texas and began depreciating away. After four years of taking $100,000 in depreciation deductions each year, their remaining basis—as we should know by now—was $1.4 million. In the meantime, there had been a fall in real estate values. The building was now worth $1.5 million. Assume that the principal amount of debt was still $1.8 million (that is, assume again an interest-only loan). At this point the taxpayers walked away, and the commercial lender foreclosed.

Here was the situation from the *Crane* footnote: the project was "under water," with no equity. The taxpayers received no cash when they simply walked away from the project. The investors then simply ignored the end game for tax purposes. The IRS argued, and the Supreme Court (reversing the 5th Circuit Court of Appeals) agreed, that the logic of *Crane*—indeed, the logic of tax—governed. On discharge of their debt, the taxpayer/investors had an *amount realized* of $1.8 million under IRC Section 1001. Subtracting their adjusted basis of $1.4 million meant that they had $400,000 of gain—to be taxed at capital gains rates under Section 1221.

The taxpayers were upset with this result. My students often puzzle over it. But it is unquestionably correct as a matter of tax logic. Further, *the entire transaction, viewed as a whole, is significantly pro taxpayer.* How so? Consider what happened.

The taxpayers borrowed a large amount of cash, no money down, and bearing no economic risk on the downside because of the nonrecourse nature of the loan. The interest owed on the debt roughly equaled the rents from the office building, so little money changed hands, and the inclusion in income for rents received under Section 61 was wiped out by the deduction for interest expense paid under Section 163. Yet the borrowed money generated tax basis for them. The taxpayers were able to use that basis to generate depreciation deductions—at ordinary income tax rates—of $100,000 a year for four years. These deductions—from a paper loss, the economic effects of which they would never feel—helped to wipe out their salaries as taxable income on their Form 1040s. At the end of four years, the taxpayers walked away, at which point they had $400,000—of capital gain.

At the time, marginal tax rates on ordinary income were as high as 50 percent; capital gains rates were 20 percent. So, on a transaction with virtually no cash outlay and no downside risk, the taxpayers in essence saved $50,000 a year for four years, $200,000 total, and then "paid back" the government with $80,000 in Year 5. Table 4 summarizes these results.

On a deal with virtually no money down, no economic risk, no real cash flow, the taxpayers made a net profit of $120,000, all because of tax benefits. And they *complained* about this tax treatment, not wanting to pay capital gains taxes in Year 5. (Justice O'Connor, in an interesting concurrence, actually argued that the

TABLE 4 Tax Consequences of *Tufts* Transaction at 50 percent and 20 percent Tax Rates

Year	Income or (Loss)	Tax Savings (or Tax Owed)
1	($100,000)	$50,000
2	($100,000)	$50,000
3	($100,000)	$50,000
4	($100,000)	$50,000
5	$400,000	($80,000)
Net	**$0**	**$120,000**

government should have been arguing for ordinary income treatment on the discharge of debt, although there is little support in the law for this position.) Here we have an acceleration of losses, a deferral of gain, and a conversion into capital gains. Nice work if you could get it—and any highly paid wage earner could get in, easily enough, in the 1970s and pre–Tax Reform Act 1980s, subject only to a common law challenge in the case of an abusive making-up-of-the-numbers, as in *Estate of Franklin*.

7.3.1 A Quick Look to Hollywood

Perhaps because I happen to live in Hollywood, I feel obligated to correct some common mistakes about tax planning found in the movies.

In the comedy *Slapshot*, Paul Newman plays the coach of a minor league hockey team. The team struggles on the ice and at the ticket booth until three "goon" brothers start attracting large crowds by engaging in multiple acts of gratuitous violence. Thinking that he has saved the franchise, Newman visits the owner, who informs him that he is in fact messing with the plan: the owner's accountant had told her to lose money for tax purposes.

In point of fact, that is a bad idea. One should always, rationally, want to make real money on a tax shelter. In the facts of *Tufts*, for example, the taxpayers would have been better off if the property had gone up in value, say to $2.5 million. Had they sold then, they would have gotten $700,000 cash plus the discharge of the $1.8 million loan. True, they would have had to pay tax, at a capital gains rate, on the $700,000 (as well as on the gain from the discharge of debt, the $400,000 already discussed, which would not change in this example). This would be $140,000 in tax, 20% of $700,000. But the taxpayers would also have been left with $560,000, cash, in their pockets, in addition to the tax benefits chronicled above. Why would the taxpayers not want this? If a taxpayer really has no motive at all to make money, something very wrong is going on.

A related note: many people think that the Mel Brooks play/ movie *The Producers* involved a tax scam. It does not. The trick there was an *oversubscription* scam, whereby the would-be dramatists oversold shares in their play—they gave away more than 100 percent of the profits. If you do that, you do, in fact, want to lose money: to have a horrible play shut down on opening night. I had to correct the *Wall St. Journal* a few years back on this one.

7.4 What the Tax Reform Act of 1986 Did, and Did Not Do

7.4.1 What the Law Did

The traditional view of tax sees the choice of broad-based systems as one of income versus consumption. The influential *Blueprints for Basic Tax Reform*, beginning in a Treasury Department analysis from the 1970s, traced out the two perceived forks in the road: perfecting the income tax or moving toward a consistent consumption tax. The Tax Reform Act of 1986 ostensibly took the income-tax path. This epochal legislation's general strategy was to widen the income tax base by eliminating scores of exemptions, exclusions, and deductions, in order to bring tax rates down. In particular, the 1986 Act took aim at and effectively shut down all the shelters mentioned above, with the exception of those already shut down.

There is thus no longer a general deduction for personal interest under IRC Section 163. Investment interest is subject to a "netting" rule under 163(d) as we saw in Chapter 3. The interest dodge is dead. Susie can still borrow money, but she cannot use the interest to offset her salary for tax purposes.

Pure straddles had already been attacked, in the rather technical provisions of IRC Section 1092 and 1256, and the capital loss offset rules of IRC Section 1211 generally limit the usefulness of Joe's simple straddle idea. Joe cannot deduct the loss from his losing "tails" position against his salary from his day job; he must wait until he shows gains from a sale or exchange of his winning "heads" position.

The sweeping passive activity loss rules of Section 469 effectively shut down the classic shelter in most of its incarnations. This major piece of legislation in essence creates a massive netting rule. All income or profit-seeking activities are put into one of three "baskets":

1. active trade or business, meaning an activity in which one "materially participates;"
2. passive activities, meaning profit-seeking ventures relative to which one does not materially participate; and
3. portfolio, essentially meaning stock, bond, and other securities investments.

Passive activity losses (PALs) can only be taken against passive activity income, category 2. Otherwise, these passive losses must be held in abeyance, until the activity is closed out. Sara can still run a rundown hotel, but she cannot use the tax losses generated thereby to subtract from her salary as a doctor on her tax forms. (She may also not get basis for certain forms of nonrecourse debt, principally those not involving a commercial lender, under the somewhat complex "at risk" rules of IRC Section 465.)

In the case of *Tufts*, the taxpayer/investors would have to hold their $400,000 in depreciation deductions in suspense until they closed out the activity: in which case the $400,000 in what is called "minimum gain," from the discharge of indebtedness, would wash it out in Year 5. The economic $0 in Table 4, above, becomes a tax $0, too.

The Section 469 rules are very complex—and also very effective— at taking away the incentive to engage in the classic form of sheltering from the 1970s and early 1980s.

Recall *Nickerson*, the case with the Chicago advertising executive turned dairy farmer that we considered in Chapter 3. Mr. Nickerson was using depreciation deductions and other tax losses from his farm to offset his wage income from his day job as an advertising executive in Chicago. The government attacked the transaction using IRC Section 183, arguing that the dairy farming was an "activity not engaged in for profit," that is, a hobby, such that the excess losses would be nondeductible personal matters under the general principles of Section 262. That argument lost. In fact Mr. Nickerson, like the hockey club owner in *Slapshot*, should have been trying to make a profit. Section 183 was the wrong tool to attack Mr. Nickerson's activity. The Section 469 passive activity loss rules *might* shut down this kind of shelter, unless Mr. Nickerson could prove he "materially participated" in the dairy farm—basically putting in something like 500 hours a year—in which case it would be an "active trade or business," category 1 above.

The Tax Reform Act of 1986 also gave us the "kiddie tax" that we considered in Chapter 5. This statute killed Tom's clever idea, again in most instances, by putting his children in the same marginal tax bracket as their parents for unearned income. Tom can still give his office to his children and pay them rent, but he will find them paying the same tax he otherwise would.

In sum, the Tax Reform Act of 1986 was systematic in curtailing tax shelters, thereby stopping the bleeding in tax and enabling lower tax rates on a broader tax base.

7.4.2 What the Law Did Not Do

But—and herein lies the rub—the watershed 1986 Act did *nothing* about Tax Planning 101 or any of its three simple steps. The Act did not touch the realization requirement of *Macomber*, although Congress clearly has the power to do so. "Buy" still works. The Act did not make debt taxable, or a deemed realization event for people with appreciated assets. "Borrow" still works. The Act did not alter or repeal the stepped-up basis rule of IRC Section 1014 for assets acquired on death. "Die" still works.

It is true that the Act repealed the capital gains preference, which resulted in an interim rise in its rate. Capital gains had for a significant period of time been set at 40 percent of the ordinary income tax rate; thus the top capital gains rate was 28 percent when Reagan took office with a 70 percent top ordinary rate bracket. When Reagan oversaw his first major tax-cutting bill, the Economic Recovery Tax Act (ERTA) of 1981, the ordinary rate fell to 50 percent. The capital gains rate fell in step, to 20 percent. The 1986 Act, which instituted a marginal rate bracket of 28 percent on the highest incomes, eliminated any further and specific capital gains rate preference, thus, in essence, restoring the pre-ERTA rate of 28 percent on capital gains. Interestingly, this created a natural experiment to see if capital transactions were responsive to the tax rate; there was, indeed, a spike in sales under the outgoing 20 percent regime.

But recall that the capital gains rate is a reaction to the very existence of Tax Planning 101. Since the 1986 Act left Tax Planning 101 unchecked, its elimination of the capital gains preference was fragile from the start. Indeed, a preferential rate soon enough reappeared, with the elder George Bush maintaining the top rate at 28 percent when ordinary income tax rates went up. Bill Clinton then reduced the capital gains rate, first to 20 then later to 18 percent. The younger George Bush brought it down to its current (as I write) 15 percent, where Barack Obama has maintained it. As this saga of capital gains preferences played itself out, the simple advice of buy/borrow/die lived on.

Thus what the Tax Reform Act of 1986—one of the most sweeping acts of tax legislation ever passed, and the subject of laudatory volumes from the popular press—did was simple. It shored up the status of the "income" tax as a wage tax. Shelters for wage earners were shut down or drastically curtailed. Yet people with capital could still buy, borrow, and die to their hearts' content. Tax remains voluntary for those with financial capital.

7.5 Common Law and Judicial Doctrines

One of the most interesting and very much open questions in tax is whether or not the Internal Revenue Code, alone, is enough to shut down tax shelters and other perceived abuses. A great deal of tax history suggests that it is not. Rich taxpayers are well advised and highly motivated to exploit any and all gaps or loopholes in the statutory language or in the judicial interpretations of it. We need go no further than *Macomber*, again: a seemingly innocent decision, to wait until some realization event to tax gain, gave a blueprint to generations of tax practitioners as to how to avoid all taxation.

Taxpayers always seem to be at least one step ahead of the statute. The constant attempts to plug up legislative loopholes lead to further complexity and more unintended consequences. Further, taxpayers have the distinct advantage of being the first movers in most tax planning, and to be able to put their own labels and spins on things: calling transactions "gifts," "sales," "leases," or something else altogether to get the best tax result.

To give the government some tools in this ongoing game, to help level the playing field, the law has developed a series of common law doctrines to help break down clever taxpayer attempts to avoid tax: "substance over form," "economic substance," "business purpose," "step transaction," and "sham" are the most common.

All of these judicial creations are set against a backdrop wherein many judges—including many powerful Supreme Court Justices through the years—believe that a taxpayer is entitled to rely on the literal language of the Internal Revenue Code. After all, it would be abhorrent to notions of justice to have common law *crimes*— to accuse, convict, and incarcerate someone on the basis of some action that was not *literally* prohibited by express statute. Yet taxes have a punitive dimension to them. "[T]here is not even a patriotic duty to increase one's taxes," Judge Learned Hand famously wrote in the case of *Gregory v. Helvering*, 69 F.2d 809 (2nd Cir. 1934), affirmed, 293 U.S. 465 (1935), one of the most important cases, at both the circuit and Supreme Court levels, for articulating common law doctrines against tax avoidance. (Tax academics tend to use "tax avoidance" to refer to arguably legal attempts to reduce one's taxes; they use the more pejorative "tax evasion" to refer to outright cheating, such as simply not reporting income one received.)

The basic strategy of the common law doctrines is to mediate the tension between the government's need to collect some revenue and the taxpayer's right to enjoy the benefits as well as the obligation to bear the burdens of the existing written law. Most of the doctrines thus look at what the taxpayer claims to have done, and to recharacterize it as something else: this is the key to the "substance over form" doctrine. The taxpayer in *Duberstein* may have said that the Cadillac was a "gift," and even created paperwork to back up this claim, but the government could successfully argue that, in "substance," it was a payment for services rendered, whatever its "form" may have been.

In *Gregory v. Helvering*, the statute said that certain liquidations of corporations would be tax-free nonrecognition events, whereas an ongoing corporation's distribution of appreciated stock would trigger double-taxation (to the corporation and the shareholder) as a dividend. To get around this result, the taxpayer:

(1) created a new corporation,
(2) "spun off" certain stock holdings into it, and
(3) dissolved and completely liquidated the new corporation.

All of this happened within minutes, or at most hours. The government successfully argued that, whereas the taxpayer was entitled to the benefits of the statutes that made each of the three steps taken nontaxable, in and of themselves, what was "really" done, in "substance," was a taxable dividend, not the kind of "reorganization" that the law meant to accomodate. *Gregory* is also an illustration of the "step transaction" doctrine, which gives the power to the government to collapse certain literally separate steps and ignore them. Doing so in *Gregory* leads to the view that the stock went from ongoing corporation to individual shareholder, a taxable transaction.

Knetsch v. United States, 364 U.S. 361 (1960), illustrates a variant, dealing with "sham transactions," though the Supreme Court did not use this exact phrase. Mr. Knetsch was—no surprise—a high wage-earning executive. He purported to buy $4 million worth of annuities, an insurance product, in the 1950s. Trouble was that he did not have $4 million. So Knetsch borrowed it—from the insurance company selling him the annuities. Each year, the annuities were guaranteed to rise in value by 2½ percent, or $100,000. The interest on the loan was 3½ percent, or $140,000. Each year when the interest came due, Knetsch would borrow another $100,000 against the rise in value of his annuities and write a check for the additional $40,000 of interest.

Now why would a smart executive like Knetsch do such a thing? At any moment in time, his debt was *exactly equal* to the annuity amount: each started at $4,000,000; each was $4,100,000 at the end of Year 1, $4,200,000 at the end of Year 2, and so on. This meant that if Knetsch were to die, his heirs would get nothing: the amounts received from the annuity would have to go straight back to the company to pay off the debt. For this— that is, nothing—Knetsch was paying $40,000 a year. Why, you ask again?

Because this was a time, prior to the 1986 Act, when all interest was income-tax deductible. Knetsch was able to deduct $140,000 a year, while not including the rise in value of the annuities as income, because of *Macomber*. If, as he may well have been, Knetsch was in the 90 percent bracket, the deduction for interest paid would save him $126,000 in taxes. In a transaction in which Knestch acquired no real asset and had no risk whatsoever, he was able to make $126,000, in the form of saved taxes, on an outlay of $40,000, *every year*. This was a net gain of $86,000, annually, for nothing! Nice work if you can get it.

Ultimately, the game did not work, although it took the Supreme Court to say so this time. (Congress later made a change to shut down single-premium annuity policies.) The Court actually struggled a bit with its reasoning, but the key to the holding was the conclusion that the $140,000 was not "really" interest: the whole thing was a "sham."

This is easy enough to see if you follow the money, or lack thereof. I ask my students to tell me where, exactly, the $4 million was located—who had it? After they struggle for a bit with the puzzle, I explain to them that it was a trick question—that there was *no real money* in *Knetsch*. The company supposedly "lent" the $4 million to Knetsch, who supposedly turned around and gave it back to them for the annuities. For both Knetsch and the company, this was a wash. The money never existed. There was no real cash, and no real annuity. There was only nothing. There were accounting entries that, at any moment in time, literally offset each other. That is not real money.

A recent round of highly sophisticated, largely "corporate" tax shelters have featured intricate transactions tracking literal language in the Code or regulations, matters surviving the Tax Reform Act of 1986. These are especially prevalent as "capital loss generators," designed to offset large capital gains that Internet and other entrepreneurs have been encountering of late. The government has had some considerable success shutting these down with the doctrines of "business purpose" or "economic substance." The latter, which has evolved a bit over the years, maintains that a transaction must have some reasonable possibility of profit, *independent of taxes saved and in excess of professional fees paid*, in order to qualify for any tax benefits. See *ACM Partnership v. Commissioner*, 157 F.3d 231 (3rd Cir. 1998), affirming 73 T.C.M (CCH) 2189 (1997), cert. denied, 526 U.S. 1017 (1999). The possibility of profit must be both subjectively believed and objectively believable. The doctrine has now been "codified" in IRC Section 7701(o)(3).

Time will tell how this attempt to put a common law doctrine into the statute will fare, but there is little doubt that the IRS feels it needs such help to compete with the highly sophisticated and dynamic world of tax planning.

✳ 7.6 Ethics

Tax ethics is a very important and much neglected subject. Unfortunately, there is not much room in this short introduction for a lengthy discussion. The essential problem is that a tax lawyer or other adviser is caught between two duties: to zealously represent her client, saving taxes where possible, and to the government and society at large to uphold the law.

In almost all cases where relevant *facts* are being hidden or misrepresented by the taxpayer, there is an ethical problem—documents are being backdated, transactions are taking place "off the books" or "under the table." But in matters of legal interpretation, things are far more often gray than black or white. Plenty of cases that we have considered, such as *Cottage Savings* on realization, *Brooke* on income shifting, *Starker* on deferred like-kind exchanges under Section 1031, and *Tufts* on the classic real estate shelter pre–Tax Reform Act of 1986, featured clever and aggressive tax planning that ended up working in the end. See also *Frank Lyon Co. v. United States*, 435 U.S. 561 (1978) (upholding a tax strategy whereby depreciation deductions were shifted to a high-bracket financial company, an early example of a "sale-leaseback" transaction.)[1] Not to advise your clients on such possibilities can be malpractice. And of course Tax Planning 101 constitutes perfectly legal advice.

In other cases, however, such as *Estate of Franklin*, *Knetsch*, or *Gregory v. Helvering*, the clever planning did *not* work and in fact arguably constituted fraud, especially in the first two cases.

How does one tell what side of the line one is on? In the world of tax compliance and reporting—other very important subjects largely out of our scope here—tax advisers are often in the position

---

1. The just-departed (as I write) Professor Wolfman was highly critical of the *Frank Lyon* case. *See* Bernard Wolfman, "The Supreme Court in the Lyon's Den: A Failure of Judicial Process", 66 *Cornell Law Review* 1075 (1980-81).

of *disclosing* arguable positions on returns. Other times, tax advisers write *opinion letters* that set forth, in probabilistic terms, their sense of the likely success of an arguable position if litigated: that the taxpayer has a "reasonable basis," that the position is "more likely than not" to prevail in court, or that it "should" do so, for example. Practitioners disagree among themselves over what these standards even mean, and also disagree as to how they apply in particular cases. Penalties to taxpayers and/or their advisers can apply to those who get these matters wrong, or neglect them altogether. The Treasury Department and IRS also have broad powers to sanction tax professionals acting outside the lines, and to require advisers to keep lists and disclose the names of their clients engaging in tax shelter transactions.

These are difficult matters. I wish I could give readers a clear sense of what is "right" and "wrong" here, but, alas, I cannot. But any reader considering a career in tax—or considering taking an aggressive position on any taxing matter—would do well to pause and reflect over his or her ethical obligations, and to think through all the consequences, legal and moral, of being on the wrong side of the line, and to talk through any dilemmas faced with responsible others.

※ 7.7 Summary

In rounding up the details of tax in this chapter, we have learned:

- The general strategy of a tax shelter is to get some or all of the benefits of tax planning—escape, defer, shift, convert—to wage income, using the tools of the capital classes;
- Capital holders typically do not need to shelter, because Tax Planning 101 offers a simple and perfectly legal way to avoid all taxes for those with financial capital;
- Debt, or other people's money, is key to sheltering for wage earners who lack their own capital to play tax Planning 101;

- Many surprisingly simple shelters existed for many years before the law shut them down; the unlimited interest deduction allowed before the Tax Reform Act of 1986 alone was enough to put the entire tax system at risk;
- Many "classic" shelters prior to the 1986 Act involved debt, especially nonrecourse debt for which the borrower bears no real economic risk. The *Crane* case allowed taxpayers borrowing even on a nonrecourse basis to get tax basis, thereby generating depreciation deductions. *Tufts* showed how this could lead to significant sheltering, even with an obligation ultimately to pay capital gains on the seemingly inevitable discharge of debt at the end stage;
- While tax shelters can be abusive, as in the cases of *Estate of Franklin* or *Knetsch*, many were indeed perfectly legal;
- The Tax Reform Act of 1986 was systematic in shutting down wage shelters—limiting interest deductions, adding the "kiddie tax," and, most importantly, the passive activity loss rules of Section 469. This latter provision was systematic in creating "baskets" of income subject to "netting rules," for active, passive, and portfolio income;
- In addition to the statute, various common law doctrines—substance over form, step transaction, sham, business purpose, and economic substance—have been used by the government and courts to plug up leaks. Economic substance has now been codified in IRC Section 7701(o)(3);
- Ethics matter, and there are various rules and regulations governing the conduct of taxpayers and tax advisers—as well as monetary penalties and fines, possible criminal penalties, and professional sanctions—that all must consider before engaging in any aggressive or arguable tax reporting position;
- The truly rich—those who can live on the capital side of the great divide—do not need any of this stuff. The games played by taxpayers in the past and today tend to concern the sheltering of labor income. For capital income, see Tax Planning 101

and its variants. Neither the Tax Reform Act of 1986 nor the prevalent common law doctrines cast any doubt whatsoever on Tax Planning 101's key planks, and any adviser who is not aware of this basic planning advice is committing malpractice almost every day of her professional life.

PART THREE

Whither Tax?

✎ EIGHT

The Once and Future Tax System

WE HAVE COME TO THE END. Now it is time to return to the beginning: a discussion of tax policy. In between, I hope I stayed true to my aim to keep things short as we got a sense of tax's forest.

The circle is coming full. We began in Part I with a preliminary consideration of tax policy, getting a sense of the basic analytic structure of tax. We did this in order to help better see the choices that have been made in the practical evolution of the U.S. income tax system, to better understand what tax is today. This sense of policy and structure helped to convey the "big picture" of tax. A basic sense of tax policy also helped to keep matters reasonably brief and to steer clear of getting lost in details in Part II.

Now it is time to return to policy as a way to consider what tax might *become*. Change is constant in tax. The U.S. income tax as it exists is very different from the system of three, four, five decades ago. I have no doubt that the tax system of the mid-twenty-first century will be far different from what it is today. A major reason to contemplate policy now, at the end of this short introduction, is to put you in a position to be ahead of the curve—to be able to predict and understand change as and when it occurs. A second reason is that tax is and always has been about policy: reviewing the policy currents that point to tax's future help to review and shore up our understanding of tax's past and present. I will be quick, in part because I and many others have written elsewhere at great length about tax policy and ideas for the future of tax; I list some among many possible sources in the Notes for Further Reading at the end of this volume. Here, I intend simply to touch on the major themes.

Of course, the major theme of this short introduction has been that the U.S. "income" tax is not an income tax at all. Not only does it fail to "double-tax" savings or the yield to savings, as an income tax is supposed to do, it also systematically fails to tax savings at all in many cases. This makes the income tax a wage tax in practice. If all income comes from labor or capital, and we are not taxing capital, we are only taxing labor. Much can be learned from accepting that fact.

Throughout this book we have seen that it is difficult to escape, defer, shift, or convert income from labor, but that all these essential tax-planning goals are readily, even trivially, available to those with financial capital in hand to play the games beginning with Tax Planning 101. We carry that understanding of the status quo with us as we explore possible futures for tax. There are several strategies, forks in the road, that the law might pursue as it evolves. We will look quickly at the major ones.

8.1 The Lay of the Land

The most important fact to consider in thinking about future tax reform is that the U.S. government needs more revenue. Lots of it. Massive deficits run as far as the eye can see, and show no real signs of abating. Even assuming modest spending cuts that seem as unlikely as tax increases under the income tax, the U.S. government needs more revenue, and fast. Deficits are running around one trillion dollars per year—that is $1,000,000,000,000 for those who think in terms of numerals. More-or-less locked-in entitlement programs—social security, Medicare, prescription drug benefits, and then some—are set to grow exponentially. The labor force, already burdened with high taxes, is shrinking relative to the base of retirees entitled to benefits. The possibility of a fiscal catastrophe in the mid-term future cannot be ruled out, with precise consequences unknown. The recent crisis over the latest expansion of the federal debt ceiling, and the downgrading of the U.S. government's credit rating, is just a tip of an iceberg. In order to bring the books into balance, the government must raise revenue. This is not going to be easy to do.

Recall the first equation we looked at in Chapter 1, namely that:

$$Tax = Base \times Rate$$

If we are going to raise revenues under the *income* tax, we must expand the tax base, raise rates, or do both. All of this seems unlikely. The income tax as structured seems close to being "tapped out." It is hard to imagine its base significantly widening or its rates significantly increasing under its current design. Nonetheless, we can consider incremental reform of the income tax as an Option 1. The other choices for revenue-raising seem to come down to:

(2) increasing other taxes;
(3) adding on a new tax; or
(4) fundamental reform of the income tax.

The balance of this chapter tracks these options.

🏛 8.2 Incremental Reform

One obvious strategy is to patch up the income tax, so let us count this as Option 1.

What we see at any moment—and there are lots of moments in tax—is incremental reform. This means keeping the basic income tax, along with its deepest features, intact. It means not attacking Tax Planning 101, but nonetheless attempting to raise more revenue, as the times call for.

Recent commissions and panels considering tax reform have followed this incremental approach. There is thus for a leading example a growing focus on tax expenditures, which largely mean the personal deductions and exclusions considered in Chapters 2 and 3. Limiting business expenses is not a strong option even for a government deeply concerned with its own tax revenue. Indeed, incremental tax reform legislation of late has tended to feature more, not fewer, "breaks" for business, as the government continues to attempt to spur economic growth—which is in turn good for the business of collecting taxes.

The personal deductions most discussed or most at risk of repeal or limitation are:

- the mortgage interest deduction under IRC Section 163(h),
- employer-provided health care under Sections 105–106,
- pension plans and retirement savings under Section 401 and following and elsewhere,
- personal dependency exemptions under Sections 151–152,
- charitable contributions under Section 170, and
- state and local taxes under Section 164.

Some of these are already limited by the alternative minimum tax (AMT), others have been subject to various phase-outs or phase-downs. There has been talk of further limiting the value of any or all of these deductions to a certain fixed marginal tax rate, one below the top rate—the Obama administration has proposed a 28 percent ceiling. Other proposals have the personal deductions being replaced with credits, set at lower percentages than the top marginal rate, or eliminated altogether.

Yet even a quick list of these items shows both that change here is going to be difficult politically and unlikely to yield great revenue economically. The mortgage interest deduction is a highly sacred cow. While a case can be made to get rid of Sections 105 and 106, which allow for employer-provided health care to be tax-free, now that we have some form of universal health insurance, it is hard to count on this. Health-care reform took place in the light of employer-provided health insurance, and failed to take on this Titanic of a policy mistake, as Michael Graetz has called it. It seems extremely unlikely that Congress would cut back on pension or retirement plans, given our continued need for savings on all levels (personal and national), and the trend toward adding new savings provisions. The other "tax expenditures" are limited in their dollar magnitude and also rather entrenched.

Yet if we are not going to take on the personal deductions, it is hard to see where else to go with incremental income tax reform. Of course, we could see tax rates go up. But that has not happened in over a decade; President Barack Obama failed to deliver on his campaign commitment to allow the George W. Bush tax cuts "simply" to expire for the highest income earners, meaning a return to 35 and 39.6 percent from the current 33 and 35. That is hardly radical, yet the difficulty of getting it across only underscores the near impossibility of raising income tax rates during peacetime.[1] You can ask the first George Bush with his quivering lips about that one.

If rates stay the same and personal deductions are left largely untouched, what else is there to do with the income tax? The rules on timing (Chapter 4), attribution (Chapter 5), and capital gains (Chapter 6) are well evolved by now, and rather good—at keeping *wage* income in the tax base, at current ordinary income rates. Wage tax shelters have largely been shut down, as we considered in Chapter 7. This leaves, then, some attempt to bring capital back into the fold—some attack on some or all of the planks of Tax Planning 101. But such a strategy hardly counts as "incremental" reform. We discuss it below, under a different heading.

8.3 More Taxes?

Assume that "major" incremental reform of the existing tax, if the very term is not an oxymoron, is unlikely to raise significant revenue. What then?

---

1. *See* Edward J. McCaffery and James R. Hines, Jr., "The Last Best Hope for Progressivity in Tax," 83 *Southern California Law Review*, 1031 (2010).

Option 2 is to raise other taxes. But looking at federal revenues, we see the individual income tax as number one, and the payroll tax – the combined Social Security/Medicare "contribution" system – as a close number two. As I have noted above, payroll taxes are the most burdensome one for most Americans. Until President Obama reduced the employee share of these taxes by lowering the flat rate by 2% in 2010, this was also the one major American tax that had *never* been cut. Since World War II, while the income tax as a percentage of GDP has remained fairly constant, payroll taxes have increased more than seven-fold. They seem tapped out. In any event, they fall on wages, and only wages. They do not address the fundamental flaw in today's income tax, whereby wage earners are highly burdened, and capital owners are lightly taxed if at all – payroll taxes *add* to that problem.

Dropping below payroll taxes, there simply is not much else. Corporate income taxes could be shored up here and there, but the U.S. faces international competition to keep rates low, and the equities and efficiencies of taxing corporations – which must ultimately pass on taxes, just like any other cost they face, to some real persons, likely workers and consumers – are unclear at best. What else? President Obama has already raised various excise taxes, such as on alcohol and cigarettes. We simply run out of specific options when it comes to raising more revenue from exisiting taxes pretty quickly.

And so we think of Option 3, some new tax. The most likely new tax is a national sales or Value-Added Tax (VAT). A VAT is essentially a sales tax paid by businesses in the course of producing goods: various interim manufactures "add value" to a good as it moves through the production chain toward its ultimate sale to consumers. VATs are common in Europe. A VAT or national sales tax may seem to be the subject for another book, and it largely is— sources listed in the Notes for Further Reading consider such options. But the very topic is connected to our consideration of the income tax, both because the need for another tax grows out of the limitations of the income tax, and because any new tax will add to the burdens of the income tax. That is not necessarily a good thing. Just as we mentioned other taxes in Chapter 2, because one needs to situate the income tax in a wider context to see the deeper themes of tax, so other taxes are relevant to the income tax's future, and vice versa. At some point, we cannot keep squeezing blood from middle-class stones, whether by explicit wage taxes or wage taxes in drag.

This is the principal problem with a VAT: it would not alter the fundamental theme of this book. A flat sales tax or VAT—and flat is highly likely to be what we would see in the United States, as we see around the world—is economically equivalent to a wage tax, as explained in Chapter 1. A VAT would *add* to the significant payroll tax and the income-qua-wage tax to put an even larger burden on middle-class working Americans, while essentially allowing capital to remain off the social hook.

We may still see a VAT. Such a new tax may be necessary to prevent a worse outcome, namely a fiscal crisis on a national, indeed global, scale. We should not let the perfect be the enemy of the good. Incremental reform of the income tax combined with an add-on VAT may be as good as we can get here on earth. But it is still worth being conscious of the defects in these approaches, and how far they fall short of perfection.

With these themes in mind, the balance of this chapter considers Option 4 as set out above: the case for fundamental reform.

8.4 Comprehensive Reform: A Better Direction

The influential volume *Blueprints for Basic Tax Reform* began with a U.S. Treasury Department study in the 1970s and laid out two comprehensive directions for tax reform.

One was to perfect the income tax by widening its base and lowering its rate structure. A motivation for the latter point was that, at high tax rates, the incentives to avoid or evade taxes, legally or otherwise, was so great that high rates actually *cost* the government revenue. In crude form, this is the "Laffer curve" argument—that revenues decline when tax rates rise above a certain level. In more sophisticated form, virtually all economists and public policy types now agree that overly high marginal tax rates under an income tax are counterproductive, although there would be a fierce fight about what "overly high" means, exactly.

This road of base broadening and rate lowering was the one taken in the important Tax Reform Act of 1986. This law went further than most observers would have imagined in advance it would go. As we saw in Chapter 7, the Act effectively shut down most tax shelters. It widened the tax base, and it dramatically lowered taxes. But we also saw that the Act did *nothing* about the capital side of the great divide, leaving untouched each of the planks in Tax Planning 101's buy/borrow/die. It left us with, in essence, a wage tax. Never mind that much of the simplification of the Act has unraveled in the ensuing decades, which have witnessed a rise in ordinary tax rates and a fall in capital gains ones. The Act, best understood, should help us to see the limits of the income tax and of potential further incremental income tax reform.

The second road sketched by *Blueprints* was to abandon the income tax and move toward a consumption tax, specifically a "cash-flow" or "postpaid" consumption tax—what we can and have called a spending tax.

This was the road not taken. But it is worth a good hard look—again. This new look involves rethinking some aspects of the analytics and effects of a *progressive* spending tax. Recall that a flat spending tax, such as a VAT, is essentially equivalent to a wage tax. Can we get something else?

ℳ 8.5 A New View: Three Types of Tax

I sketched the traditional view of tax policy in Chapter 1. To summarize, most tax theorists presumed that the very point of any consumption tax was the nontaxation of the yield to capital, in the spirit of John Stuart Mill's critique of the income tax as a "double tax" on savings. Under this way of thinking, both forms of consumption tax—wage and spending—turned out to be the same. The income tax, alone, gets at savings.

Income tax advocates, who included the initial proponents of the tax in the beginning decades of the twentieth century, *wanted* an income tax, Mill be damned, because they wanted to get at the rich capitalists hanging out on Wall Street. As time went by, however, the income tax expanded in both scale and scope; more and more people fell under its jurisdiction. The double-tax sting on middle-class savings bothered many. Rather than giving up the attempt to tax savings at all, we added on patches to the existing income tax, in the pension and IRA provisions and so on.

Policymakers continued to believe that the two basic forms of consumption tax, wage and spending, were created equal. Followers of Mill—opponents of double-taxation—began to pick and choose between a flat wage tax or a flat spending tax, based on matters such as administrative convenience. Aspects of each form of consumption tax leaked into the income tax. The system became a hybrid, an incoherent mishmash of income, wage, and spending tax features.

Now ready for another surprise? The traditional view of things is wrong.

The income-versus-consumption-tax debate, centered on the yield to savings, in essence eliminated an important type of tax from further analysis.[2] Those who wanted to tax the return to savings came to favor an income tax; those who thought it unfair or

---

2. I explore this argument with Jim Hines, an economist, in Edward J. McCaffery and James R Hines, The Last Best Hope for Progressivity in Tax, *Southern California Law Review* 1031 (2010). The remainder of this chapter borrows on our analysis there.

inefficient or both to ever tax savings favored a wage or a flat spending tax. For under *variable* marginal rates, the analytic equivalence of wage and spending taxes disappears. The tax rate at the time of initial earnings may not be the same as that at the time of spending. Savings could be "subsidized" or "penalized" vis-á-vis an income or a wage tax.

This analytic fact has led many to argue for flat or constant-rate spending taxes, such as a VAT, because they thought it to be a goal not to tax capital or its yield *at all*. This argument presumes once more that the reason for choosing a consumption tax turns on the principled nontaxation of the yield to savings. It need not be so. Policymakers might desire a *progressive spending tax* for reasons unrelated to the nontaxation of capital or its yield, or at least not precommitted to such nontaxation.

With varying marginal tax rates, there are *three* distinct choices for a comprehensive tax base: income, wage, and spending. Each affects the taxation of savings differently. Specifically:

- An income tax double-taxes all saving, whatever their use.
- A wage tax exempts all savings, whatever their use.
- A spending tax splits the difference.

To understand this point, we need a richer understanding and vocabulary of different types of savings.

8.5.1 A New Look at Savings

The equivalence of wage and spending taxes holds only for wage and *flat* spending taxes. The three bases differ under progressive rates. We must consider each, especially as to how they affect savings.

To get a sense of how to characterize the savings that a progressive spending tax does and does not tax, we need a better understanding of the uses of savings.

Consider in financial terms how most of us live out our lifetimes. As any parent knows full well, we spring forth into the world nearly fully formed as consumers: we cost money from the get-go. But (as any parent also knows) we do not earn anything for quite some time. When we do start earning, we have to earn more than we spend (let us hope!), to pay off the debts of our youth, including school loans, and to set aside funds for our retirement, so that we do not have to keep working all the days of our lives.

Our lives look like one fairly steady consumption profile, from cradle to grave, financed by a lumpy period of labor market earnings concentrated in midlife. If we lived as islands, unto ourselves, we would have to balance the books on our own account, borrowing in youth, first paying off our debts and later saving for retirement in our midlife, spending down in old age. Financial intermediaries such as banks and insurance companies would help us to effect these results. In practice, many families work as more or less informal annuities markets, between generations. Thus our parents pay for our youths, and we pay for our children's youths; we also stand ready to pay our parents back, should their needs exceed their resources in their old age, and so on.

Figure 2 is meant to be a very simple picture of this pattern. The curved line indicates earnings from work. The straight horizontal lines represent spending. The lower, solid horizontal line is a crude approximation of a fully self-financed taxpayer, whose lifetime

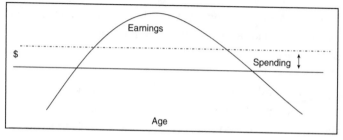

FIGURE 2 Earnings and Spending over Time

spending equals, in present value terms, her lifetime earnings. The dotted straight line above that solid one represents a taxpayer who has been able to live "better"—a more expensive lifestyle— than her labor earnings alone, smoothed across time, would seem to allow.

In this perhaps atypical characterization of a typical life, note three broad uses of savings. One is to *smooth* out consumption profiles, within lifetimes or across individuals—to translate uneven labor market earnings into even consumption flows. We do this by borrowing in youth and saving for retirement in midlife. We can do this using third-party financial intermediaries, or within the family. Economists tend to call this *life-cycle savings*.

A second use of savings, after life-cycle or smoothing uses, is to provide for periods of emergency, such as heightened medical or educational needs, or times of low income due to un- or under-employment. We can imagine that these are exceptional needs, off the usual plan for living shown in Figure 2. Economists call this *precautionary savings*. Such savings are significant because provisions in the tax's base may carve out the attendant uses for lower or even no taxation—the deduction for extraordinary medical expenses under IRC Section 213 is an example.

This leaves as a third use of savings essentially all else, the analytic complement of smoothing. Capital transactions can *shift* consumption profiles, up or down. An upward shift occurs when the fruits of our own or another's savings (through gifts or bequests) allow us to live a more expensive lifestyle than we could on the basis of our own labor market earnings, alone, smoothed out over time. Suppose that we inherited wealth, or got lucky in the capital markets and made a high return on our investments: our spending could increase. This is what the dotted line in Figure 2, above, illustrates.

A downward shift in parallel contrast occurs when our own beneficence or bad fortune means that we will live at a lower lifestyle than we otherwise could, again on the basis of our smoothed out labor market earnings profile alone.

Economists tend not to have a handy phrase for this type of shifting transaction, in part because the issue has not arisen under the traditional income-versus-consumption-tax debate. Economists write instead about *bequest* savings, which is private capital handed over to the next generation. But this phrase does not necessarily get at the initial motivation for such saving. Individuals may be saving for life-cycle or precautionary reasons, and simply end up with left-over funds to pass on. The vocabulary of smoothing/precautionary/shifting works perfectly well intra- as well as inter-generationally: capital passed between generations can be used to smooth out familial spending patterns, provide for emergencies, or enable later generations to live more expensive lifestyles than they other-wise could. Hence I use the smoothing/precautionary/shifting vocabulary.

An Aside on Debt, Again

Note again that a spending tax consistently subtracts savings, under the simple formula:

$$\text{Consumption} = \text{Income} - \text{Savings}$$

This means that a spending tax will include debt within its base, as a form of *negative* savings. Debt that is used to save ends up being a "wash": an inclusion for the debt minus a deduction for the sav-ings. But debt that is used to finance spending is taxed currently.

This may sound odd, but need not: consider a basic sales tax. You pay this tax when you buy an item on credit, as with a credit card; you do not pay the tax again when you pay off your balance. So, too, debt to finance personal spending is within a spending tax base; repayments of principal of debt, which in fact reflect positive savings, are not.

Students and others often consider that this means a progres-sive spending tax will hurt them, but, in fact, allowing the tax to come due in the period of spending lowers average tax rates across a lifetime for students, under progressive rates, compared to the income tax treatment of ignoring both debt and its repayment. Borrowing under a progressive spending tax works like retirement savings in reverse; it pulls down the level being taxed. Just as Mr. Drescher, through his deferred annuity plan, was attempting to shift taxable income to his *later* self, when he would be in a lower tax bracket, a student borrowing and paying tax on the debt under a spending tax is shifting income to her *earlier* self, again when she is in a lower tax bracket. This is a good thing for people prudently using debt, like students building up valuable human capital.

8.5.2 Putting It All Together: Three Bases, Three Types of Savings

Return to the three basic tax systems: income, wage, and spending.

Under progressive rates, a tax is constantly increasing in the base: that is, the tax rate is rising as the amount in the base (income, wages, or spending) increases. Now we can see, visually, that the three tax systems affect different patterns of work, savings, and spending differently.

Both income and wage taxes, as *source*-based taxes, apply to the curved earnings line in Figure 2, above. Thus both penalize taxpayers with uneven earnings as compared to steady ones—highly educated professionals, for example, who must wait while their education progresses to earn back their keep, and then have a period of high earnings concentrated in midlife. Further, an ideal income tax double-taxes all savings, come what may. An ideal income tax would add to the tax on wages reflected in the curved line a second tax on the yield to the savings needed to smooth labor earnings out into retirement. An income tax would also double-tax all precautionary savings.

A wage tax simply ignores all capital transactions, again whatever their use.

But a progressive spending tax, which is a *uses*-based tax, differentiates among uses of savings. Smoothing savings *lower* the burden of taxation because they move material resources, income, from a period of high earnings into a period of a lower level of spending – both in youth and in old age. So, too, precautionary savings—presuming that the precautionary use, such as for medical or educational needs, is tax-favored, somehow—also bring down the level of taxation. Upward shifts, in contrast, *increase* the level of tax, measured off the baseline of the smoothed consumption pattern. The taxpayer living out the dotted line in Figure 2 is in a higher tax bracket, *under a spending tax*, than the taxpayer living out the solid line. A wage tax ignores this difference. In other words, a progressive spending tax includes the yield to capital or savings in its base when this yield is used to finance a greater material lifestyle.

ℳ 8.6 The Case for a Progressive Spending Tax

This small taste of theory is meant to signal a big point: that a progressive spending tax is an exciting option for comprehensive tax reform.

Such a tax is not a radical departure from the status quo. We would still have annual returns: this is not a tax levied at the cash register. It follows the simple form of the rearrangement of the Haig-Simons definition, namely:

$$\text{Consumption} = \text{Income} - \text{Savings}$$

Hence we need only allow unlimited deductions for savings, along the lines of traditional IRAs under Section 408, and find a way to include debt in the tax base. These two steps change the "what" of taxation. They give us a base as to which we could apply progressive rates – ones that are more progressive than we have today, because they fall on spending, and can be avoided by savings, an activity that helps us all. If Ant makes $1 million but only spends $100,000, she will be taxed on $100,000: the tax on her $900,000 of savings can wait until she pulls money out of her account. If Grasshopper makes $1 million, in contrast, and spends even more than that, say

$1.2 million, because he borrows, he will be taxed on $1.2 million. We can put back in place tax rates of 50% or higher, falling on such high-end consumption, say over $1 million per year. We may not want to discourage anyone from *earning* so much money, because the worker is helping out the wider society, but why should we hesitate to raise taxes on someone *spending* so much? All the more so as we could deduct certain forms of spending, such as medical or educational expenses, from the spending tax base, leaving only high-end personal discretionary spending to face high tax rates.

All savings and investment would take place inside individual savings accounts. We would no longer have any need for the tax concept of basis, since all savings, not having been taxed, would have zero basis. Nor would we need a capital gains preference as discussed in Chapter 6 or the rules on realization and recognition discussed at length in Chapter 4. Taxes would be paid when and only when money was withdrawn from the unlimited savings accounts. The base would broaden by the inclusion of debt-financed consumption and the elimination of the capital gains rates preference.

One of the most important benefits of the shift to a consistent progressive spending tax is then that *we could raise marginal tax rates*. High tax rates under an income tax discourage work and savings: two social goods that we desperately need as we the people attempt to ward off an impending fiscal crisis. High tax rates under a spending tax, in contrast, deter only high-end spending. And this we may well want to curtail, in order to generate the savings we need as a country.

Many people object right away that consumption is good, the engine of our economy. And so it is. But in addition to consumption, we also need savings. Savings and not current consumption fuels future growth in real income. *And savings is nonconsumption*, as the Haig-Simons definition helps us to see. We only have savings if some people do not consume all that they could. One question for the United States in the twenty-first century is where will we get our national savings? The poor and middle classes, the latter highly burdened by taxes, have little ability to save. The government itself has proven wholly incompetent to do so. Who is left? It is the wealthy, the rich who need not consume all that they can.

Part of the motivation for a progressive spending tax is that we can raise marginal tax rates on high-end spending, and thereby give the wealthy a choice. They can continue to spend a great deal on luxuries, and pay a high tax rate for the privilege. Or they can save, thereby avoiding current taxation under the spending tax base, but helping all through their contribution to the common pool of capital. High tax rates under a spending tax, in other words, *do not necessarily deter the productive activities of work and savings, because we are giving the rich an opt-out via unlimited deductions for savings.* We are, in short, no longer taxing the social goods of work and savings but rather the social "bad," or at least not-really-good, of high-end luxury spending.

Now many liberals object that this is unfair, because we are letting the rich build up large stores of capital, tax-free. This objection fails to understand the tax. The money saved in the unlimited savings accounts is not taxed *now*. But it will be taxed—when, as and if some individual moves to spend it. That progressive spending tax could fall on the first generation or heirs. The greater the withdrawal for private use, the higher the tax. In the meantime, the capital sits in a common pool, helping all by its contributions to lower interest rates and higher wages.

The knee-jerk criticism of a progressive spending tax as being somehow illiberal—as being too favorable to the capitalist class— misses another critical point. *It is the existing income tax system that fails to tax capital.* A progressive spending tax *does* tax capital and its yield, and at potentially sharply progressive rates—when, but only when, individuals go to spend the yield on their own personal wants and preferences. This would be a dramatic improvement over the status quo.

8.6.1 The Progressive Spending Tax and Tax Planning 101

Unlike any incremental reform we have seen enacted or proposed with the income tax, a systematic progressive spending tax would also—and most importantly—shut down Tax Planning 101. It would do so by, of all things, eliminating the middle plank in buy/borrow/die. There would be no need for a realization requirement. Just as today inside an IRA or pension plan, taxpayers could sell and buy assets without tax.

There need be no estate tax; taxpayers could pass on their savings accounts on death, with their zero bases, and have their children or other heirs pay tax when and if *they* withdrew funds. The logic of a progressive spending tax is to tax people when and only when they spend, not when they work or save. This logic can work straight through death, for the simple reason that dead men don't spend.

The key is that *borrowing* will become taxable, just as it is under the regular, more commonly understood sales tax. Rich Dad cannot get any personal consumption benefit out of his savings and investments without paying some tax. This is as it should be.

The case for a progressive spending tax rests on broaching the capital-labor divide in a sensible, principled way. We need not and should not double-tax all savings. But neither should we ignore all savings. We should tax the yield to capital when but only when it allows individuals to live a better material lifestyle than they otherwise could. This, I submit, is what our seemingly incoherent practices as evident in the actual tax code have been trying to tell us for years. We should listen.

8.6.2 The New Achilles' Heel

Way back in Chapter 1, at the beginning of our journey, we learned about *Macomber* and the realization requirement and how it was the Achilles' Heel of the income tax. And so it was. The realization requirement gave us Tax Planning 101, and led to a plethora of non-cash producing assets and financial instruments. It led to a capital gains preference, to mitigate the lock-in effect it created. It basically killed the income tax as any kind of effective tax on capital or its yield.

But now at the end of our journey comes another twist. We know the three steps in Tax Planning 101: buy, borrow, die. We know that no income Tax reform over the century of the tax's existence has meaningfully attacked any of its planks. I have been advocating a progressive spending tax as a way to cure the income tax's ills, to get at capital and its yield in some cases. And a progressive spending tax does shut down Tax Planning 101. But it does so, not by attacking the realization requirement, but by changing the nontaxation of debt.

Under the lights of the progressive spending tax and its underlying theory, debt is the Achilles' heel. And we can say, in ending, that it is not just the Achilles' heel of the *tax* system: it is the Achilles' heel of the United States. We are borrowing too much, on individual and national levels. Eventually, the chickens will come home to roost, the piper must get paid. We have to start saving more, which, *necessarily*, means borrowing less. And yet we have a tax system that encourages us to borrow away. That ought to change, before we as a nation suffer the fate of Achilles.

⌘ 8.7 Summary

In this our final chapter, we return to where we started with a consideration of tax policy. We need to do this because, whatever happens, there will be change. The well-grounded student of tax will understand what has been and could be as a way to navigate a lifetime of change in tax. More specifically, we learned:

- Any discussion of tax reform today must take into account the federal government's dramatic need for more revenue; deficits are mounting, threatening our present and future;

- There are four broad paths for tax reform: (1) incremental reform within the individual income tax, (2) increasing other exisiting taxes, (3) adding a new tax such as a VAT; and (4) fundamental reform of the income tax, as by moving systematically toward a consumption tax;
- There are good reasons to believe that the income tax as presently structured is essentially tapped out as a major source of revenue;
- The most likely form of a new or "add-on" tax is a flat national sales tax or a VAT: neither would do much to change the basic theme of this short introduction, as each is essentially equivalent to wage tax;
- The traditional view of tax pits an income tax against consumption taxes of one of two forms, flat wage or spending taxes; this analytic mapping comes about because it is assumed that a consumption tax is desired for its principled nontaxation of the yield to capital;
- Under progressive rates, wage and spending taxes are not equivalent;
- An income tax double-taxes all savings, for whatever use; a wage tax ignores all savings, for whatever use;
- A progressive spending tax splits the difference: it allows savings for "ordinary" uses such a retirement and other smoothing transactions to lower taxes, but savings that lead to more luxurious living get taxed, and at progressive rates;
- A progressive spending tax need not be a radical change. We must only allow unlimited deductions for savings and pick up debt in the tax base. This will allow us to get rid of all rules about tax bases (there will be none), realization and recognition, and capital gains. It would broaden the base by including debt-financed consumption and repealing the capital gains preference;
- Rates under a progressive spending tax could increase, because they would only fall on spending, not work or savings—the theme is to tax social bads, not goods;

- Under the lights of a progressive spending tax, it is debt, and not the realization requirement, that is the Achilles' heel, and we conclude by saying that borrowing is the Achilles' heel not just of the tax system but of the United States more generally;
- Tax is fun (remember?).

Appendix

TABLE A-1 Top 100 Code Sections

General Topic	Code Section	Brief Description
Tax rates	1	Tax rates (including kiddie tax and capital gains rate)
Credits	21	Child-care credit
	24	Child credit
	25A	Hope and lifetime learning credits
	32	Earned income tax credit (EITC)
Alternative minimum tax	55	Alternative minimum tax (AMT) rates and exemption
	56	Adjustments in calculating AMT
	57	AMT preference items
Definitions	61	Gross income defined
	62	Adjusted gross income (AGI) defined
	63	Taxable income defined
	64	Ordinary income defined
	67	2 percent floor on miscellaneous itemized deductions
	68	Overall limit on itemized deductions (suspended)
Specific inclusions in income	71	Alimony and separate maintenance
	72	Annuities
	73	Services of child
	74	Prizes and awards

(*Continued*)

TABLE A-1 Top 100 Code Sections (*Cont'd*)

General Topic	Code Section	Brief Description
	83	Property transferred in connection with performance of services
	86	Social security benefits
Specific exclusions from income	101	Insurance and certain death benefits
	102	Gifts and inheritance
	103	Interest on state and local bonds
	104	Compensation for injuries or sickness
	105	Amounts received under accident and health plans
	106	Employer contributions to accident and health plans
	108	Income from discharge of indebtedness
	111	Tax benefit rule
	117	Qualified scholarships
	119	Meals or lodging furnished for the convenience of the employer
	121	Exclusion of gain from sale of principal residence
	125	Cafeteria plans
	127	Educational assistance programs
	129	Dependent care assistance programs
	132	Certain fringe benefits
State and local (tax-exempt) bonds	141	Private activity bonds
Personal exemptions/ dependents	151	Allowance of deductions for personal exemptions
	152	Dependent defined

Itemized deductions—individuals and corporations	161	Allowance of deductions
	162	Trade or business expenses
	163	Interest
	164	Taxes
	165	Losses
	166	Bad debts
	167	Depreciation
	168	Accelerated cost recovery system
	170	Charitable contributions and gifts
	179	Election to expense certain depreciable business assets
	183	Activities not engaged in for profit
	195	Start-up expenditures
	197	Amortization of goodwill and certain intangibles
Itemized deductions for individuals	211	Allowance of deductions
	212	Expenses for production of income
	213	Medical, dental deductions
	215	Alimony payments
	217	Moving expenses
	219	Retirement savings
	221	Interest on education loans
	222	Qualified tuition and related expenses
	223	Health savings accounts
Items specifically not deductible	261	General rule for disallowance of deductions
	262	Personal, living, and family expenses
	263	Capital expenditures
	263A	Uniform capitalization (UNICAP) rules
	265	Expenses and interest relating to tax-exempt income

(*Continued*)

TABLE A-1 Top 100 Code Sections (*Cont'd*)

General Topic	Code Section	Brief Description
	267	Losses, expenses, and interest with respect to transactions between related taxpayers
	274	Disallowance of certain entertainment, etc. deductions
	280A	Disallowance of certain expenses in connection with business use of a home, etc.
Pensions and IRAs	401	Qualified pension, profit-sharing, and stock bonus plans
	408	IRAs
	408A	Roth IRAs
Accounting	441	Accounting period
	442	Change in annual accounting period
	446	General rule for methods of accounting
	451	General rule for taxable year of inclusion
	453	Installment method
	461	General rule for taxable year of deduction
	465	Deductions limited to amounts at-risk
	469	Passive activity losses and credits limited
	482	Allocation of income and deductions among taxpayers
Charitable organizations	501	Exemption from tax on certain charities
	509	Private foundation defined
	511	Imposition of tax on unrelated business income of charitable organizations

Educational savings accounts	529	Qualified tuition programs
Property	1001	Determination of amount of and recognition of gain or loss
	1011	Adjusted basis for determining gain or loss
	1012	Basis of property cost
	1014	Basis of property acquired from decedent (stepped-up basis)
	1015	Basis of property acquired as gift (carryover basis)
	1016	Adjustments to basis
	1031	Like-kind exchanges
	1032	Exchange of stock for property
	1033	Involuntary conversions
	1041	Transfers of property between spouses or incident to divorce
	1091	Loss from wash sales of stocks or securities
Capital gains and losses	1211	Limitation on capital losses
	1221	Capital asset defined
	1222	Other terms relating to capital gains or losses
	1231	Property used in a trade or business and involuntary conversions
Claim of right	1341	Computation of tax where taxpayer restores substantial amount held under a claim of right

TABLE A-2 Top 10 Code Sections

Code Section	Description
1	Tax rates
32	Earned income tax credit
61	Definition of income
102	Gifts (not taxable income)
162	Ordinary and necessary active trade or business expenses deductible
212	Expenses for production of income (not active trade or business) deductible
262	No general deduction for "personal, family, or living expenses"
1001	Gain or loss on disposition of property = f.m.v. of amount realized minus basis
1014/15	Stepped-up basis on death/carryover basis on gifts
1221	Capital asset defined

Table of Cases

ACM Partnership v. Commissioner, 157 F.3d 231
(3d Cir. 1998), aff'g 73 T.C.M. (CCH) 2198 (1997),
cert. denied, 526 U.S. 1017 (1999) 197
Alice Phelan Sullivan Corp. v. United States, 381 F.2d 399
(Ct. Cl. 1967) 140
Arkansas Best Corp. v. Commissioner, 485
U.S. 212 (1988) 171–172n1, 172–173, 179

Blair v. Commissioner, 300 U.S. 5 (1937) 154–155
Bliss Dairy, Inc. v. United States, 704 F.2d 1167
(9th Cir. 1983)..140
Brooke v. United States, 468 F.2d 1155 (9th Cir. 1972)...........153, 160, 198
Bruun, Helvering v., 309 U.S. 461 (1940)...................... 122, 128–129
Burnet v. Logan, 283 U.S. 404 (1931)....................................135
Burnet v. Sanford & Brooks, See *Sanford & Brooks, Burnet v.*

Clifford, Helvering v., 309 U.S. 331 (1940)..............................155
Corn Products Refining Co. v. Commissioner, 350
U.S. 46 (1955)...............................171–172n1, 171–173, 179
Cottage Savings Ass'n v. Commissioner, 499
U.S. 554 (1991) 125–126, 142, 172, 198
Crane v. Commissioner, 331 U.S. 1 (1947) 185–187, 200

Davis, United States v., 370 U.S. 65 (1962)................123–125, 128–130
Drescher, United States v., 179 F.2d 863 (2d Cir. 1950),
cert. denied, 340 U.S. 821 (1950)..................... 74–75, 77–78, 123,
133, 135–136, 159
Duberstein, Commissioner v., 363
U.S. 278 (1960) 64–69, 86, 102, 195

Eisner v. Macomber, See *Macomber, Eisner v.*

Encyclopaedia Britanica v. Commissioner, 685
    F.2d 212 (7th Cir. 1982) 103, 109

Frank Lyon Co. v. United States, 435 U.S. 561 (1978) 198, 198n1

Franklin, Estate of, 554 F.2d 1045 (9th Cir. 1976) 185, 187, 189, 198, 200

Gilbert v. Commissioner, 552 F.2d 478 (2d Cir. 1977)...................... 80

Glenshaw Glass, Commissioner v., 348 U.S. 426 (1955)......... 36, 38–42,44,
                46–47, 54, 58, 62, 74, 78, 80–81, 85, 114, 128, 136, 142

Gregory v. Helvering, 69 F.2d 809 (2d Cir. 1934),
    aff'd, 293 U.S. 465 (1935)................................. 194–195, 198

Helvering v. Bruun, See *Bruun, Helvering v.*

Helvering v. Clifford, See *Clifford, Helvering v.*

Helvering v. Horst, See *Horst, Helvering v.*

Hillsboro Nat'l Bank v. Commissioner, 460
    U.S. 370 (1983) 140, 143

Horst, Helvering v., 311 U.S. 112 (1940)....................... 154–155, 174

Hort v. Commissioner, 313 U.S. 28 (1941)..............................175

Knetsch v. United States, 364 U.S. 361 (1960).............. 183, 196–198, 200

Lewis, United States v., 340 U.S. 590 (1951)............................139

Lucas v. Earl, 281 U.S. 111 (1930)....................... 146, 148, 153, 160

Macomber, Eisner v., 252 U.S. 189 (1920).............12, 33, 36–37n3, 36–40,
            44, 46, 48, 51, 58–59, 61, 64, 73, 84–85, 108–110, 112, 121–123,
            122n1, 125, 127, 136, 141–142, 166, 174, 177, 192, 194, 196, 222

Miller v. Commissioner, 299 F.2d 706 (2d Cir. 1962),
    cert. denied, 370 U.S. 923 (1962)....................................173

Nickerson v. Commissioner, 700 F.2d 402 (7th Cir. 1983) ... 110, 114, 119, 191

Old Colony Trust Co. v. Commissioner, 279
    U.S. 716 (1929) 82, 82n11, 96n3

Olk v. United States, 536 F.2d 876 (9th Cir. 1976),
    cert. denied, 429 U.S. 920 (1976)................................. 66–67

P.G. Lake, Inc., Commissioner v., 356 U.S. 260 (1958).......... 174–176, 179

Poe v. Seaborn, 282 U.S. 101 (1930)................................ 148, 152

Pollock v. Farmers Loan & Trust Co., 157 U.S. 429,
     aff'd on rehearing, 158 U.S. 601 (1895)................................33

Sanford & Brooks, Burnet v., 282 U.S. 359 (1931)....................138–139
Smith v. Commissioner, 40 B.T.A. 1038 (1939), aff'd without
     opinion, 113 F.2d 114 (2d Cir. 1940) 107, 107n6
Solicitor's Opinion 132, I-1 C.B. 92 (1922) 44–45, 47, 63, 124
Starker v. United States, 602 F.2d 1341 (9th Cir. 1979) 130, 131–132, 198
Stephens v. Commissioner, 905 F.2d 667 (2d Cir. 1990)....................99

Taft v. Bowers, 278 U.S. 470 (1929)......................... 71–72, 123, 129
Tufts, Commissioner v., 461 U.S. 300 (1983) 187–189, 191, 198, 200

Welch v. Helvering, 290 U.S. 111 (1933) 102, 104, 121

Glossary of Key Terms

appreciation: The rise in the value of an asset. Appreciation can be merely due to inflation or can represent a real gain in value. Appreciation is not consistently taxed under the current U.S. income tax.

after-tax dollars: Dollars that have already been taxed. If you earn $10,000 at work and your taxes come to $1,500, you are left with $8,500 in after-tax dollars. You should not be taxed on this amount again. See also *basis*.

average tax rate: The tax rate that an average dollar bears in taxes. Under an income tax, the average tax rate is calculated by dividing one's total taxes by one's total income. See also *marginal tax rate*.

base: See *tax base*.

basis: After-tax dollars. If you invest with money that has already been subject to the income tax, you have basis in the investment equal to its cost: that value cannot be taxed again. If, on the other hand, you get a tax deduction for an investment, you have no basis in the investment, so its value can still be subject to tax. Our present tax code allows you to receive certain types of income tax-free: cash gifts, Section 102; tax-exempt interest, Section 103; the proceeds of life insurance, Section 101; and so on. Because you cannot be taxed on these types of income, they have basis. See also *after-tax dollars*, *carryover basis*, *stepped-up basis*.

built-in gain: Appreciation that has not yet been taxed. If you buy a share of stock for $100 and it rises in value to $150, you will have $50 of built-in gain, also called unrealized appreciation.

capital asset: Property under IRC Section 1221 that has been held for over one year. Investments can be capital assets; inventory and certain self-created assets, such as books and paintings, cannot.

capital appreciation: The rise in value of a capital asset.

capital gain or loss: The gain or loss that occurs when a capital asset is sold. IRC Section 1001(a).

capital gains tax rate: The tax rate applied to a capital gain or loss, IRC Section 1(h). The capital gains tax rate is lower than the rate applied to ordinary income; currently it stands at a maximum of 15 percent, much lower than the top rate of 35 percent for ordinary income. See also *ordinary income.*

carryover basis: The basis that a new owner of an asset takes over from its prior owner. If Jack buys stock for $100, it appreciates in value to $150, and Jack then gives the stock to Jill as a gift, Jill will take a carryover basis of $100 in the stock. In this way, both the basis and the built-in gain stay with the stock and its new owner. A leading example is IRC Section 1015's carryover basis for gifts. See also *basis, built-in gain.*

consumption: Income or wealth that is spent rather than saved. According to the Haig-Simons definition, Consumption = Income − Savings.

consumption tax: Any tax that does not directly fall on savings.

credit: A dollar-for-dollar reduction in tax owed. Under the current system, if you are eligible for the per-child tax credit, your tax is reduced by $500 per child. Unlike deductions, credits do not add regressivity to the tax system. See also *deduction, nonrefundable credit, refundable credit.*

deduction: A subtraction from the relevant tax base. Under the present system, if you make charitable contributions worth $10,000, you can deduct this amount from your income; that amount of your income will not be taxed. Deductions have a regressive effect in a progressive system. See also *credit.*

effective tax rate: See *average tax rate.*

estate tax: See *gift and estate tax.*

exemption level: See *zero bracket.*

flat tax: Literally, a tax that imposes a single rate or sum on all taxpayers. In practice, all modern flat-tax proposals involve two rates because they feature some kind of exemption level or zero bracket. See also *zero bracket.*

gift and estate tax: A tax that falls on the estate or wealth holdings of decedent or certain gifts made by them. Also called the unified wealth transfer system or, colloquially, the death tax.

Haig-Simons definition of income: The principle that Income = Consumption + Savings, named after the economists Henry Simons and Robert Haig.

income: According to the Haig-Simons definition, Consumption plus Savings. See also IRC Section 61, *Elenshaw class.*

income tax: In theory, a tax on both consumption and savings.

inflation: The general rise in a price level.

indexing for inflation: Adjusting a price or tax system so that it uses real, or inflation-adjusted, values. For example, a zero bracket that is to be indexed for inflation will increase at the rate of inflation. If inflation is 5 percent, a $10,000 bracket for Year 1 will become a $10,500 bracket in Year 2.

IRA: Individual Retirement Account, a tax-favored savings account that operates on a spending tax model: savers deposit pretax dollars and do not pay taxes until they withdraw the money. IRC Section 408. See also *Roth IRA.*

lock-in effect: The present law's tendency to discourage the sale of capital assets that have built-in gain. The lock-in effect breeds inefficiency because wealth holders retain assets that might otherwise be sold.

marginal tax rate: The rate of tax one pays on the next dollar of income. If you are in the 28 percent marginal tax bracket and you earn $1,000 next week, you will pay a tax of $280 on those earnings. See also *average tax rate.*

national retail sales tax: See *sales tax.*

nonrecognition: The non-taxation of a realized gain because of an explicit statute, such as section 1031 (like-kind exchanges).

nonrefundable credit: A refund or credit that is limited to the amount of taxes paid. The $500 per-child tax credit of IRC Section 24 is nonrefundable. If a taxpayer with two children owes only $800 in taxes before the credit is applied, her tax will be reduced to zero; she will not benefit from the additional $200 of the credit. See also *credit, refundable credit.*

ordinary income: Income from wages, interest, dividends, and other usual inflows. Ordinary income does not include proceeds from the sale of capital assets. IRC Section 64. See also *capital gain or loss.*

payroll tax: A tax levied on labor earnings and typically remitted by the employer. The Social Security and Medicare contribution system is a leading example.

pension plan: A retirement savings vehicle, typically maintained or established by one's employer, that is tax-favored under present law.

progressive tax system: A system of taxation in which higher earners or spenders pay a higher average tax rate than lower earners or spenders. See also *average tax rate, regressive tax system*.

rate: See *tax rate*.

rate bracket: The range of income over which a certain marginal tax rate applies. If the marginal rate is 15 percent for earnings between $10,000 and $30,000, a taxpayer will pay 15 percent on every dollar she earns over $10,000 but under $30,000.

rate schedule: The full range of tax rates and rate brackets in a tax system.

real value: Value that is held constant over time. Real value reflects actual purchasing power. Because of inflation, a coat that you can buy for $100 in Year 1 will cost more the following year. The value of your dollars will have eroded.

realization requirement: The rule, seen in the important Supreme Court case of *Eisner v. Macomber*, that an asset holder need not pay tax until the asset is sold or exchanged—until the underlying built-in gain is realized. See also *built-in gain*.

recognition: What occurs when a realized gain is actually taxal. See non recognition realization requirement.

refundable credit: A refund or credit that can exceed the amount of taxes paid. The Earned Income Credit under IRC Section 32 is refundable. If a taxpayer owes $800 in taxes before the credit is applied, and her credit is $1,000, she will receive a refund of $200. See also *credit, nonrefundable credit*.

regressive tax system: A system in which higher earners or spenders pay a lower average tax rate than lower earners or spenders. See also *average tax rate, progressive tax system*.

Roth IRA: An Individual Retirement Account that operates on the wage tax model: savers deposit after-tax dollars and do not pay taxes on withdrawals. IRC Section 408A. See also *IRA*.

sales tax: A tax levied on consumer purchases, typically collected from sellers but borne effectively by buyers.

savings: Nonconsumed, or unspent, wealth. Income minus Consumption under the Haig-Simons definition of income.

stepped-up basis: An adjustment of basis to fair market value, which the current income tax allows for assets acquired after a death. A decedent might have had only $1,000 of basis in an investment valued at $10,000; when his heirs receive the asset, it will have a new level of basis that matches its current value—$10,000. IRC Section 1014. See also *basis, carryover basis*.

taxable unit: The "who" of taxation; the person or persons responsible for paying a tax. Currently the taxable unit can be an individual, a married couple, or a household.

tax base: The "what" of taxation; the value that is subject to tax. Income is the base of an income tax; purchased goods are the base of most sales taxes; consumption is the base of a Consumption tax.

tax expenditure: A way to refer to the revenue that Congress "spends" by including provisions in the income tax code not constitutionally or otherwise required; leading examples include the "personal" deductions for home mortgage interest, employer-provided medical care, charitable contributions, and retirement savings.

tax rate: The "how much" of taxation, or the percentage of a tax base that is collected by the government. See also *average tax rate, marginal tax rate*.

unrealized appreciation: See *built-in gain*.

value-added tax (VAT): A tax levied on the value that is added at different stages of a production process; in essence, a sales tax that is collected gradually.

zero bracket: The amount of a tax base that is not subject to tax.

Notes for Further Reading

There are many good income tax texts, treatises, and handbooks. I list here a few sources for further reading, mostly those with a bit of a policy twist. This list is by no means exclusive, but each source mentioned will point the way toward others.

The late David Bradford wrote or largely wrote two important volumes, *Blueprints for Basic Tax Reform, 2d edition*, Arlington Va.: Tax Analysts (1984) (with the staff of the U.S. Treasury) and *Untangling the Income Tax*, Harvard University Press (1986).

Paul Caron edited a fun volume with chapters on many of the cases considered in this volume, *Tax Stories*, Thomson/Reuters/Foundation Press (2009).

Marvin Chirelstein is the author of the classic student guide to the U.S. income tax, *Federal Income Taxation, 11th edition*, New York: Foundation Press (2009).

Professor Michael Graetz has been leading commentator on the income tax. He is the author of two important and interesting books, *The U.S. Income Tax: What It Is, How It Got That Way, and Where We Go From Here*, New York: Norton (1999) and *One Hundred Million Unnecessary Returns: A Simple, Fair and Competitive Tax Plan for the United States*, Yale University Press (2007).

I have written two books, *Taxing Women*, Chicago: University of Chicago Press (1997) and *Fair Not Flat: How to Make the Tax System Simple and Better*, Chicago: University of Chicago Press (2002). For readers interested in scholarly details, see my law review article, "*A New Understanding of Tax*," Michigan Law Review 103: 807 (2005), complete with many footnotes and references.

Joel Slemrod and Jon Bakija have written a very useful book, *Taxing Ourselves: A Citizen's Guide to the Debate over Taxes, 4th edition*, MIT Press (2008).

Gene Steurle has been a participant in various tax reform efforts and an astute observer of the scene, his *Contemporary U.S. Tax Policy, 2d edition*, Urban Institute Press (2008) is an excellent account of recent (and multiple!) changes.

Interested readers should also check out a wonderful blog, maintained by Paul Caron, TaxProf Blog, http://taxprof.typepad.com/. The weekly *Tax Notes* published by Tax Analysts out of Washington, D.C., is a must-read periodical for any reader really serious about taxes.

Index

A

Accounting methods, 121, 133–135, 137, 142
  cash, 133, 142
  accrual, 134, 142
  installment sales. *See* installment sales accounting method
  inventory. *See* inventory accounting method
Accounting period. *See* Annual accounting rule
Alimony, 156–157
Alternative minimum tax (AMT)
  deductions, 92, 96, 98, 115–117, 119, 208
  inflation, 116
Andrews, William, 12
Annual accounting rule, 137–140, 143
Annuity, 74–77, 135–137, 159, 196–197, 218
Anticipatory income, 174–176, 179. *See also* Recharacterization of income; "Fruits and Trees"
Appreciated property
  gifts, 64, 70–73, 97
  divorce, 123–124, 130
  realization requirement, 50–54, 58, 85, 122*n*1
  tax "time bombs," 50–54
  tax deferral, 15, 24, 49, 61, 127, 158, 178, 192

Attribution of income
  generally, 145–147, 160–161
  bonds, 154–156
  children, 152–153, 160–161
  divorce, 156–157
  "fruit and tree" distinction, 153–156, 161
  head of household status, 151
  marriage bonuses, 149–151
  marriage penalties, 149–151
  property, income from, 153–156, 161
  same-sex couples, 151–152
  spouses, 147–152, 160
  trusts, 155
Average tax rates, 21
Avoidance. *See* Tax avoidance
Aykroyd, Dan, 171

B

"Balance sheet" test. *See* Definition of income
Base. *See* Tax base
Basis
  generally, 14, 68, 73, 83
  annuity, 76–77
  debt, 58, 83
  business expenditure deductions, 100, 105, 105*n*4
  carryover basis, 50*n*5, 71
  divorce, 123–124
  charitable contributions, 54

Basis (*Cont.*)
  gain, 45–47
  gifts, 70–73
  loss, 59–60, 95, 113
  Macomber, 50–52, 85
  noncash benefits, 76–77
  retirement savings, 18
  spending taxes, 84
  stepped-up basis, 14, 53, 59, 62,
    84, 117, 179, 192
  substituted basis, 50n5
  transferred basis, 50n5
Bequests,
  exclusion, 62
  savings, 216, 217
Blueprints for Basic Tax Reform
    (Treasury Department), 190,
    211–212
Bonds
  generally, 155–156,191
  municipal, 50, 63
  zero-coupon, 122, 122n1
  original issue (OID), 122, 122n1
Boortz, Neal, 6, 6n3
Boot, 132
Borrowing. *See* Debt
Brooks, Mel, 190
Buffet, Warren, 15, 117, 127
Built-in gains, 14, 16, 51, 54, 70, 72,
    85, 97, 109, 121, 124, 128,129,
    131–132, 134, 142, 164, 166
Bush, George H.W., 193, 209
Bush, George W., 19, 193, 209
Business expenditures
  generally, 33, 88–91, 98–100,
    118, 200
  AMT, 116
  basis, 100–101, 104–105, 105n4
  capitalization, *See*
    capitalization
  deduction, 99–105, 153, 168, 184
  depreciation, 104–105
  timing considerations, 100–104
  tips or tokes, 67

Business purpose doctrine, 194, 197,
    200. *See also* Tax shelters

C
Capital. *See also* Savings
  appreciation, 17, 49
  assets, 15, 56, 109, 164, 165,
    167–170, 178
  progressive spending tax, 221
  self-supplied capital, 55–57.
    See also Imputed income
Capital gains
  generally, 20, 163, 177–179
  anticipatory income, 174–176,
    179
  Arkansas Best, 171–174
  "bunching" effect, 165
  capital property, 173–174
  carried interest, 176–177, 179
  Corn Products, 171–174
  divorce, 130
  "double taxation," 165–166
  gift, 72
  inclusions, 33, 44–47
  inflation, 164–165
  inventory exception, 170
  ordinary income distinguished,
    167–170
  policy considerations, 164–167
  real estate, 170, 178–179
  realization requirement,
    166–167
  securities, 170, 178–179
  statutory provisions, 167–170
  stock in trade exception, 170
  tax rates, 16, 20, 23, 163–164, 188,
    192–193
  tax shelters, 192–193
Capitalization
  business expenditures, 102–104
  timing considerations, 141, 143
Capital-labor divide
  generally, xviii–xx, 24–25, 84
  AMT, 117

income taxes, 33
Macomber, 37, 48
progressive spending tax, 222
Capital loss
  generators, 182, 197
  offset rule, 60, 170, 178
Cardozo, Justice Benjamin, 102
Carried interest, 13, 176–177, 179.
    See also Recharacterization
    of income
Carryover basis, 14*n*6, 50*n*5, 71–72,
    129, 142, 153, 169
Carter, Jimmy, 14*n*6
Cash equivalence, 133, 135–137,
    142–143
Casualty loss, 95, 113, 118, 119, 127
Charitable contributions
  basis, 54, 85
  deductions, 97–98, 118
  proposals to eliminate
    deductions, 208
Child care expenses
  credit, 56–57
  deductions. *See* Mixed business-
    personal expenditure
    deductions
Children
  attribution of income, 152–153,
    160–161
  credit, 152
  deduction, 152
  gifts to, 153, 184
  "kiddie tax." *See* "Kiddie tax"
  shifting of income, 152–153,
    160–161, 184
Child support, 69, 156–157
Claim of right doctrine, 139–140, 143
"Clearly realized accession to
    wealth." *See* Definitions
    of Income
Clinton, Bill, 17, 19, 93, 193
Clothing expenses. *See* Mixed
    business-personal expenditure
    deductions

Commuting expense. *See* Mixed
    business-personal expenditure
    deductions
Constructive receipt, 135–137,
    142–143
Consumption
  Definition of income, 6–8, 47–48,
    219–220
  progressive spending tax,
    220–221
Consumption taxes
  generally, 8–9, 224
  income taxes, 87–88, 213–214
  progressive spending tax, *See*
    Progressive spending tax
  proposals, 212
  spending taxes. *See* Spending
    taxes
  wage taxes. *See* Wage taxes
Conversion of income. *See*
    Recharacterization of income
Copyrights, 169
Corporations
  "double-taxation." *See* Double-
    taxation
  gifts, 65
  proposals to increase income
    tax, 210
  realization, 126
  shifting of income, 158, 159, 161
"Coupon clippers," 154
Credits
  child, 152
  child care, 56–57, 107, 107*n*6
  earned income tax credit (EITC),
    93–94, 99, 118
  education, 106. 106*n*5
  generally, 21, 92–93, 117

D
Debt
  basis, 83
  generally, 42–43
  discharge of. *See* Discharge of debt

Debt (*Cont.*)
  nonincome, 13–14, 58, 86
  nonrecourse debt, 185–187, 200
  progressive spending tax,
      217–218, 224–225
  spending taxes, 83–84, 86
  tax shelters, 185–189, 199–200
Deductions, 87–119
  generally, 87–90, 117–119
  "above the line," 34, 34*n*1, 90
  AMT, 92, 96, 98, 115–117, 119, 208
  business expenditures. *See*
      Business expenditures
  business use of home, 107
  calculation, 91–92
  casualty losses. *See* Casualty
      losses
  charitable contributions. *See*
      Charitable Contributions
  child-care expenses. *See*
      Child-care
  clothing expenses, 107
  commuting expenses, 107
  credits compared, 92–94
  earned income tax credit, 93–94,
      99, 118
  education expenses, 106, 106*n*5
  employer-provided health care,
      92, 208
  exclusions compared, 92*n*1
  401(k) plans, 92, 96, 208
  gambling losses, 114–115
  home mortgage interest, 92, 96,
      112–113, 208
  interest expenses. *See* Interest
      deductions
  IRAs, 18, 26. 92, 96, 159, 219
  itemized deductions. *See*
      Itemized deductions
  losses, 95, 113–114, 119
  mechanics, 90–94
  medical expenses, 95
  mixed business-personal
      expenditures. *See* Mixed

        business-personal expenditure
        deductions
  net operating losses (NOLs), 139*n*3
  pension plans, 78, 86, 92, 96, 209
  personal dependency deduction,
      98, 116, 118, 119, 208
  personal expenditures. *See*
      Personal expenditures
  progressive spending tax. *See*
      Progressive spending tax
  property taxes, 4, 96
  proposals to eliminate, 208
  regressive nature, 92
  Roth-style IRAs, 10–11, 19, 26, 96
  sales taxes, 96
  standard deduction, 90, 93, 94,
      98, 118
  state and local income
      taxes, 96, 208
Defense of Marriage Act (DOMA),
      151–152
Deferring tax liability, 23–25.
      See also Timing considerations
Definition of income
  generally, 31–32, 84–85
  academic, 47–48
  "balance sheet" test, 40–42
  "clearly realized," 39–42
  Constitutional definitions, 33–36
  consumption, 6–8, 47–48,
      219–220
  debt, 42–44
  "dominion,",39–42
  Glenshaw Glass, 38–42
  gross income, 33–36
  Haig-Simons definition, 6–7,
      39–40, 47–49, 58, 78, 85–86, 94,
      219–220
  judicial definitions, 36–40
  Macomber, 36–40
  sources of income, 37–38
  statutory definitions, 33–36
  "undeniable accession to wealth,"
      39–42

Depreciation
    accrual method of accounting, 134
    deductions, 83, 89, 104–105
    tax shelters, 186–189, 200
    timing considerations, 141, 143, 168
Devises, 62. *See also* Exclusions
Discharge of debt
    inclusions, 43–44, 81–83, 86
    statutory exclusion, 63
    tax shelters, 187–189
Divorce
    attribution of income, 156–157
    nonrecognition rules, 129–130,
        142
DOMA (Defense of Marriage Act),
    151–152
"Dominion over accession to
    wealth." *See* Definitions of
    Income
"Double taxation"
    capital gains, 165–166
    gifts, 68–69
    savings, 5, 18, 26, 206, 213–214, 224
Douglas, Justice William O., 175

E

Earned income tax credit (EITC),
    93–94, 99, 118
Economic benefit, 135–137,
    142–143
Economic Recovery Tax Act of 1981
    (ERTA), 193
Economic substance doctrine, 182,
    194, 197, 200. *See also* Tax
    shelters
Education expense deductions. *See*
    Mixed business-personal
    expenditure deductions
Effective tax rates, 21
Emotional distress, 47
Employer-provided health care
    deductions, 63, 78–79, 92
    proposals to eliminate
        deductions, 208

Escaping tax liability, 23. *See also*
    Deductions; Exclusions
Estate taxes, 62–63n7
Evasion, *See* Tax evasion
Excise taxes, 210
Exclusions. *See also* Deductions
    bequests, 62
    deductions compared, 92n1
    devises, 62
    gifts. *See* Gifts
    health care. *See* employer-
        provided health-care
    life insurance proceeds, 62
    municipal bond interest, 63
    pension plans. *See* Personal
        expenditures deductions
    personal injuries, 44–45, 63
    proposals to eliminate, 208

F

Federal Savings and Loan
    Insurance Corporation
    (FSLIC), 126
First in, first out (FIFO). *See*
    Inventory accounting method
"Flat taxes"
    proposals, 5
    value-added tax, *See* Value-added
        tax
    wage taxes, xviii, 5–6, 5n1, 8, 13.
        See also Wage tax
Forgiveness of debt. *See* Discharge of
    debt
401(k) plan deduction
    generally, 92, 96
    proposals to eliminate, 208
Fringe benefits, 34, 73, 77–79, 86
"fruits and trees"
    characterization of income,
        174–176, 179
    attribution of income, 153–156,
        161
FSLIC (Federal Savings and Loan
    Insurance Corporation), 126

G

Gambling loss, 114–115
Gates, Bill, 15, 117, 127
Gifts
  generally, 64, 86
  appreciated property, 70–73
  business-personal distinction,
    65–68
  children, 152–153, 184
  defined, 64–68
  "double taxation," 68–69
  nonrecognition rules,
    128–129, 142
  shifting of income, 153, 160–161
  statutory exclusion, 62
  tax, 62–63n7
  tips, 66–67
  tokes, 66–67
The Glen Miller Story (film), 173
Graetz, Michael, 78, 208
The Grifters (film), 115
Gross income, 33–36, 89, 93

H

Haig, Robert Murray, 6
Haig-Simons, 6–7, 47–49, 52, 58, 78,
    81, 85–86, 94, 219–220
Hall, Robert, 6
Hand, Learned, 194
Head of household, 151
Health care
  deductions, 92, 92n1
  proposals to eliminate
    deductions, 208
  reform, 208–209
  statutory exclusion, 63, 78–79
Hedge funds, 13, 176–177, 179
Hines, James R., 209n1, 213n2
Holmes, Oliver Wendell, 146–148
Home
  business deduction. *See* Mixed
    business-personal expenditure
    deductions
  equity loans, 112

imputed income. *See* Imputed
    income
  mortgage interest deduction. *See*
    Mortgage interest deduction
Homosexual couples, 151–152
Husband and wife. *See* Spouses
Huston, Angelica, 115
"Hybrid" taxes, 10–11, 26

I

Illegal income, 80–81
Imputed income, 55–57, 150. *See
    also* Nonincome
Imputed rent, 57
Inclusions, 31–86
  generally, 31–32, 84–86
  capital gains, 44–47
  discharge of debt, 43–44,
    81–83, 86
  fringe benefits, 77–79, 86
  gifts. *See* Gifts
  illegal income, 80–81
  noncash benefits. *See* Noncash
    benefits
  nonincome. *See* Nonincome
  statutory exclusions, 62–63
  tax planning, 59–62
Incremental reform of tax system,
    207–209, 224
Indebtedness. *See* Debt
Individual retirement account (IRA)
  generally, 26
  deductions, 17–18, 92, 96, 159
  progressive spending tax, 219
  spending taxes, 10–11
Inflation
  AMT, 116
  capital gains, 164–165
Installment sales accounting
    method, 134–135, 142
  closed method, 135
  open method, 134
Insurance proceeds
  life insurance, 62

nonrecognition rules, 128–129, 142

Interest
carried interest, 13, 176–177, 179
municipal bond, 50, 63

Interest deductions
generally, 89, 111–113, 119
investment interest, 112, 119, 190
mortgage interest, 14*n*6, 57, 89, 91, 96, 112–113, 118–119, 208. *See also* Mortgage interest deduction
tax shelters, 183, 190, 200

"Interest dodge," 183, 185, 190. *See also* Tax shelters

Interspousal transfers. *See* Spouses

Inventory
accounts receivable, 169
exception, 170, 173
notes receivable, 169

Inventory accounting method, 134, 142
first in, first out (FIFO), 134
last in, first out (LIFO), 134

Involuntary conversions. *See* Recognition of income

IRA. *See* individual retirement account (IRA)

Itemized deductions
generally, 90–91, 99
casualty loss, 95, 113. *See also* Casualty loss
charitable contributions. *See* Charitable Contributions
home mortgage interest, 96, 112–113. *See also* Mortgage interest deduction
medical, 95
"phase out" of, 99
property tax, 96
sales tax, 96
state and local income tax, 96

J
Joint filing, 149, 152

K
Kennedy, John F., 146
"Kiddie shift," 184. *See also* "Kiddie tax," Tax shelters
"Kiddie tax"
shifting of income, 72*n*9, 153, 157–158, 161
tax shelters, 184, 192, 200
King Lear, 154, 159
Kiyosaki, Robert, 12, 26, 56
Kleinbard, Edward D., 171–172*n*1

L
Laffer curve, 212
Last in, first out (LIFO). *See* Inventory accounting method
Life-cycle savings, 216–217
Life insurance, 62
Like-kind exchanges
boot, 132
nonrecognition rules, 50, 75, 129–132, 142
Linder, John, 6
Losses
capital. *See* Capital loss
deductions, 95, 113–114, 119
passive activity loss rules, 108–111, 119, 191–192, 200
realization requirement, 125–126

M
Macomber
basis, 50–51, 85
income, defined. *See* Definition of Income
realization requirement, 37–38
tax "time bombs," 50–54, 85
tax *versus* economics, 48–49

Marriage. *See also* Spouses
  bonuses, 149–151
  divorce, 44, 123–124, 129–130,
    142, 156–157
  penalties, 149–151
  same-sex couples, 151–152
Marx, Karl, xviii, 38
Meals and entertainment. *See* Mixed
    business-personal expenditure
    deductions
Medical expenses. *See* Deductions
Medicare taxes
  generally, 5, 84, 206
  proposals to increase, 210
Mill, John Stuart, 5, 8, 17, 38, 68,
    165, 213
Miller, Glen, 173, 179
Minors. *See* Children
Mixed business-personal
    expenditure deductions
  generally, 89, 105–107,
    118–119
  child care, 107
  clothing, 107
  commuting, 107
  education, 106, 106*n*5
  for-profit activities, 108–110
  home business use, 107
  meals and entertainment, 100
  tax planning, 110–111
  travel, 100
Mortgage interest deduction
  generally, 91–92, 96, 112–113
  proposals to eliminate, 208
Mortgage swaps, 126, 172
Municipal bonds. *See* Bonds
Murphy, Eddie, 171

N
Negative savings, 58, 217
Net operating loss (NOL)
    deductions, 139*n*3
Netting rules
  interest expenses, 112, 119

  mixed business-personal
    expenditures, 109, 119
  tax planning, 61
  tax shelters, 190–191, 200
Newman, Paul, 189
Noncash benefits
  generally, 73–75, 86
  basis, 76–77
  fringe benefits, 77–79, 86
  valuation, 75–77
Nonincome
  generally, 54, 85
  debt, 13–14, 58, 86
  imputed income, 55–57
  psychic income, 55
  self-supplied capital, 57
  self-supplied labor, 55–57
  unrealized income, 58
Nonrecognition rules. *See*
    Recognition of income
Nonrecourse debt, 185–187, 200

O
Obama, Barack, 14*n*6, 19, 79, 152,
    177, 193, 208–210
O'Connor, Sandra Day, 188–189
Opinion letters, 199

P
Partnerships. *See* Shifting of income
Passive activity loss rules.
    See Losses
Patents, 169
Payroll taxes
  generally, 5*n*1, 15, 84
  proposals to increase, 210
Pension plans
  deductions, 92, 96
  deferred income, 25
  income taxes, 17
  proposals to eliminate
    deductions, 208
Personal dependency deduction
  generally, 98, 118–119

proposals to eliminate, 208
Personal expenditure deductions,
    67, 87–88, 94–99, 118
    casualty loss, 95, 113
    charitable contributions. *See*
        Charitable Contributions
    home mortgage interest, 96,
        112–113
    IRA, 96
    pension plan, 96
    property taxes, 96
    medical expenses, 95
    sales taxes, 96
    state and local income taxes, 96
Personal injuries, 44–45, 63
Planning. *See* Tax planning
Posner, Judge Richard, 103, 109
Precautionary savings, 216, 218–219
Presley, Elvis, 174, 179
Presley, Priscilla, 174, 179
The Producers (play/film), 190
Progressive marginal tax rates
    generally, 6, 20–21, 117, 145, 160
    progressive spending tax, 220–221
Progressive spending tax
    borrowing, 225
    capital, 221
    consumption, 220–221
    debt, 217–218, 224–225
    deductions, 219, 224
    individual savings accounts,
        220–221
    progressive marginal rates,
        220–221
    realization requirement, 222–223,
        225
    savings, 214–219, 220–221
    tax base, 218–219
    tax planning, 222
    tax rates, 220–221, 224
Property
    anticipatory income, 174–176, 179
    attribution of income, 153–156,
        160–161

taxes. *See* Personal expenditure
    deductions
Proposals for tax reform. *See*
    Reform of tax system
Psychic income, 23, 55, 85. *See also*
    Nonincome

R
Rabushka, Alvin, 6
Rates. *See* Tax rates
Reagan, Ronald, 14*n*6, 19, 193
Real estate
    characterization of income, 170,
        178–179
    tax planning, 13, 16–17, 56
Realization requirement
    analysis of transaction, 124–125
    appreciated property, 50–54, 58,
        122*n*1
    capital gains, 166–167, 177–178
    income taxes, 73–75, 119
    losses, 125–126
    Macomber, 37–38, 108–110,
        122*n*1
    progressive spending tax,
        222–223, 225
    realization events, 122–123,
        126–127
    recognition compared, 127–128
    spending taxes, 73–75
    tax planning, 12–14, 16, 18, 59–62,
        83–86
    timing considerations, 122–127,
        142
    valuation, 124
Recharacterization of income,
    163–179. *See also* Capital gains
    generally, 23–24, 27, 48, 163,
        177–179
    anticipatory income, 174–176, 179
    Arkansas Best, 171–174
    capital property, 173–174
    carried interest, 176–177, 179
    Corn Products, 171–174

Recharacterization of income (*Cont.*)
    inventory exception, 170
    policy considerations, 164–167
    real estate, 170, 178–179
    securities, 170, 178–179
    statutory provisions, 167–170
    stock in trade exception, 170
    tax rates, 163–164
Recognition of income
    divorce, 129–130, 142
    gifts, 129, 142
    insurance proceeds, 128–129, 142
    interspousal transfers, 129–130,
        142
    involuntary conversions, 129, 142
    like-kind exchanges, 129–132, 142
    realization compared, 127–128
    timing considerations, 127–130,
        142
Recommendations for tax reform.
    See Reform of tax system
Reform of tax system
    generally, xix–xx, 22, 92, 96, 118,
        148, 205–206
    comprehensive reform, 211–212
    deficits, effect of, 206–207, 223
    incremental reform, 207–209, 224
    progressive spending tax. *See*
        Progressive spending tax
Retirement benefits
    income taxes, 18–20
    IRAs. *See* individual retirement
        accounts (IRAs)
    pension plans. *See* Pension plans
    Roth-style IRAs. *See* Roth-style
        IRAs
    shifting of income, 159
Rich Dad/Poor Dad (Kiyosaki), 12,
    12n5, 13, 26, 56
Roth-style IRAs
    generally, 26
    deductions, lack of, 96
    income taxes, 19
    wage taxes, 10–11

S
Sales taxes
    generally, 5, 9
    deductions, 96
    value-added taxes (VAT).
        See Value-added taxes (VAT)
Same-sex couples, 151–152
Savings. *See also* Capital
    ad hoc deviations, 17–18
    bequest savings, 217
    "double taxation," 5, 18, 26, 206,
        213–214, 224
    earnings, relation to, 215–216
    life-cycle savings, 216
    negative savings, 217
    precautionary savings, 216
    progressive spending tax,
        214–222
Securities, *See* Recharacterization
    of income
Self-supplied capital, 55, 57.
    See also Nonincome
Self-supplied labor, 55–57.
    See also Nonincome
Sham transaction doctrine. *See*
    Tax shelters
Shelters. *See* Tax shelters
Shifting of income. *See also*
    Attribution of income
    generally, 23–25, 72, 145–147, 160
    children, 152–153, 160–161
    corporations, 158, 161
    deferred retirement benefits, 159
    "fruit-tree" distinction, 153–155,
        161, 174–176, 179
    gifts, 153, 160–161
    "kiddie tax," 72n9, 157–158, 161
    partnerships, 158, 161
    property, income from, 153–155,
        161
    spouses, 147–152, 160
    tax shelters. *See* Tax shelters
    trusts, 155, 158, 161
Simons, Henry, 6, 6n4

"Simple straddle," 183–184, 190–191.
    See also Tax shelters
Sixteenth Amendment, 6, 33, 37, 84,
    128
Slapshot (film), 189, 192
Smith, Adam, 166–167
Social Security taxes
    generally, 5, 15, 84
    proposals to increase, 210
Sources of income, 3, 7–8, 26
Spending. *See* Consumption
Spending taxes
    generally, 5, 26, 217
    basis under, 84
    borrowing under, 83–84, 86
    consumption taxes, 8–9
    progressive spending tax. *See*
        Progressive spending tax
    realization requirement, 73–75
    wage taxes distinguished,
        213–214, 224
Spouses
    interspousal transfers,
        nonrecognition rules, 129–130,
        142
    joint filing, 149
    shifting of income, 147–152, 160
    spousal support, 156–157
Spouses, attribution of income
    generally, 56–57, 147–150, 160
    marriage bonuses, 150–151
    marriage penalties, 150–151
    same-sex couples, 151–152
Standard deduction, 34n1, 90, 93, 94,
    98, 118
State and local income tax
        deductions
    generally, 96, 116, 118–119
    proposals to eliminate, 208
Stepped-up basis, 14, 14n6, 179, 192
Step transaction doctrine, 194, 195,
    200. *See also* Tax shelters
Stock in trade exception, 167–168,
    170, 178

Stock-on-stock dividends, 36–37,
    36–37n3
Substance over form doctrine,
    194–195, 200. *See also*
        Tax shelters
Substituted basis, 131, 132, 50n5
Supremacy Clause, 151–152
"Sweat equity," 55–56, 111

T
Taxable gain, 45, 53–54
Taxable income, 21, 44, 146
Taxable unit, 147, 152, 160
Tax avoidance, 194–195
Tax base
    generally, 3–4, 25–26, 207
    under progressive spending tax,
        218–219
    proposals to increase, 211–212
Tax benefit rule, 139–140, 143
Tax evasion, 194–195
Taxing Women (McCaffery), 56, 56n6,
    94n2, 107n6, 148n1, 150–151
Tax planning
    generally, xix, 11, 15
    attribution of income. *See*
        Attribution of income
    deductions. *See* Deductions
    deferring tax liability, 23
    escaping tax liability, 23
    exclusions. *See* Exclusions
    goals, 22–24, 27
    inclusions, 59–62
    mixed business-personal
        expenditure deductions,
        110–111
    netting rules, 61
    progressive spending tax, 222
    real estate, 16–17
    realization requirement, 12–13,
        59–62
    recharacterization of income.
        See Recharacterization of
        income

Tax planning (*Cont.*)
  shifting of income. *See* Shifting
    of income
  tax shelters, 182–183
  timing considerations.*See* Timing
    considerations
Tax rates
  generally, 3–5, 207
  average rates, 21
  capital gains, 16, 163–164, 193
  effective rates, 21
  progressive marginal rates, 20–21,
    220–221
  progressive spending tax,
    220–221, 224
  proposals to decrease, 211–212
Tax reform. *See* Reform of tax
    system
Tax Reform Act of 1986
  capital gains, 163–164
  itemized deductions, 99
  "kiddie tax," 157, 161
  mixed business-personal
    expenditure deductions, 111
  tax base, 212
  tax rates, 212
  tax shelters, 181–183, 185,
    190–193, 197, 200–201
Tax shelters
  generally, 181, 199–201
  business purpose doctrine, 194,
    197, 200
  capital gains, 192–193
  classic shelters, 184–190, 200
  common law doctrines,
    193–197
  Crane case, 185–187
  debt, role of, 185–189, 199–200
  depreciation, 187–189
  discharge of debt, 187–189
  economic substance doctrine,
    182, 194, 197, 200
  ethical considerations, 198–200
  "interest dodge," 183, 190

interest expense deductions, 183,
    190, 200
  judicial doctrines, 193–197
  "kiddie shift," 184
  "kiddie tax," 192, 200
  legal malpractice, 198
  nonrecourse debt, 185–187, 200
  passive activity loss rules,
    191–192, 200
  sham transaction doctrine, 194,
    196–197, 200
  "simple straddle," 183–184,
    190–191
  step transaction doctrine, 194, 200
  substance over form doctrine,
    194–195, 200
  tax planning, 182–183
  Tax Reform Act of 1986, 181–183,
    185, 189, 190–193, 197, 198,
    200–201
  Tufts, 187–189
"Time bombs," 50–54, 59, 85
Timing considerations
  generally, 90, 121
  accounting, 132–134
  accounting methods, 133–135, 142
  annual accounting rule, 137–139,
    143
  business expenditure deductions,
    100–104
  capitalization of expenses, 141, 143
  cash equivalence, 135–137, 142–143
  claim of right doctrine, 139–140,
    143
  constructive receipt, 135–137,
    142–143
  depreciation, 141, 143
  economic benefit, 135–137,
    142–143
  like-kind exchanges, 130–132
  realization requirement, 122–127,
    142
  recognition, 127–130, 142
  tax benefit rule, 139–140, 143

Tips, 66–67
Tokes. *See* Tips
Trading Places (film), 171
Transferred basis, 50*n*5
Travel expenses. *See* Mixed
    business-personal expenditure
    deductions
Treasury Regulations
    generally, 35*n*2
    income, defined, 35–36, 38, 40
Trusts. *See* Shifting of income

U
"Undeniable accession to wealth."
    See Definitions of income
Unrealized income, 58

V
Valuation
    noncash benefits, 75–77

realization requirement, 124
Value-added taxes (VAT)
    generally, 224
    "flat taxes," 210–211, 214
    proposals, 210–211, 214
    wage taxes, 211, 224
Venture funds, 176–177, 179

W
Wage taxes
    generally, 5, 5*n*1, 26–27
    consumption taxes, 8
    "flat taxes," 5–6
    income taxes, 11–20
    retirement benefits, 18–20
    spending taxes distinguished,
        213–214, 224
    value-added taxes,
        211, 224
"Workfare," 93